CIVIL LITIGATION

CIVIL LITIGATION

Charlotte Hart LLB, Solicitor

2001

Published by
Jordan Publishing Limited
21 St Thomas Street
Bristol BS1 6JS

© The College of Law 2001

All rights reserved. No part of this publication may be
reproduced, stored in a retrieval system, or transmitted in
any way or by any means, including photocopying or recording,
without the written permission of the copyright holder,
application for which should be addressed to the publisher.

British Library Cataloguing-in-Publication Data
A catalogue record for this book is available from the British Library.

ISSN 1352-4496
ISBN 0 85308 709 1

Printed in Great Britain by Hobbs the Printers Ltd of Southampton

PREFACE

This Resource Book is intended as a basic guide to procedure for students taking the Legal Practice Course at The College of Law. It is anticipated that students will have studied the substantive law and remedies at the academic stage of training, and this text therefore deals mainly with the practice and procedure of the courts under the Civil Procedure Rules 1998.

The objective is to explain as simply as possible the way to conduct an action in the civil courts so that students can go on to consult the Civil Procedure Rules, together with the standard practitioners' guides with some understanding of the procedures involved. Although parts of particular Rules or Practice Directions have been quoted, this is not intended to be a substitute for looking at the full text.

In the interests of brevity, the masculine pronoun has been used throughout to include the feminine.

Although I am responsible for this edition of the Resource Book, it remains very much the work of my predecessors. In particular, I wish to acknowledge the contributions of Mike Waring and Graham Beecher. Mike had the unenviable task of preparing the first edition to appear after the introduction of the Civil Procedure Rules and it is on his original text that this edition is based. Graham, who prepared last year's edition, sadly died in September 2000. He taught at The College for 26 years and is greatly missed.

CHARLOTTE HART
The College of Law
London

CONTENTS

PREFACE	v
TABLE OF CASES	xi
TABLE OF STATUTES	xiii
TABLE OF STATUTORY INSTRUMENTS AND CODES OF PRACTICE	xv
TABLE OF EUROPEAN LEGISLATION	xxi
TABLE OF ABBREVIATIONS	xxiii

Chapter 1		INTRODUCTION TO CIVIL LITIGATION	1
	1.1	The Woolf reforms	1
	1.2	The Rules	2
	1.3	An overview of a civil action	3
	1.4	Human rights	4
Chapter 2		CONSIDERATIONS AT THE FIRST INTERVIEW AND FUNDING THE ACTION	5
	2.1	Purpose of the first interview	5
	2.2	Limitation	5
	2.3	Viability and burden of proof	7
	2.4	Remedy sought	8
	2.5	Funding	10
	2.6	Ethics and conflict of interest	15
	2.7	Foreign element and choice of forum	16
	2.8	Alternatives to a civil action	18
	2.9	Human rights	20
Chapter 3		EARLY ACTION	23
	3.1	Writing to the client	23
	3.2	Interviewing witnesses	23
	3.3	Preserving documents	24
	3.4	Obtaining expert evidence	24
	3.5	Site visits	26
	3.6	Instructing counsel	26
	3.7	Pre-action protocols	28
	3.8	Sending the letter of claim	28
	3.9	Pre-action disclosure	29
	3.10	Settlement	30
	3.11	Researching the law	30
Chapter 4		COMMENCING PROCEEDINGS	31
	4.1	Choice of court	31
	4.2	Court personnel	32
	4.3	Issuing proceedings	33
	4.4	Parties to the action	35

	4.5	Service	39
	4.6	Time for service of claim form	42

Chapter 5	**RESPONDING TO PROCEEDINGS AND JUDGMENT IN DEFAULT**	45
	5.1 Introduction	45
	5.2 Computation of time	45
	5.3 Acknowledgement of service	46
	5.4 The defence	47
	5.5 Admissions	47
	5.6 Default judgments	50
	5.7 Human rights	51

Chapter 6	**STATEMENTS OF CASE**	53
	6.1 Introduction	53
	6.2 Contents of the particulars of claim	53
	6.3 The defence	60
	6.4 Reply to defence	63
	6.5 Amendments to statements of case	63
	6.6 Requests for further information	65

Chapter 7	**PART 20 PROCEEDINGS AND PART 8 CLAIMS**	67
	7.1 Introduction	67
	7.2 Procedure	68
	7.3 Part 8 claims	73

Chapter 8	**CASE MANAGEMENT AND ALLOCATION OF CASES**	75
	8.1 Introduction	75
	8.2 The court's powers	75
	8.3 Striking out	76
	8.4 Relief from sanctions	78
	8.5 Allocation	79
	8.6 Allocation to a track	82
	8.7 Human rights	90

Chapter 9	**APPLICATIONS TO THE COURT**	91
	9.1 Introduction	91
	9.2 Applications generally	91
	9.3 Costs	93
	9.4 Appeals against an interim order	96
	9.5 Particular types of application	96
	9.6 Interim remedies	100
	9.7 Interim payments	101
	9.8 Security for costs	103
	9.9 Human rights	103

Chapter 10	**DISCLOSURE AND INSPECTION OF DOCUMENTS – PART 31 OF THE CPR 1998**	107
	10.1 Purpose of disclosure and inspection	107
	10.2 Definition of 'disclosure'	107
	10.3 Definition of 'documents'	107
	10.4 Standard disclosure	107
	10.5 Disclosure of copies	108
	10.6 The duty to search	108
	10.7 The right of inspection	108

	10.8 Procedure for standard disclosure	109
	10.9 The disclosure statement	109
	10.10 Continuing obligation	110
	10.11 Withholding inspection	110
	10.12 Withholding other documents	113
	10.13 Failure to disclose	114
	10.14 Subsequent use of disclosed documents	114
	10.15 Applying for specific disclosure	114
	10.16 Pre-action disclosure	115
	10.17 Non-party disclosure	115
	10.18 Human rights	116
Chapter 11	EVIDENCE	117
	11.1 Introduction	117
	11.2 Witness evidence	117
	11.3 Form of witness statements	118
	11.4 Use of witness statements at trial	118
	11.5 Witness summaries	119
	11.6 Sanctions for non-service of witness statements	119
	11.7 Affidavits	120
	11.8 Opinion evidence	120
	11.9 Hearsay evidence	121
	11.10 Use of plans, photographs and models as evidence	124
	11.11 Notice to admit facts	125
	11.12 Notice to admit or prove documents	125
	11.13 Expert evidence	125
	11.14 Assessors	129
	11.15 Human rights	129
Chapter 12	SETTLEMENT	131
	12.1 Negotiations	131
	12.2 Pre-action settlements	132
	12.3 Settlements reached after the issue of proceedings	132
	12.4 Part 36	133
	12.5 Claims involving children and patients	141
	12.6 Discontinuance	141
Chapter 13	FINAL PREPARATIONS FOR TRIAL, TRIAL AND ASSESSMENT OF COSTS	143
	13.1 Final preparations for trial	143
	13.2 Trial	145
	13.3 Costs	149
	13.4 Human rights	156
Chapter 14	ENFORCEMENT OF MONEY JUDGMENTS	157
	14.1 Introduction	157
	14.2 Interest on judgment debts	157
	14.3 Tracing the other party	158
	14.4 Investigating the judgment debtor's means	158
	14.5 Methods of enforcement	160
Chapter 15	ALTERNATIVE DISPUTE RESOLUTION	169
	15.1 The nature of ADR	169
	15.2 Advantages of ADR	170

15.3	Disadvantages of ADR	171
15.4	Types of ADR	172
15.5	Organisations providing ADR	174
15.6	Using ADR	174
15.7	Choosing ADR	175
15.8	Summary	175

Appendix A	COURT FORMS	177
Appendix B	OTHER DOCUMENTS	219
Index		231

TABLE OF CASES

References are to paragraph numbers.

Airey v Ireland (1979–80) 2 EHRR 305, ECHR	2.9.2
Amber v Stacy [2001] 2 All ER 88, CA	12.4.7
Andronicou and Constantinou v Cyprus (1998) 25 EHRR 491, ECHR	2.9.2
Arrow Nominees Inc v Blackledge (1999) *The Times*, December 8, ChD	8.3.2
AXA v Swire Fraser (2000) *The Times*, January 19	8.3.2
Baron v Lovell [1999] CPLR 630, CA	8.6.3(3)
Beathem v Carlisle Hospitals NHS Trust (1999) *The Times*, May 20, QBD	4.4.1
Biguzzi v Rank Leisure plc [1999] 1 WLR 1926, CA	8.3.2
Breeze (Norman Roger) v John Stacey & Sons Ltd (1999) *The Times*, July 8, CA	10.11.5
Channel Tunnel Group Ltd and France Manche SA v Balfour Beatty Construction Ltd [1993] 2 WLR 262, HL	15.3.1
Chapple v Williams [1999] CPLR 731, CA	9.9.2
Daniels v Walker [2000] 1 WLR 1382, CA	1.4, 8.7, 11.13.8, 11.15.2
Daryanami v Kumar & Co and Another (2000) Lawtel, 15 March, CA	8.4
Field v Leeds City Council (2000) *The Times*, January 18	11.13.1
Ford v GKR Construction and Others [2000] 1 All ER 802	12.4.5
Habib Bank v Abbeypearl Ltd and Others [2001] 1 All ER 185	8.3.2
Hunt v RM Douglas (Roofing) Ltd [1990] 1 AC 398, HL	13.2.7
Hyams v Pender [2000] 1 WLR 32, ECHR	13.4
IBM Corporation and Another v Phoenix International (Computers) Ltd [1995] 1 All ER 413, ChD	10.11.5
Mars UK Ltd v Teknowledge Ltd (No 2) [1999] Masons CLR 322, ChD	13.3.2, 13.3.7
Matthews v Tarmac Bricks and Tiles Ltd [1999] CPLR 463, CA	8.5.1
McGinley and Egan v UK (1998) 27 EHRR 1, ECHR	10.18
Mealey Horgan plc v Horgan (1999) *The Times*, July 6, QBD	11.6
Molins plc v GDSA (2000) *The Times*, March 1	4.5.1(5)
Nanglegan v Royal Free Hampstead NHS Trust (2001) *The Times*, February 14, CA	4.5.5, 4.6
Negati v Metropolitan Police Commissioner (2001) LTL, 19 January	8.3.2
Petrograde Inc v Texaco Ltd [2000] CLC 1341	12.4.7
Practice Statement (Alternative Dispute Resolution) (No 2) [1996] 1 WLR 1024, QBD	15.2, 15.9

R v Marylebone Magistrates' Court ex parte Andrew Clingham (2001) LTL, 22 January   11.15.1

Satwinder Kaur v CTP Coil Ltd (2000) unreported, 10 July   4.6
Scammell and Others v Dicker [2001] 1 WLR 631, CA   12.4.3
Smith v Probyn (2000) *The Times*, March 29   4.6
Stevens v Gullis [1999] BLR 394, CA   11.13.1
Stubbings and Others v The United Kingdom [1997] 1 FLR 105, ECHR   2.9.1

Tolstoy Miloslavsky v UK (1995) 20 EHRR 442, ECHR   9.9.3

UCB Corporate Services Ltd v Halifax (SW) Ltd [1999] 1 Lloyd's Rep 154, CA   8.3.2

Van de Hurk v Netherlands (1994) 18 ECHR 481, ECHR   13.4
Vinos v Marks & Spencers plc (2000) Lawtel, 8 June   4.6

Winer v UK 1998 48 DR 154   2.9.2

TABLE OF STATUTES

References are to paragraph numbers.

Access to Justice Act 1999	2.5.6
Administration of Justice Act 1920	14.5.7
Arbitration Act 1996	2.8.1, 15.3.1, 15.4.6
s 66	2.8.1, 15.3.2
Children Act 1989	
s 96(2)	13.2.4
Civil Evidence Act 1972	
s 3(1)	3.4.3
(2)	11.8
Civil Evidence Act 1995	11.9.2, 11.9.3(5), 11.15.1, 13.1.3
s 1	11.9.2
(2)(a)	11.9.1
s 2	11.9.2
(1)(a)	11.9.2
s 3	11.9.3(2)
s 4	11.9.3(1), 11.15.1, 13.2.3
s 5	11.9.3(3), 11.9.3(4)
s 6	11.9.3(5)
Civil Jurisdiction and Judgments Act 1982	2.7.1, 4.5.6(1)
Civil Procedure Act 1997	
s 7	9.6
Consumer Credit Act 1974	5.6.1, 14.5.1(1)
County Courts Act 1984	
s 52	3.9, 9.6
s 53	9.6
s 69	2.4.3(1), 2.4.3(2), 7.2, 12.2.1, 13.2.7
Courts and Legal Services Act 1990	
s 58	2.5.2
Foreign Judgments (Reciprocal Enforcement) Act 1933	14.5.7
Human Rights Act 1998	1.4, 4.3, 9.9.2
s 3(1)	1.4
s 4	4.1, 4.4.5
s 5(1)	1.4
Judgments Act 1838	
s 17	13.2.7
Late Payment of Commercial Debts (Interest) Act 1998	2.4.3, 6.2.1, 12.2.1, 13.2.7
Limitation Act 1980	2.2, 2.9.1
s 2	2.2.1, 2.2.5
s 5	2.2.1, 2.2.5
s 11	2.2.2, 2.2.5
s 14	2.2.2, 2.2.3
s 14A	2.2.3, 2.2.5
s 14B	2.2.3
Mental Health Act 1983	2.2.4, 4.4.1
Pt VII	1.2, 4.4.1(1), 4.4.1(2)
Road Traffic Act 1988	2.8.5
Supreme Court Act 1981	
s 33	3.9, 9.6
s 34	9.6
s 35A	2.4.3(1), 2.4.3(2), 12.2.1, 13.2.7
s 51	8.3.2
Torts (Interference with Goods) Act 1977	
s 4	9.6

TABLE OF STATUTORY INSTRUMENTS AND CODES OF PRACTICE

References are to paragraph numbers and the Appendix.

Access to Justice (Membership Organisations) Regulations 2000, SI 2000/693	2.5.6
Civil Procedure Rules 1998, SI 1998/3132	1.1 *et seq*
Pt 1 Overriding Objective	2.6.4
r 1.1	1.1, 1.4, 10.15, 11.1
(2)(c)	10.6
r 1.2	1.1
r 1.3	1.1, 2.3
r 1.4	1.1, 8.1
(2)(b)	8.6.3
(e)	15.7
Pt 2 Application and Interpretation of the Rules	
r 2.3(1)	8.5
r 2.8	4.5.2, 5.2
Pt 3 The Court's Case Management Powers	4.2, 8.1, 8.3.1, 9.5.2
r 3.1(2)	8.2
(5)	8.2
r 3.4	
(2)(a)–(c)	8.3
r 3.8	8.4
r 3.9	8.3.1, 8.3.2, 8.4
(1)(a)–(i)	8.4
Practice Direction – Striking Out a Statement of Case	8.3
Pt 6 Service of Documents	4.5
r 6.3(1)	4.5.3
r 6.5	4.5.4, 6.3
rr 6.13–6.16	4.5.5
r 6.15	4.5.5
r 6.16	4.5.5
r 6.19	4.5.6(1)
r 6.20	4.5.6(1)
rr 6.24–6.26	4.5.6(2)
Practice Direction 6B	4.5.6(1)
Pt 7 How to Start Proceedings – The Claim Form	
r 7.5	4.6
r 7.6	4.6
Practice Direction – How to Start Proceedings – The Claim Form	
para 2.4	4.1
para 5.1	4.3
Pt 8 Alternative Procedure for Claims	4.4.1(4), 5.6.1, 6.1, 7.3, 7.3.1, 7.3.2, 12.5
Practice Direction – Alternative Procedure for Claims	7.3.1
Pt 11 Disputing the Court's Jurisdiction	2.7.1(6)
Pt 13 Setting Aside or Varying Default Judgment	9.5.1
r 13.2	9.5.1
r 13.3(1)	9.5.1
Pt 14 Admissions	5.5
Practice Direction – Admissions	
para 6.1	5.5.7
Pt 16 Statements of Case	6.1
r 16.2(1)	4.3.1

Civil Procedure Rules 1998 *cont*
  Pt 16 Statements of Case *cont*
    r 16.4(1) — 6.2.1
      (1)(a)–(e) — 6.2.1
      (2) — 6.2.1
    r 16.5 — 6.3, 8.3
      (1)(a)–(c) — 6.3
      (2)(a), (b) — 6.3
      (3)(a), (b) — 6.3
      (4) — 6.3
      (5) — 6.3
      (6)(a), (b) — 6.3
      (7), (8) — 6.3
    r 16.7(1) — 6.4
    Practice Direction – Statements of Case — 6.1, 6.2.1
      para 8.3(1), (2) — 6.2.1
      para 8.4 — 6.2.1
      para 8.5 — 6.2.1
      paras 9.1–9.2 — 6.2.1
      para 9.2 — 6.2.1
        (1)–(3) — 6.3
        (1)–(8) — 6.2.1
      para 14.1 — 6.3
      para 16.4(2) — 6.2.1, 6.3
  Pt 17 Amendments to Statements of Case — 6.5
    r 17.2 — 6.5.7
  Pt 18 Further Information — 6.6, 6.6.1, 8.6.1, 9.5.3
    r 18.1(1)(a), (b) — 6.6.1
    Practice Direction – Further Information
      para 1 — 9.5.3
      para 5.5(1) — 9.5.3
  Pt 19 Addition and Subtraction of Parties — 4.4.5
    r 19.2 — 4.4.5
    r 19.4(2) — 4.4.5
    r 19.5 — 4.4.5
  Pt 20 Counterclaims and Other Additional Claims — 6.3, 7.1, 7.2.3, 7.2.4, 7.2.5, 7.2.6, 7.2.7, 8.5.1, 8.6
    r 20.2 — 7.1
      (1)(a)–(c) — 7.1
      (2) — 7.1
    r 20.4 — 7.2.1
    r 20.6 — 7.2.2
    r 20.7 — 7.2.3
    r 20.9(2)(a), (b) — 7.2.4
      (c)(i), (ii) — 7.2.4
    Practice Direction – Counterclaims and Other Part 20 Claims
      para 5.3 — 7.2.7
      para 7.1–7.6 — 7.2.8
  Pt 21 Children and Patients — 4.4.1
    r 21.6 — 4.4.1(1)
    Practice Direction – Children and Patients
      para 2.1 — 4.4.1(1)
      para 6.2 — 4.4.1(4)
  Pt 22 Statements of Truth — 4.3, 6.3
    Practice Direction – Statements of Truth
      para 3.8 — 4.3
      para 3.10 — 4.3

Civil Procedure Rules 1998 *cont*
    Pt 23 General Rules About Applications for Court Orders   9.1
        r 23.2   9.2.1
        r 23.6   9.2.2
        Practice Direction – Applications   9.2.3, 9.2.4, 9.2.8
            para 3   9.2.7
    Pt 24 Summary Judgment   8.5.2, 9.5.2, 14.5.7, 15.3.2
        r 24.2   9.5.2
            (a)(i), (ii)   9.5.2
            (b)   9.5.2
        Practice Direction – The Summary Disposal of Claims
            para 1.3   9.5.2
            para 2.3   9.5.2
            para 5.1   9.5.2
            para 5.2   9.5.2
    Pt 25 Interim Remedies   9.6, 9.8
        r 25.1   9.6
            (1)(a), (b)   9.6
            (a)–(n)   9.6
            (c)(i)–(vi)   9.6
        r 25.6   9.6
        Practice Direction 25B
            para 2.1   9.7.1
    Pt 26 Case Management – Preliminary Stage   8.5
        r 26.2   8.5
        r 26.7(3)   8.6
        r 26.8(1)(a)–(i)   8.6
        Practice Direction – Case Management – Preliminary Stage: Allocation and Re-
        allocation
            para 2.4   8.5.2
            para 6.5   8.5.2
            para 6.6   8.5.2
            para 11   8.6
    Pt 27 Small Claims Track   8.6.1
        r 27.14   8.6.1
        Practice Direction – Small Claims Track
            Appendix A   8.6.1
            Form A   8.6.1
    Pt 28 The Fast Track
        r 28.4   8.6.2(2)
        Practice Direction – The Fast Track   8.6.2(4)
            para 3.9   11.13.8
            para 3.12   8.6.2(1)
            para 4.2(1), (2)   8.6.2(2)
            para 8.1   13.1
    Pt 29 The Multi-Track   8.6.3
        Practice Direction – The Multi-Track
            para 2.2   4.1
            para 2.6   8.5.1
            para 4.10   8.6.3(1)
                (1)–(8)   8.6.3(1)
            para 5.1   8.6.3(2)
                (1)–(3)   8.6.3(2)
            para 5.6   8.6.3(3)
                (1)–(4)   8.6.3(3)
            para 10.1   13.1
    Part 30 Transfer   4.1
        r 30.3(2)   4.1

Civil Procedure Rules 1998 *cont*
    Pt 31 Disclosure and Inspection of Documents ..... 8.6.1, 10.1 *et seq*, 11.12, 13.1.3
        r 31.2 ..... 10.2
        r 31.3 ..... 10.7
        r 31.4 ..... 10.3
        r 31.6 ..... 10.4
        r 31.10 ..... 10.9
        r 31.16(3) 3.9
        r 31.20 ..... 10.11.5
        Practice Direction – Disclosure and Inspection 10.6, 10.9
            para 2 ..... 10.6
            para 3.2 ..... 10.8
    Pt 32 Evidence 8.6.1, 11.1
        r 32.1 ..... 11.1
            (1)(a)–(c) 11.1
            (2), (3) 11.1
        r 32.2 ..... 13.1.3
            (1) 11.2
        r 32.4(2) 11.2
        r 32.9 ..... 11.5
        r 32.18 ..... 11.11
        r 32.19 ..... 11.12
        Practice Direction – Written Evidence
            paras 17–20 ..... 11.3
    Pt 33 Miscellaneous Rules About Evidence 11.1, 11.9.2
        r 33.3 ..... 11.9.2
            (1)(a), (b) 11.9.2
        r 33.4 ..... 11.9.3(2)
        r 33.5 ..... 11.9.3(4)
        r 33.6 ..... 11.10, 13.1.3
    Pt 34 Depositions and Court Attendances by Witnesses 13.1.2
    Pt 35 Experts and Assessors 6.3, 8.6.1, 11.13
        r 35.1 ..... 3.4.4
        r 35.3 ..... 11.13.1
        r 35.4 ..... 11.13.2
        r 35.10 ..... 11.13.5
            (3) 11.13.3
            (4) 11.13.3
                (a), (b) 11.13.3
        r 35.12 ..... 11.13.7
        r 35.15 ..... 11.14
        Practice Direction – Experts and Assessors 11.13.5
    Pt 36 Offers to Settle and Payments into Court ..... 3.10.2, 8.6.1, 12.4 *et seq*, 13.3.2
        r 36.6 ..... 12.4.2
        r 36.10 ..... 3.10.2, 12.4.1
        r 36.20 ..... 12.4.2
        r 36.21 ..... 12.4.1, 12.4.4, 12.4.5, 12.4.7
        Practice Direction – Offers to Settle and Payments into Court
            para 3.4 ..... 12.4.2
            para 5 ..... 12.4.2
    Pt 38 Discontinuance 12.6
    Pt 39 Miscellaneous Provisions Relating to Hearings 9.9.4, 13.1.3
        Practice Direction – Miscellaneous Provisions Relating to Hearings
            para 3.2 ..... 13.1.3
            para 3.9 ..... 13.1.3
    Pt 40 Judgments, Orders, Sale of Land etc
        r 40.6 ..... 12.3.1
    Pt 44 General Rules about Costs 13.3.2

Civil Procedure Rules 1998 *cont*
  Pt 44 General Rules about Costs *cont*

r 44.3(1)	13.3.2
(2)(a)	13.3.1
(4)(c)	12.4.7
r 44.3B	13.3.7
r 44.4	13.3.3
r 44.5	13.3.3, 13.3.4
r 44.8	9.3
r 44.15	2.5.2, 13.3.7
Pt 45 Fixed Costs	4.3, 5.6.3, 9.3, 9.5.2
Pt 46 Fast Track Trial Costs	13.3.6
Pt 47 Procedure for Detailed Assessment of Costs and Default Provisions	
r 47.8	13.3.7
r 47.9	13.3.7
r 47.13	13.3.7
r 47.20	13.3.7
Pt 52 Appeals	9.4, 13.3.7
r 52.3(6)	9.4
r 52.11	9.4
Practice Direction – Appeals	13.4
Practice Direction – Costs (Parts 43–48)	13.3.7
s 4	
para 4.6	13.3.7
s 11	13.3.7
s 14	9.3.1
s 32	13.3.7
s 47	13.3.7
s 48	13.3.7
Practice Direction Pre-action Protocols	3.7
para 2	3.7
para 4	3.7
para 4A	2.5.2
Sch 1	1.2, 14.1
RSC Ord 23	1.2
RSC Ord 46	14.5.1
RSC Ord 48, r 1	14.4.2
RSC Ord 49	14.5.4
RSC Ord 50	14.5.2
RSC Ord 71, r 28	14.5.7
r 36	14.5.7
Sch 2	1.2, 14.1
CCR Ord 25, r 3	14.4.2
CCR Ord 26, r 1	14.5.1
CCR Ord 27	14.5.5
CCR Ord 30	14.5.4
CCR Ord 31	14.5.2
Forms	
N1 and N1A Claim form and Notes for Claimant	App A(1)
N1C Notes for Defendant on Replying to the Claim Form	5.1, App A(3)
N9 Response Pack	5.1, 5.3, 5.4, 5.5, App A(4)
N9A	5.5.1, App A(4)
N9B	5.4, App A(4)
N9C	5.4, App A(4)
N9D	App A(4)
N150 Allocation Questionnaire	8.5, 8.5.1, 8.5.2, App A(6)
paras (c)–(j)	8.5.1
N170 Listing Questionnaire	8.6.2(6), 8.6.3(6), App A(9)

Civil Procedure Rules 1998 *cont*
    Forms *cont*
        N208 — 7.3.2
        N211 Pt 20 Claim Form — 7.2.3, App A(5)
        N242A Notice of Payment Into Court — App A(7)
        N243A Notice of Acceptance and Request for Payment — App A(8)
        N244 Application Notice — 9.2, App A(10)
        N251 Notice of Funding — 2.5.2, 13.3.7, App A(2)
        N252 Notice of Commencement of Assessment of Bill of Costs — 13.3.7, App A(13)
        N260 Statement of Costs — 9.3, App A(11)
        N265 List of Documents — 10.8, 10.9, App A(12)
Conditional Fee Agreements Regulations 2000, SI 2000/692 — 2.5.2
    reg 3 — 13.3.7
    reg 3(2)(b) — 13.3.7
County Courts (Interest on Judgment Debts) Order 1991 — 13.2.7

Guide to Commercial Court Practice — 4.1
Guide to the Professional Conduct of Solicitors 7th edn 1996 — 2.10
    principle 20.01 — 3.4.1

Solicitors' Practice Rules
    Rule 1 — 2.6.4
    Rule 8 — 2.5.3
    Rule 15 — 2.5, 3.1

TABLE OF EUROPEAN LEGISLATION

References are to paragraph numbers.

Brussels Convention on Jurisdiction and the Enforcement of Judgments in Civil and Commercial Matters 1968	2.7.1, 2.7.1(1), 2.7.1(3), 2.7.1(4), 2.7.1(5), 4.5.6(1), 5.7, 14.5.7
Art 2	2.7.1
Art 5	
(1)	2.7.1
(3)	2.7.1
Art 6	2.7.1
Art 16	2.7.1
Art 17	2.7.1
Art 18	2.7.1
Art 26	14.5.7
European Convention on Human Rights and Fundamental Freedoms 1950	1.4, 8.3.2
Article 6	1.4, 10.18, 11.15.2
(1)	1.4, 2.9, 2.9.1, 5.7, 9.9.3, 9.9.4, 11.15.1, 13.4

TABLE OF ABBREVIATIONS

ADR	alternative dispute resolution
CEDR	Centre for Dispute Resolution
CFA Regulations 2000	Conditional Fee Agreement Regulations 2000
CICA	Criminal Injuries Compensation Authority
CLS	Community Legal Service
CLSF	Community Legal Service Fund
CPR 1998	Civil Procedure Rules 1998
LA 1980	Limitation Act 1980
LSC	Legal Services Commission
MIB	Motor Insurers Bureau
RCJ	Royal Courts of Justice
RICS	Royal Institution of Chartered Surveyors
RSC	Rules of the Supreme Court 1965
T/A	trading as

Chapter 1

INTRODUCTION TO CIVIL LITIGATION

1.1 THE WOOLF REFORMS

The nature of civil litigation in England and Wales changed fundamentally on 26 April 1999, when the Civil Procedure Rules 1998, SI 1998/3132 (CPR 1998) came into force. These Rules are the courts' attempt to implement the 'Woolf Reforms', as set out in Lord Woolf's report, *Access to Justice*, which was published in 1996. The philosophy behind this report was that the litigation system at the time was too expensive, too slow, alarming to litigants because of the unknown quantity of time and cost that they might need to spend and, indeed, incomprehensible to many litigants. Furthermore, because the system was almost entirely adversarial, it did not necessarily operate in the interests of justice as a whole.

Lord Woolf hoped that his proposed reforms, now enshrined in the CPR 1998, would lead to a civil justice system that was just in the results it delivered, fair in the way it treated litigants, and easily understood by users of that legal system. It was hoped that the new system would also provide appropriate procedures at a reasonable cost which could be completed within a reasonable time-scale. In particular, he thought it necessary to transfer the control of litigation from the parties to the court. The court would then determine how each case should progress by making appropriate directions, setting strict timetables and ensuring that the parties complied with them, backed up by a system of sanctions which the court could impose itself without the need for an application by any party. The overriding objective of the reforms is set out in r 1.1 of the CPR 1998:

> '(1) These Rules are a new procedural code with the overriding objective of enabling the court to deal with cases justly.
> (2) Dealing with a case justly includes, so far as is practicable –
>   (a) ensuring that the parties are on an equal footing;
>   (b) saving expense;
>   (c) dealing with the case in ways which are proportionate –
>   (i) to the amount of money involved;
>   (ii) to the importance of the case;
>   (iii) to the complexity of the issues; and
>   (iv) to the financial position of each party;
>   (d) ensuring that it is dealt with expeditiously and fairly; and
>   (e) allotting to it an appropriate share of the court's resources, while taking into account the need to allot resources to other cases.'

The overriding objective must be borne in mind at all times when conducting civil litigation, both by the court, because r 1.2 states:

> 'The court must seek to give effect to the overriding objective when it –
> (a) exercises any power given to it by the Rules; or
> (b) interprets any rule.'

Chapter 1 contents
The Woolf reforms
The Rules
An overview of a civil action
Human rights

and by the parties and their legal advisers, because r 1.3 states:

'The parties are required to help the court to further the overriding objective.'

In a sense, all the other rules in the CPR 1998 are designed to try to achieve the overriding objective. It is important to note that solicitors have a positive duty, pursuant to r 1.3, to help the court to further the overriding objective.

Before the introduction of the CPR 1998, the speed at which cases progressed was largely determined by the parties' solicitors. Under the CPR 1998, the court has a duty to manage cases and will therefore determine the pace of the litigation. Rule 1.4 states:

'(1) The court must further the overriding objective by actively managing cases.

(2) Active case management includes –

(a) encouraging the parties to co-operate with each other in the conduct of the proceedings;
(b) identifying the issues at an early stage;
(c) deciding promptly which issues need full investigation and trial and accordingly disposing summarily of the others;
(d) deciding the order in which issues are to be resolved;
(e) encouraging the parties to use an alternative dispute resolution procedure if the court considers that appropriate and facilitating the use of such procedure;
(f) helping the parties to settle the whole or part of the case;
(g) fixing timetables or otherwise controlling the progress of the case;
(h) considering whether the likely benefits of taking a particular step justify the cost of taking it;
(i) dealing with as many aspects of the case as it can on the same occasion;
(j) dealing with the case without the parties needing to attend at court;
(k) making use of technology; and
(l) giving directions to ensure that the trial of a case proceeds quickly and efficiently.'

Case management by the court is considered in further detail in Chapter 8.

1.2 THE RULES

The CPR 1998 apply to all proceedings in the county courts, High Court and the Civil Division of the Court of Appeal, except:

– insolvency proceedings;
– family proceedings;
– adoption proceedings;
– proceedings within the meaning of Part VII of the Mental Health Act 1983;
– non-contentious probate proceedings;
– proceedings where the High Court acts as a Prize Court (eg Admiralty proceedings).

Therefore, the CPR 1998 apply to virtually all types of civil litigation proceedings in England and Wales.

In addition to the CPR 1998 (which are contained currently in 54 Parts), in order to understand and interpret the Rules correctly, it is necessary also to look at the Practice Directions which supplement the Rules.

In some cases, the Practice Direction for a particular Rule is more expansive than the Rule itself. In a sense, the Practice Direction puts clothes on the bare bones of the Rule.

Reference is made to the Rules and Practice Directions throughout this book. Sometimes a Rule or Practice Direction has been quoted in full, at other times it is paraphrased. When conducting civil litigation, it is essential always to check the wording of any relevant Rule or Practice Direction. The 'official' version of the CPR 1998 is contained in a three-volume looseleaf folder – the 'Blue Book'. Because it is a looseleaf service, it can be kept up to date as the Rules and Practice Directions are amended or added to. The Rules can also be accessed on the Internet, via the Lord Chancellor's website (www.lcd.gov.uk). In addition, various publishers have produced their own guides to the Rules, such as *Civil Court Service* (Jordans) and its Website at www.civilcourtservice.co.uk. (See also *Civil Procedure* (Sweet & Maxwell) and *Civil Court Procedure* (Butterworths).)

The Lord Chancellor's Department provides further information and guidance via the Court Service. The Court Service website (www.courtservice.gov.uk) provides access to court forms, leaflets and details of current court fees (amongst other things).

When the CPR 1998 were drafted to replace the old High Court and county court rules, there was insufficient time to draft new Rules for every aspect of the civil litigation process. For that reason, some of the 'old' Rules have been retained and are contained in two Schedules to the CPR 1998. Schedule 1 contains the Rules of the Supreme Court. Unless otherwise stated, these apply only to proceedings in the High Court.

Schedule 2 contains the old County Court Rules. Again, unless otherwise stated, these apply only to proceedings in the county court.

An example of 'old' rules which still apply are those which deal with enforcement of court judgments, which are dealt with in Chapter 9.

1.3 AN OVERVIEW OF A CIVIL ACTION

Appendix B contains a flowchart showing the structure of a defended claim ('Overview of the five stages of litigation'). It can be seen that, after a defence is filed, the court will allocate a case to one of the three 'tracks' – small claims track, fast track or multi-track. Allocation to a track is primarily based on the value of the case:

Small claims track	–	up to £5,000
Fast track	–	£5,001–£15,000
Multi-track	–	£15,001 and above

This allocation process is part of the scheme of case management by the courts, whereby the court, rather than the parties or their lawyers, control the manner and speed of the progress of the case up to its conclusion. After allocation, the court will manage the case by bringing it to trial as quickly and efficiently as possible.

It should always be borne in mind that the purpose of case management by the court is to achieve the overriding objective.

Chapter 4 looks at the way in which court proceedings are commenced. Before that, Chapters 2 and 3 identify various matters which have to be considered prior to the issue of proceedings.

1.4 HUMAN RIGHTS

The Human Rights Act 1998 came into force on 2 October 2000. Section 3(1) requires that, so far as possible, primary and subordinate legislation must be read and given effect in a way which is compatible with the European Convention for the Protection of Human Rights and Fundamental Freedoms 1950 (the Convention). Where legislation is incompatible with the Convention, this may result in the courts making a declaration of incompatibility under s 4 of the Act.

The requirement in s 3(1) is, of course, applicable to the CPR 1998 (which are secondary legislation). The provision of the Convention that is most relevant to the interpretation of the Rules is Article 6(1). This states that:

> 'In the determination of his civil rights and obligations everyone is entitled to a fair and public hearing within a reasonable time by an independent and impartial tribunal established by law.'

Arguments under Article 6(1) have already been raised in civil proceedings. It is too early to tell how common such arguments will become, or whether they will have much impact.

The Court of Appeal has, however, already made clear (*Daniels v Walker* [2000] 1 WLR 1382) its reluctance to allow human rights issues to intrude unnecessarily into case management decisions. The Court of Appeal commented that, since the overriding objective in r 1.1 requires the courts to deal with cases justly, it was unnecessary and undesirable for the consideration of such issues to be complicated by arguments based on Article 6. Judges should, therefore, be robust in resisting such arguments. Further, the onus was on legal representatives to take responsibility for when it was appropriate to raise such issues.

Chapter 2

CONSIDERATIONS AT THE FIRST INTERVIEW AND FUNDING THE ACTION

2.1 PURPOSE OF THE FIRST INTERVIEW

The first interview between the solicitor and client is very important from both parties' points of view. The client will be anxious that the solicitor appreciates his problem and will want to be assured that there is a satisfactory solution to it. At the same time, the solicitor needs to be able to extract relevant information from the client in order to be able to give preliminary advice on such issues as liability and quantum.

There is no comprehensive list of those matters which need to be dealt with at first interview because each case is different. However, the following matters do require consideration.

2.2 LIMITATION

The Limitation Act 1980 (LA 1980) (as amended) prescribes fixed periods of time for issuing various types of action. If this period of time elapses without proceedings being issued, the case becomes statute barred. The claimant can still commence his action, but the defendant will have an impregnable defence. If the defendant wishes to rely on this defence it must be specifically stated in his defence (see Chapter 6).

2.2.1 Actions founded on contract or tort (LA 1980, ss 2 and 5)

The basic rule is that the claimant has 6 years from the date when the cause of action accrued to commence their proceedings.

In contract the cause of action accrues as soon as the breach of contract occurs.

In tort the cause of action accrues when the tort is committed. In the tort of negligence, as damage is an essential element, the cause of action accrues only when some damage occurs. This may be at a date considerably later than when the breach of duty itself occurred.

This basic rule is modified in the case of certain specific types of action.

2.2.2 Personal injury actions (LA 1980, s 11)

Where in any action (whether for negligence, nuisance or breach of duty, statutory, contractual or otherwise) the claimant claims damages which 'consist of or include damages in respect of personal injuries' the basic period of limitation is only 3 years. This reduced time-limit runs from:

Chapter 2 contents
Purpose of the first interview
Limitation
Viability and burden of proof
Remedy sought
Funding
Ethics and conflict of interest
Foreign element and choice of forum
Alternatives to a civil action
Human rights

(a) the date on which the cause of action accrued; or
(b) the date of knowledge (if later) of particular facts.

Therefore, in a simple road traffic accident, generally the claimant has 3 years from the accident itself in which to commence the action. However, in more complex claims the claimant may be able to rely on the subsequent date of knowledge, which may enable him to commence the action more than 3 years after the event which caused the injury.

The date of knowledge is defined in s 14 of LA 1980.

2.2.3 Latent damage

In a non-personal injury action based on negligence, where the damage is latent at the date when the cause of action accrued, s 14A of LA 1980 provides that the limitation period expires either:

(a) 6 years from the date on which the cause of action accrued; or
(b) 3 years from the date of knowledge of certain material facts about the damage, if this period expires after the period mentioned in (a). The definition of 'material facts' is similar to the 'date of knowledge' definition in s 14 – see above.

In theory, these rules could mean that a defendant is indefinitely open to the risk of proceedings being issued in latent damage cases. In order to avoid this there is a long-stop limitation period of 15 years from the date of the alleged breach of duty (LA 1980, s 14B). This long stop can bar a cause of action at a date earlier than the claimant's knowledge; indeed, it can even bar a cause of action before it has accrued.

2.2.4 Persons under disability

A person under a disability is either a child, ie someone who has not yet attained the age of 18, or a patient, ie a person of unsound mind within the meaning of the Mental Health Act 1983 and who is incapable of managing and administering their property and affairs.

Where the claimant is a person under a disability when a right of action accrues, the limitation period does not begin to run until the claimant ceases to be under that disability. Therefore, for example, if the claimant is injured in an accident at the age of 16 years, the limitation period does not commence until the claimant is 18 years old and, accordingly, the claimant has until his twenty-first birthday to commence the action, ie 3 years from his eighteenth birthday.

2.2.5 Summary

Type of action	Limitation period
Contract (excluding personal injury)	6 years (LA 1980, s 5)
Tort (excluding personal injury and latent damage)	6 years (LA 1980, s 2)
Personal injury	3 years from date of knowledge (LA 1980, s 11)
Latent damage	6 years or 3 years from date of knowledge (LA 1980, s 14A)

2.3 VIABILITY AND BURDEN OF PROOF

2.3.1 Viability

The overall viability of pursuing a claim against a potential defendant needs to be considered at the earliest possible stage with the client.

Viability involves a number of issues of which the claimant needs to be aware.

(1) Defendant's solvency

There is little point in suing a defendant who is on the verge of either bankruptcy or liquidation. Enforcement of any judgment obtained would be impossible. If there is doubt as to the liquidity of the prospective defendant, then further enquiries should be made. For example, if the proposed defendant is a company, a company search should be carried out. For an individual, an inquiry agent could be instructed, although the costs of doing this must be considered.

(2) Defendant's whereabouts

Clearly, the defendant needs to be traceable and his whereabouts known in order to issue and serve proceedings. Again, an inquiry agent may be able to help.

(3) The claim itself

This involves balancing the merits of the claim itself against the overall cost of pursuing it and the prospects of a successful outcome. The client may believe he has a good claim but will be concerned as to the costs of litigation. Finance is discussed below (see **2.5**), but the client must be advised at this stage on the law, and any possible defences to the claim should be anticipated. The client must be told of the requirement in r 1.3 that parties must help the court further the overriding objective.

(4) Alternative remedies

The solicitor should consider whether there are any alternative remedies available to the client for resolving the problem and advise the client accordingly. For example, the dispute may concern a contract which contains an arbitration clause, or the client may wish to use one of the forms of alternative dispute resolution (see Chapter 15).

2.3.2 Burden of proof

There are two questions of proof which need to be considered.

(1) Legal burden

The party asserting a fact must prove it unless it is admitted by his opponent. For example, a claimant who alleges negligence must prove all the elements of the tort, ie a duty existed between the parties, the defendant breached that duty and the claimant sustained damage as a result. Similarly, a claimant alleging breach of contract must prove that a contract existed between the parties, the defendant broke the contract and the claimant suffered loss as a result.

(2) Balance of probabilities

In civil cases the claimant is required to prove a fact on a balance of probabilities. This simply requires the judge to be persuaded that the claimant's version of events is more likely to be true than the defendant's.

2.4 REMEDY SOUGHT

There are a number of alternative remedies which a claimant can pursue against the defendant assuming liability can be established. The most common remedy sought is damages.

2.4.1 Damages

The rules as to quantum of damages in civil cases depend on the type of action being pursued.

(1) Contract

A claim for damages arises when one party to the contract has failed to perform an obligation under the contract. The purpose of damages in such a situation is to place the injured party in the position he would have been in if the contract had been properly performed.

For example, damages can be recovered for either the repair of defective goods or repayment of the purchase price. In addition, there may be a claim for general damages in respect of physical discomfort and/or inconvenience. However, damages for injured feelings or mental distress are not generally recoverable. There is an exception where the subject matter of the contract was to provide enjoyment, peace of mind or freedom from distress (eg a contract for a holiday). In such cases, damages for mental distress and loss of enjoyment are recoverable.

The test for the recovery of damages for breach of contract is that they must not be too remote from the breach, ie did the loss flow naturally from the breach or was the loss within the reasonable contemplation of the parties at the time the contract was made as being the probable result of the breach?

(2) Tort

A claim for damages arises where injury, loss or damage is caused to the claimant or the claimant's property. The aim of damages is, so far as possible, to place the claimant in the position he would have been in if the damage had not occurred. Damages are therefore compensatory in nature and as a result the claimant can seek compensation for any direct loss and consequential loss providing the rules on remoteness are not broken. The rules on remoteness require that in order to be recoverable the loss must be a reasonably foreseeable consequence of the tort.

(3) Reduction in damages – duty to mitigate

Any potential claim for damages for either breach of contract or tort can be reduced if it can be shown that the claimant has failed to mitigate his loss.

2.4.2 Debt

A debt action is a particular type of contract claim. Instead of claiming damages for breach of contract, the claimant is claiming a sum which the defendant promised to pay under the contract.

For example, in a sale of goods case, if the buyer wrongfully rejects the goods (and the seller accepts this as repudiation of the contract) the seller has an action for damages for breach of contract. However, if the buyer takes delivery but then fails to pay then the action is for debt. The significance is that in the latter case the claimant has no duty to mitigate their loss.

2.4.3 Interest

Where the remedy sought by the claimant is either damages or the repayment of a debt, the court may award interest on the sum outstanding. The rules vary according to the type of claim. A claimant seeking interest must specifically claim interest in the particulars of claim.

(1) Breach of contract (including debt claims)

In contract cases, there are three alternative claims to interest:

(a) the contract itself may specify a rate of interest payable on any outstanding sum. This will be the rate negotiated between the parties. The court will usually apply this rate;
(b) if there is no contractual rate then the court has a discretion to award interest either under s 35A of the Supreme Court Act 1981 in respect of High Court cases or under s 69 of the County Courts Act 1984 in respect of county court cases. The current rate of interest awarded by the courts is 8 per cent per annum;
(c) it may be possible to claim interest under the Late Payment of Commercial Debts (Interest) Act 1998.

The interest is awarded from the date on which the cause of action accrued until either the date of judgment, or payment if sooner.

Since a debt claim is for a specified amount of money, interest must be claimed precisely giving as a lump sum the amount of interest which has accrued from breach of contract up to the date of issue of the proceedings and a daily rate thereafter. In a damages claim, the request for interest is not set out in detail if the claim is for an unspecified amount of money.

THE LATE PAYMENT OF COMMERCIAL DEBTS (INTEREST) ACT 1998

This Act gives a statutory right to interest on commercial debts which are paid late if the contract itself does not provide for interest in the event of late payment. The term 'commercial debt' includes debts arising from the supply of goods and services.

Although it is intended that all businesses will eventually be able to claim interest under the Act, it currently applies only to debts owed to small businesses (defined as those which have employed an average of 50 or fewer staff in the previous financial year).

Interest under the Act can be claimed at a rate of 8 per cent above the Bank of England's base rate, but is only payable if court proceedings are commenced to recover the debt. The interest accrues from the expiry of any period of credit under the contract. If the contract does not provide for any such period, interest can be claimed from 30 days after the latest of:

(i) delivery of the bill;
(ii) delivery of the goods;
(iii) performance of the service.

(2) Tort

The court has a general discretion to award interest on damages in any negligence action. This power is derived from the Supreme Court Act 1981, s 35A in respect of High Court claims and the County Courts Act 1984, s 69 in respect of county court claims. Generally speaking, if interest has been properly claimed the court will normally exercise its discretion to award interest for such period as it considers appropriate. The current rate of interest awarded by the courts is 8 per cent per annum.

In a personal injury case, the rules as to interest are slightly more complex. There are special rules which are outside the scope of this book.

When interest is claimed in a tort claim, it must be claimed generally if the claim is for an unspecified amount of money.

2.5 FUNDING

On taking instructions, the solicitor should give his client the best information they can about the likely cost of the matter, in accordance with Rule 15 of the Solicitors' Practice Rules. This includes advising the client on the different types of funding available.

In litigation cases, it is usually not possible to agree a fee or give an estimate of costs at the outset. But the client should be told how the solicitor's fee will be calculated (eg who is going to do the work and the hourly charging rate of that person). Often a payment on account will be required immediately and interim bills may be delivered as the case progresses. The client should be advised of any foreseeable disbursements (eg court fees) and that he can set a limit on the costs to be incurred.

The solicitor should also consider whether the client's liability for costs may be covered by insurance, and whether the likely outcome of the matter justifies the expense involved.

In addition, the solicitor should advise the client of the risk that he may be ordered to pay the opponent's costs if the case is lost.

2.5.1 Solicitor and client costs and costs between the parties

In litigation cases, the solicitor should explain to the client the distinction between solicitor and client costs (ie the sum the client must pay to his own solicitor) and costs awarded between the parties

If the client loses the case, he will have to pay his own solicitor's costs and, in addition, he will normally have to pay his opponent's costs. The opponent's costs are not necessarily all the costs incurred by the opponent.

The court will assess what costs the client must pay towards the opponent's costs (unless there is agreement on this amount between the parties). The client will only have to pay to his opponent such costs as are ordered by the court or agreed between the parties.

If the client wins the case, he will still have to pay his own solicitor's costs. He will normally receive from his opponent his costs. Again, this will be such sum as is approved by the court or agreed between the parties as being payable on a 'between the parties' basis. The client will, of course, use the costs that he receives to help towards payment of his own solicitor's bill. But, if his own solicitor's charges are more than the costs between the parties that he receives, the client will have to make up the shortfall.

However, if the client wins the case but recovers no costs from his opponent (for example, if he goes bankrupt or simply disappears) the client still has to pay his own solicitor's costs.

2.5.2 Conditional fee agreements

A conditional fee agreement (CFA) is one under which the solicitor receives no payment (or less than normal payment) if the case is lost, but normal, or higher than normal, payment if the client is successful.

A CFA is only enforceable if it meets the requirements of s 58 of the Courts and Legal Services Act 1990. This provides that a CFA:

(a) may be entered into in relation to any civil litigation matter, except family proceedings;
(b) must be in writing; and
(c) must comply with the Conditional Fee Agreements Regulations 2000 (the CFA Regulations 2000).

The CFA Regulations 2000 contain detailed requirements with which the CFA must comply, including that:

(a) The agreement must be signed by the client and his solicitor.
(b) The solicitor is obliged to provide the client with certain information and advice before the CFA is entered into much of which must be provided orally as well as being included in the written agreement. The information includes:

   (i) the circumstances in which the client will be liable for the solicitor's fees;
   (ii) the client's entitlement to have the reasonableness of those fees assessed by the court;
   (iii) whether other methods for financing the litigation are available; and
   (iv) whether insurance is appropriate (see below).

(c) The CFA must specify:

   (i) the proceedings to which it relates;
   (ii) the circumstances in which the solicitor's fees are payable;
   (iii) the amounts payable under the CFA and whether they are limited by reference to the damages recovered by the client;
   (iv) that the information at (b) above has been provided.

(d) Where the CFA provides for a success fee (see below), the agreement must briefly specify the reasons for setting the percentage uplift at the agreed level.

Drafting the CFA

It is of course essential that the CFA is carefully drafted. Consider, for example, the importance of a clear definition of the term 'win'. Does the client win if he succeeds on all aspects of his claim or is it enough that he recovers some damages (even if they represent only a small percentage of his claim)? The Law Society provides assistance in the form of a model CFA for personal injury cases, which can be adapted for other types of work. Precedents are also available in practitioner works.

The success fee

Where it is agreed that the solicitor should receive higher than normal payment if the case is won, the increase in his normal fees (known as a success fee) cannot exceed 100 per cent of the solicitor's normal charges.

If the client wins the case and his opponent is ordered to pay his costs, these will include the success fee. The opponent will, however, only be required to pay the success fee to the extent that it is reasonable (see further **13.3.8**). Where part (or all) of the success fee is disallowed, the solicitor is not entitled to recover the remainder from his client unless the court orders otherwise.

Whenever he enters into a CFA the solicitor takes a financial risk. The solicitor who regularly acts on this basis will only stay in business if the success fees he recovers on his 'wins' outweigh the fees sacrificed on his 'losses'. It is therefore essential that before entering into a CFA or agreeing the level of the success fee with a client, the solicitor should perform a thorough risk assessment. Relevant factors would include:

(i)   the chances of the client succeeding on liability;
(ii) the likely amount of the damages;
(iii) the length of time it will take for the case to reach trial;
(iv) the number of hours the solicitor is likely to have to spend on the case.

The solicitor may need to spend some time gathering evidence and information about the client's case before he can perform a full risk assessment. For example, it may be appropriate to obtain an expert opinion and/or interview witnesses (see Chapter 3). It is, of course, essential to discuss with the client what work will have to be performed before a decision can be reached about whether the solicitor is prepared to enter into a CFA and how that work is to be funded.

Funding disbursements and liability for the other side's costs

If the CFA client loses the case, he will not usually have to pay his own solicitor's fees, but will nevertheless be liable for his opponent's costs. In addition, the client will, during the course of the litigation, have to fund disbursements such as the fees of counsel and expert witnesses, as well as items such as travelling expenses. Many CFA funded clients are not in a position to pay these disbursements and/or may be concerned by the fact that they will not know until the end of the litigation whether they are liable to their opponent for costs and, if so, for how much.

In such circumstances, the client may benefit from purchasing after-the-event insurance, which provides cover for the other side's costs and his own disbursements in the event of losing the case. The premium payable depends on the strength of the client's case and the level of cover required. If the client wins, the premium, like the success fee, is recoverable from his opponent to the extent that it is reasonable. As stated above, the CFA Regulations 2000 require the solicitor to discuss with his client whether insurance is appropriate before the CFA is entered into.

Before recommending after-the-event insurance, the solicitor should check with the client whether he has the benefit of any existing legal expenses insurance (known as before the event or pre-event insurance) and, if so, on what terms. Similarly, the client should be asked whether he is a member of any trade union or other organisation that might fund the litigation. Otherwise, the client may end up paying for unnecessary after-the-event cover. A solicitor who does not make adequate enquiries in this regard may well be negligent.

Of course, obtaining after-the-event insurance to cover the client's disbursements in the event that he loses, does not solve the problem of how those disbursements are to be paid for during the course of the litigation. There are various solutions. As far as counsel's fees are concerned, counsel may be willing to enter into a CFA with the client. However, such an arrangement cannot be entered into with an expert witness. This is to avoid any possibility that the expert's evidence, which should be impartial, will be influenced if he is instructed on a 'no win, no fee' basis.

If necessary, many after-the-event insurers will arrange a loan to the client or his solicitors to fund both the disbursements and the cost of the after-the-event insurance premium. The loan may even be on terms that it is not repayable in the event that the client loses. If he wins, the interest on the loan is not recoverable from his opponent, but is usually deducted from the damages recovered.

Notifying the other side of a CFA

If the client enters into a CFA before proceedings have been issued, he should inform other potential parties to the dispute that he has done so (see para 4A of the Practice Direction on Pre-action Protocols).

Once proceedings are issued, the client must file with the court and serve on all parties a Notice of Funding in Form N251 (a copy appears in Appendix A). This informs the other parties of:

(i) the date on which the CFA was entered into;
(ii) the date of any relevant insurance policy and the name of the insurer.

If the information is not provided, the client will not be able to claim the success fee or insurance premium from his opponent if he wins the case (see r 44.15).

Where the client is a claimant and the CFA was entered into before the issue of proceedings, Form N251 must be filed when the claim form is issued. Where the client is a defendant and the CFA is entered into before the defendant files any documents with the court, Form N251 must be filed with the first such document. Otherwise, where the CFA is entered into later, Form N251 must be filed within 7 days of the date of the CFA.

If, during the course of the proceedings, there is any change to this information a notice of the change must be filed and served on all parties within 7 days.

2.5.3 Contingency fees

The Solicitors' Practice Rules define a contingency fee as any sum (whether fixed or calculated as a percentage of damages) which is payable only in the event that the client succeeds in contentious proceedings.

Rule 8 of the Solicitors' Practice Rules effectively prohibits all contingency fees in contentious proceedings except CFAs. In particular, it should be noted that it is not lawful to enter into an agreement with the client whereby if the case is won, the solicitor is rewarded by receiving a percentage of the damages recovered.

2.5.4 Insurance

Regardless of whether the client is going to enter a CFA, the solicitor should always check to see if the client has the benefit of a pre-event insurance policy which might fund the litigation. Such insurance is commonly purchased as part of household or motor insurance policies.

Where pre-event insurance cover is not available, the client may wish to consider purchasing after-the-event insurance even if he does not fund the litigation by way of a CFA. As discussed above, one of the disadvantages of litigation is that, if the case is lost, the loser will generally have to pay the winner's costs and this liability cannot be quantified until the end of the proceedings. By purchasing after-the-event insurance, the litigant removes this uncertainty (provided the cover bought is sufficient). Moreover, if he wins the case, he is likely to be able to recover the premium paid from the other side. Given these advantages, a solicitor who fails to discuss the possibility of such insurance with a client at the outset of litigation may well be negligent.

2.5.5 Trade unions

If a client is a member of a trade union, it may be possible to arrange for his union to be responsible for payment of his solicitor's costs. This is particularly so in the case of accidents arising at work.

2.5.6 Public funding

In limited circumstances, clients may receive public funding for civil litigation and the solicitor should always consider whether this might be available. Most civil litigation matters within the scope of this book will not, however, benefit from public funding and what follows is, therefore, no more than a broad outline.

Prior to 1 April 2000, public funding (previously called legal aid) was provided by the Legal Aid Board. As a result of the Access to Justice Act 1999, the Legal Aid Board was replaced by the Legal Services Commission (the LSC) which runs public funding schemes for both criminal and civil litigation. The civil litigation scheme is administered by the Community Legal Service (the CLS), which operates the Community Legal Service Fund (the CLSF).

The effect of the new arrangements is substantially to reduce the scope of public funding in litigation. CLS funding will not usually be available for cases that could be financed by a CFA. With very limited exceptions, claims in negligence for personal injury, death or damage to property (including intellectual property) are excluded. Nor is funding available for matters arising out of the carrying on of a business, including claims brought or defended by sole traders.

In addition to these restrictions, public funding is only open to clients whose income and capital falls within financial eligibility limits. These limits vary depending on whether the client is seeking full representation in proceedings, or merely wants assistance from a solicitor to investigate a proposed claim. By way of example, where the former applies the client will not qualify unless his disposable capital does not exceed £6,750 and his disposable income £8,067 per annum. (In calculating the disposable capital, equity up to £100,000 in the house where the client resides is disregarded.) It can be seen that only clients on welfare benefits or with very limited means will be eligible.

Furthermore, where the client is financially eligible and the claim is of a type covered by the CLSF, public funding will only be offered if a merits test is also satisfied. This involves considering the client's prospects of success and applying cost benefit criteria (ie weighing the likely cost of the proceedings against their benefit to the client). Put simply, a client who has a strong claim that will not be expensive to pursue, but which would result in substantial damages has a much better chance of securing funding than one whose prospects of winning are marginal or who wishes to pursue a claim which would involve costs that are disproportionate to its likely benefits.

Where a party is in receipt of public funding, he may be required to make a contribution from his disposable capital or his income towards the costs. Where a contribution is required from income, this is payable on a monthly basis for as long as the case is funded by the LSC. Any change in the client's circumstances must be notified to the LSC as it may affect the amount of the contribution or the client's entitlement to funding.

The statutory charge

Where a publicly funded client recovers money as a result of the proceedings, he may have to repay some or all of his legal costs to the LSC out of the money recovered. The statutory charge will only apply to the extent that the client does not succeed in recovering his costs from his opponent.

The same principle applies where the dispute involves property rather than money. Any property that is retained or transferred to the client is subject to the statutory charge. The most common example is a dispute in matrimonial proceedings over the ownership of the former matrimonial home.

The solicitor must ensure that the client has understood the statutory charge prior to accepting an offer of public funding.

2.6 ETHICS AND CONFLICT OF INTEREST

A detailed consideration of this area is contained in the LPC Resource Book *Pervasive and Core Topics* (Jordans), Part II, Professional Conduct.

The solicitor acting in civil proceedings must, in particular, have regard to the following rules of professional conduct.

2.6.1 Duty of confidentiality

The solicitor is under a duty to maintain the confidentiality of his client's affairs at all times unless the client's prior authority is obtained for disclosure.

2.6.2 Conflict of interest

A solicitor cannot act for two or more clients where there is a conflict of interest between them or a significant risk of such a conflict arising. A check for potential conflicts should be carried out before the client is interviewed for the first time.

In civil cases, such a situation could arise, for example, where a solicitor is instructed to act by two partners in a firm which has been sued for damages for fraudulent misrepresentation, where the allegation is that only one of the partners made the fraudulent misrepresentation.

The potential conflict arises because there is clearly a risk that the 'innocent' partner may have a right of action against the 'guilty' partner.

2.6.3 Solicitor's duty as advocate

As well as owing duties to the client the solicitor also has an overriding duty not to mislead the court. The duty to the court means that the solicitor must disclose all relevant legal authorities to the court such as statutory provisions or case-law even if these are not favourable to his case. The advocate is also under a duty to help the court achieve the overriding objective.

Finally, the solicitor who represents the client, either in a chambers hearing or in open court, must present the client's case as the client would do for himself if he had the requisite knowledge.

Under Part I of the CPR 1998, the parties, and therefore their solicitors, are required to assist the court in advancing the overriding objective. This creates a potential risk of conflict between the solicitor's duty to the court under CPR 1998, Part I and his duty to act in the best interests of his client pursuant to Rule 1 of the Solicitors' Practice Rules. The Law Society has recently amended Rule 1 of the Solicitors' Practice Rules to make it clear that a solicitor, in acting in the best interests of his client, must take account of his obligations to the court under the overriding objective.

2.7 FOREIGN ELEMENT AND CHOICE OF FORUM

If a solicitor is instructed by a client who is based abroad, or is instructed to take proceedings against a party based abroad, one of the first things which must be considered is the question of jurisdiction – in which country's courts can proceedings be commenced?

Different rules apply depending on whether the foreign country involved is in the EU or outside it.

2.7.1 EU Member States

The question of jurisdiction as between Member States of the EU is governed by the Brussels Convention on Jurisdiction and the Enforcement of Judgments in Civil and Commercial Matters 1968 (the Brussels Convention). This was incorporated into English law by virtue of the Civil Jurisdiction and Judgments Act 1982. The Civil Jurisdiction and Judgments Act 1982 also regulates jurisdiction as between the various parts of the UK (given that Scotland and Northern Ireland are separate jurisdictions).

(1) The basic rule (Article 2)

The basic rule under the Brussels Convention is that the defendant must be sued in his local courts. For an individual, that means the place where he is domiciled. For a company, it means its registered office or other official address or the place where it is centrally managed or controlled. However, if a company has branches in various EU States, and the dispute arises out of the activities of a particular branch, it can be sued in the State where that branch is located.

So, the basic rule states that, if you want to sue someone domiciled in France, you must do so in the French courts.

(2) Co-defendants (Article 6)

If a defendant is domiciled in an EU country, he can be sued there, and then other parties can be joined into the action even though they are domiciled elsewhere in the EU.

(3) Contract cases (Article 5(1))

The Brussels Convention confers jurisdiction in contract cases on the courts of the State where the contractual term in dispute was to be performed. This is an alternative to suing the defendant where he is domiciled. So, if a German company breaks its contract with an English company, and the relevant obligation under the contract was to be performed in England, the English company has the choice of suing the German company in England or Germany.

Many contracts contain jurisdiction clauses stating that, for example, the contract is governed by the law of England and Wales and any dispute must be resolved in the courts of England and Wales. In such a case, unless both parties agree to waive the jurisdiction clause, proceedings must take place in this country, irrespective of the defendant's domicile or where the obligation in question under the contract was to be performed (Article 17).

(4) Tort cases (Article 5(3))

The Brussels Convention confers jurisdiction in tort cases on the courts of the State where the tort was committed or the State where the harm caused by the tort occurred. Again, this is an alternative to suing a defendant where he is domiciled. So, if a Danish driver causes a road traffic accident in England, he can be sued in England or in Denmark.

(5) Exclusive jurisdiction (Article 16)

In some cases, such as disputes over land, the Brussels Convention confers jurisdiction on the courts of one State and proceedings must be taken there.

(6) Submission to the jurisdiction (Article 18)

If a defendant is sued in England and believes that the English courts do not have jurisdiction, he should simply acknowledge service of the claim and apply under Part 11 of the CPR 1998 for an order declaring that the court does not have jurisdiction. If he takes any further steps in the proceedings (eg by filing a defence), he will be taken to have submitted to the jurisdiction of the English courts.

Appendix B contains a flowchart dealing with the order in which items (1) to (6) should be applied in determining jurisdiction.

2.7.2 The rest of the world

(1) Defendant served in this country

The English courts can hear any proceedings if the claim form was served on the defendant whilst he was present in England and Wales (no matter how briefly). The defendant could then, however, object to the proceedings continuing in England on the ground that the English courts are not the most appropriate ones for resolving the dispute.

So, if an Englishman has an accident in New York caused by the negligence of a local New Yorker and then is able to serve the defendant with a claim form whilst he is in England on holiday, the defendant could object to the proceedings continuing in England on the basis that New York State was a more convenient forum.

(2) Applying for permission to serve out of the jurisdiction

If, on the other hand, the defendant cannot be served with the proceedings in England and Wales, the permission of the court needs to be obtained to serve him outside the jurisdiction (see **4.5.5**).

2.8 ALTERNATIVES TO A CIVIL ACTION

There are several alternatives to court proceedings which may produce the remedy the client wants, possibly at less cost. These alternative procedures should always be considered at first interview.

2.8.1 Arbitration

Arbitration is an adjudication operating outside the normal court process by which a third party reaches a decision which is binding on the parties. Many business contracts contain an arbitration clause requiring the parties to refer their disputes to arbitration rather than litigation. In the absence of such a clause, the parties in dispute may agree to arbitration once the dispute has arisen and may choose their own arbitrator with the relevant expertise. Arbitration itself is largely governed by statute, namely the Arbitration Act 1996 (provided the agreement to arbitrate is in writing).

The main advantages of the parties agreeing to arbitration instead of litigation are that: arbitration may be quicker than litigation; the procedures are less formal; the solutions reached are often more practical than those a court has power to order, and at the same time those decisions are binding on the parties. The winning party to an arbitration can apply to the High Court for leave to enforce the arbitration award as if it were a court judgment (Arbitration Act 1996, s 66).

On the other hand, the main disadvantages of using arbitration are that certain remedies, such as injunctions, are not available and, depending on the procedures adopted, the dispute may not receive the depth of investigation it would have done in the courts.

2.8.2 Alternative dispute resolution

Alternative dispute resolution (ADR) is a means of resolving disputes by using an independent third party to help the parties to reach a solution. The third party may suggest a solution to the parties but cannot impose one. ADR is voluntary; the parties choose the process and either of them can withdraw at any time before a settlement is reached. If either party does not like the proposed solution they do not have to accept it.

There are various types of ADR such as mediation, expert appraisal or expert determination.

The advantages of ADR are that it can be quicker and cheaper than litigation; it is very flexible; and it is likely to be less destructive than court proceedings on the relationship between the parties, who may have to continue a business relationship after the dispute is resolved.

The disadvantages of ADR are that either party may withdraw at any stage before a solution is reached; the awards are not enforceable in the same way as a court judgment; there is a risk that the parties may resolve the dispute without knowing all the facts; and it is not appropriate in certain cases, for example if the client needs an injunction or a ruling on a point of law.

Parties to a dispute can always reach an ad hoc agreement to use ADR, but very often it will be a term of a contract between them that, if any dispute does arise, they will resolve it by ADR.

Under the CPR 1998, the courts actively encourage parties to use some form of ADR. ADR is considered in more detail in Chapter 15.

2.8.3 Trade schemes

Some professional bodies and trade associations operate schemes under which an injured party may be able to pursue a remedy outside the courts. This is often cheaper and quicker than court proceedings.

2.8.4 Negotiating settlements

A solicitor should always consider at first interview whether it will be possible to negotiate a settlement with the opponent instead of incurring the expense of issuing legal proceedings. Negotiations should be commenced as soon as possible and a genuine attempt made to limit the areas of dispute between the parties. Once all reasonable attempts to settle have been exhausted, there may well be no alternative but to issue proceedings.

Negotiations are considered in more detail in Chapter 12.

2.8.5 Insurance

Many defendants in civil actions are insured. Drivers of motor vehicles are required by law to possess insurance which covers them for at least the minimum insurance (basically third party) under the Road Traffic Act 1988. Most professional bodies, such as The Law Society, require that their practising members be insured against negligence claims by clients.

The existence of insurers does not in any way affect the conduct of the proceedings and the insurers are not a party to the claim as there is no cause of action against them. However, the majority of insurance policies require the insured to notify them of any potential claim in order that the insurers can consider taking over the action on behalf of their insured. Where an insurance company is involved, they, or their solicitors, will usually deal with any negotiations or subsequent court proceedings.

In certain circumstances, a judgment against an insured defendant can be enforced against the insurers. Notice of the proceedings must be served on the insurers either before or within 7 days of commencing proceedings to invoke these provisions.

2.8.6 Motor Insurers Bureau

The Motor Insurers Bureau (MIB) operates two schemes which allow the victims of either uninsured or untraced drivers to recover compensation for certain losses sustained. The MIB is a scheme set up by the insurance companies and is also financed by them.

2.8.7 Criminal Injuries Compensation Authority

The Criminal Injuries Compensation Authority (CICA) is a body set up by the Government to provide the victims of criminal acts with ex gratia compensation for any personal injuries sustained as a result of those acts.

2.8.8 Criminal compensation order

The criminal courts have powers to order compensation in respect of any personal injury, loss or damage resulting from a criminal offence when imposing sentence at the conclusion of criminal proceedings.

2.9 HUMAN RIGHTS

The two areas most likely to lead to a human rights challenge which have been considered in this chapter are the rules relating to limitation and funding.

2.9.1 Limitation

Arguably, any time-limit on bringing court proceedings interferes with the right to a fair and public hearing. However, it is important to remember that the Convention also uses the words 'within a reasonable time' and every legal system in the world seems to recognise the concept that there comes a time when a potential defendant is entitled to assume that no claim will be made against him.

In *Stubbings and Others v The United Kingdom* [1997] 1 FLR 105, the applicants alleged that a ruling by the House of Lords that their claims were statute-barred under the Limitation Act 1980 amounted to a breach of Article 6(1). The European Court of Human Rights disagreed and held that it would not be appropriate to interfere with the limitation period unless it restricted or reduced the individual's access to the domestic court in such a way or to such an extent that the very essence of the right to access was impaired. A limitation period would only be incompatible with Article 6(1) if it did not have a legitimate aim or purpose and if there was not a reasonable relationship of proportionality between the purpose sought and the means employed to achieve it. The European Court of Human Rights recognised several legitimate aims in limitation periods: they provide legal certainty and finality; protect potential defendants from stale claims which might be difficult to challenge and prevent the injustice that might arise if the court was required to rule on events which took place so long ago that the evidence has become unreliable.

In the light of the decision in *Stubbings*, challenges to the Limitation Act 1980 are likely to be rare.

2.9.2 Funding

Fears have been expressed in some quarters that the abolition of public funding for most types of litigation will make it more difficult for those of limited means to bring a court case to trial. No doubt the government takes the view that the increased availability of conditional fee agreements, legal expenses insurance and the establishment of the Community Legal Service will have increased rather than restricted access to justice. The changes in the funding of litigation are as yet too recent to be certain whether this is the case. Even if it is, there will undoubtedly be particular individuals who are disadvantaged under the new regime and we may well see challenges from such individuals contending that they have been denied effective access to the courts.

The European Court of Human Rights has made it clear that the Convention does not guarantee public funding in civil cases (*Winer v UK* 1986 48 DR 154). Nor is public funding the only legitimate way in which governments may arrange to provide effective access to the courts (*Andronicou and Constantinou v Cyprus* (1998) 25 EHRR 491). On the other hand, the right to access must be 'practical and effective'. Thus, where legal representation is indispensible to enable the litigant to present his case satisfactorily, the lack of a funding regime which provides for such representation will be a breach of Article 6(1) (*Airey v Ireland* (1979-80) 2 EHRR 305).

Chapter 3

EARLY ACTION

After the first interview with the client, there are a number of preliminary steps the solicitor can take to advance the client's claim. The main requirements will be to confirm the client's instructions and to obtain relevant evidence to support the client's version of events. The solicitor will also have to bear in mind the necessity to comply with the pre-action protocols under the CPR 1998.

Chapter 3 contents
Writing to the client
Interviewing witnesses
Preserving documents
Obtaining expert evidence
Site visits
Instructing counsel
Pre-action protocols
Sending the letter of claim
Pre-action disclosure
Settlement
Researching the law

3.1 WRITING TO THE CLIENT

The solicitor should always confirm his instructions in writing, both in relation to the nature of the case itself and, specifically, any advice given on the question of funding the action. If a statement has been taken from the client, this should be sent to the client for approval and signature. The letter should explain the next steps which are to be taken by the solicitor and remind the client of any matters which he has agreed to undertake. The solicitor should, of course, comply with all the requirements of Rule 15 of the Solicitors' Practice Rules.

3.2 INTERVIEWING WITNESSES

The solicitor should arrange to take a statement from any witnesses as soon as possible, whilst matters are still fresh in their minds. There is no 'property' in a witness, and the solicitor may request an interview with anyone who may have information about the case. However, there is little that can be done if a witness absolutely refuses to give a statement. A witness may do this, for example, because he does not wish to say anything against his employer or simply because he does not wish to get involved.

At the eventual trial of the case a person can be compelled to attend as a witness, but the solicitor will be reluctant to call someone as a witness if he has not obtained a statement from him beforehand, because, of course, he will have no idea what the witness is going to say in the witness-box. Therefore, it is most important to persuade potential witnesses to give a statement if at all possible. If the witness refuses, the solicitor could use a witness summary (see **11.5**).

The solicitor will normally write to the witnesses initially and arrange a convenient time for an interview to take place. This may be at the solicitor's office, or the solicitor may have to go out to the witness's home or place of work.

When interviewing witnesses, the solicitor should be wary of people who try too hard to be helpful, and he should try to ensure that his story will stand up to cross-examination at the end of the day. It is better that any weakness in the case is identified at this stage rather than later on when a great deal of time and money has been spent on the case. The initial statement (which is sometimes called a proof of evidence) should be as comprehensive as possible, including background information which may not be directly relevant to the claim but which may assist in understanding the case. A more specific statement (known as a witness statement) containing only the evidence which the witness will give at the hearing will be prepared at a later stage, and this later statement is the one which will be served on the other parties before the hearing (see **11.2**). At this stage, therefore, there is no need to worry unduly if the statement contains matters which will not be admissible in evidence at the trial, although, before proceedings are commenced, the solicitor will have to ensure that he or she has or will have enough admissible evidence to prove his case at trial.

3.3 PRESERVING DOCUMENTS

The solicitor should ask the client to bring all relevant documents to him as soon as possible. A solicitor is under an obligation, both as a matter of professional conduct and under the CPR 1998, to ensure that the client understands the rules relating to disclosure of documents (see Chapter 10). A client who has little or no experience of the civil litigation process may be unaware, for example, that he is under an obligation during the course of the proceedings to disclose documents to the other side, even if those documents harm his case. Furthermore, if the solicitor reads the documents at an early stage, this should ensure that there is nothing to take him by surprise later on in the proceedings which may throw a different light on the case. In a case involving a contractual dispute, it is obviously imperative that the solicitor should see the contract as soon as possible to be able to advise the client properly. For example, the contract may include a jurisdiction clause, an arbitration clause or a provision imposing a limitation period for claims arising under the contract.

The client should also be made aware that the term 'documents' includes any method of recording information, such as video tapes and computer disks, and is not merely limited to written documents.

3.4 OBTAINING EXPERT EVIDENCE

3.4.1 Instructing an expert

There are numerous instances where a solicitor may need to obtain expert evidence to advance a client's claim. For example, in personal injury cases the solicitor will need to obtain a medical report before commencing proceedings.

As far as other experts are concerned, it is likely that the solicitor's firm regularly instructs particular experts in particular types of cases. For example, consulting engineers are regularly requested to report on accidents at the work place and on road traffic accidents. Similarly, if expert evidence is required on building work, it is likely that the solicitor's firm already has contacts with suitable architects and surveyors. If counsel is involved at an early stage, he may be able to recommend suitable experts for the case.

Specialist expertise is the vital quality required of an expert witness, but it is not the only quality. An ability to present a convincing report which can be easily understood, and to perform well as a witness, particularly under cross-examination, are equally important. There is no fixed test to qualify as an expert witness and anyone who has special expertise in an area can be considered as an expert. Expertise does not depend on qualifications alone, although frequently the expert will be highly qualified in his field. Expertise may have been acquired through years of practical experience. For example, an experienced carpenter with no formal qualifications could nevertheless be an expert on the proper seasoning of wood and so assist in deciding whether, say, an oak dining table was of satisfactory quality.

The usual method of instructing an expert is by letter, the content of which will vary depending on what is required of the expert.

It will be necessary to provide an expert with all the relevant statements and documents, together with any statements of case (if already in existence) and it may also be necessary to arrange for an inspection of the relevant machinery or site. The solicitor may need to take urgent steps to ensure that material to be inspected is preserved or, where this is not possible, to obtain the best alternative evidence, such as photographs or a video.

Where the client is to pay the expert's fees (eg if they are not covered by insurance or public funding), the solicitor would be wise to obtain an estimate of the likely fees and then clear this with the client. In such cases, the solicitor will prefer to obtain money on account to cover the expert's fees if possible. Where this is not done, the solicitor takes a risk, since he is responsible to the expert for payment of his charges. Unless the expert agrees in advance, he cannot be expected to limit his fee to the amount recovered at the end of the case when costs are assessed.

It is not only when acting for the claimant that the solicitor will be obtaining expert evidence. The defendant is also entitled to have expert evidence available. Proper facilities for inspection and observation should be granted to allow the defendant to do this. Both claimant and defendant will, later, be obliged to disclose any report on which they intend to rely at trial.

3.4.2 Experts' reports

When the expert's report is received, the solicitor should check it carefully. Mistakes can be made, even by an expert. The solicitor should send a copy to the client so that he also may check it and inform the solicitor of any errors.

Medical reports, in particular, can be difficult to follow. Resist the temptation simply to concentrate on the conclusion. Consult a medical dictionary where necessary.

Whoever the expert is, never be afraid to return to him for clarification of the report. If the solicitor does not understand it, there is a good chance that no one else will and that will defeat the object of obtaining the report.

3.4.3 Opinion

A significant advantage which the expert has over the ordinary witness (see **11.8**) is that the expert can give opinion evidence. For example, a surveyor may form the view that an earlier surveyor had been negligent in not observing certain defects in the structure of a building. All of these are matters of opinion, but nevertheless the expert is permitted to state them. Section 3(1) of the Civil Evidence Act 1972 provides that:

'... where a person is called as a witness in any civil proceedings, his opinion on any relevant matter on which he is qualified to give expert evidence shall be admissible in evidence.'

3.4.4 Restrictions on the use of expert evidence

The CPR 1998 have introduced very significant restrictions on the use of expert evidence. Although a party to an action is free to obtain as much expert evidence as his wishes, the extent to which such evidence can be used in court is strictly controlled. By r 35.1 of the CPR 1998, expert evidence shall be restricted to that which is reasonably required to resolve the proceedings. The court can therefore limit the number of expert witnesses who can give evidence, or order that a single joint expert be appointed, or restrict expert evidence to a written report rather than oral evidence in court. A solicitor advising a client on whether to obtain expert evidence should always bear in mind that the costs of doing so will be recoverable from the opponent (assuming the case is won) only if the court gives permission for the expert evidence to be used.

The use of expert evidence in proceedings is considered further in Chapter 11.

3.5 SITE VISITS

Site visits may be needed in an action, for the purpose of taking photographs or making plans. Plans and photographs are unlikely to be disputed if they are accurate, but, in the event of a dispute, the person who prepared the plan or took the photographs may have to give evidence, so ideally they should be prepared by someone other than the solicitor who will be acting as an advocate at the hearing. If a formal plan is required (eg in a boundary dispute), then this should normally be prepared by a surveyor. In some cases, a visit to the site of the incident, such as in a factory accident case, may be useful. On other occasions, it might help to visit the client's place of business to gain a better understanding of the nature of that business.

If the inspection will be expensive, it is advisable to obtain prior authorisation from the client.

3.6 INSTRUCTING COUNSEL

3.6.1 Use of counsel

It is not necessary to instruct a barrister (also known as counsel) in every case. As a highly trained lawyer, the solicitor should have confidence in his own knowledge and ability. The solicitor will be capable of forming an assessment of both the chance of success and the level of damages. Too frequent use of counsel may result in costs being disallowed on an assessment of costs at the end of a case.

Nevertheless, judicious use of counsel is sensible. If the issues are difficult, it is wise to instruct counsel to advise on liability.

Similarly, counsel's opinion on quantum may be needed at an early stage if the case is not straightforward. For example, if it appears that some element of the client's claim might arguably be too remote, it might be appropriate to check with counsel.

Even in these cases, however, the solicitor should have formulated his own view and counsel should be assisting with this. The solicitor should not be abrogating responsibility.

3.6.2 Method

Instructing counsel requires the preparation of a formal document (called 'Instructions to counsel'). It will bear the heading of the action (or proposed action) and should contain a list of the enclosures being forwarded to counsel. The enclosures will obviously vary with the case but will typically include copies of the client's statement, any other proofs of evidence, any existing statements of case, any experts' reports, and any relevant correspondence. It is not necessary to send counsel the whole file; some judgement should be exercised in deciding which papers counsel needs to have available.

The body of the instructions to counsel will identify the client and set out briefly both sides of the case. Counsel can refer to the enclosures for detail, but the instructions should contain sufficient information to enable the barrister to identify the major issues. The solicitor should indicate his own view of the case and draw counsel's attention to those areas on which particular advice is required.

The instructions will end with a formal request to counsel to carry out the required task.

The instructions must carry a back sheet endorsed with the title of the action, what the instructions are (eg Instructions to counsel to advise on quantum), counsel's name and chambers and the solicitor's firm's name, address and reference.

Sometimes, counsel may not be able to proceed without a conference (the name given to a meeting with counsel) with the solicitor and the client. This could occur, for example, because the facts of the case are too detailed and complicated to be able to cover all the aspects in the instructions. Alternatively, it may be that counsel's advice will, to some extent, depend on his assessment of the client as a potential witness, and this will have to be done face to face. A further situation where a conference would be needed is in a personal injury case where counsel needs to see the client in order to appreciate the extent of the injuries, typically with a scarring case.

If a conference is needed, counsel is still instructed in the usual way, but arrangements are then made with counsel's clerk for the solicitor and the client to visit counsel in chambers (the name given to a barrister's office) to discuss the case. Counsel will not normally expect to provide a written opinion after the conference, so the solicitor must take comprehensive notes at the conference. If a written opinion is required this should be made clear in the instructions, but the costs of both will not be recoverable from the other side unless the court thinks it was reasonable to do so.

Traditionally, instructions to counsel are prepared using the third person ('Counsel is instructed to ...', and 'Instructing Solicitors seek Counsel's advice on ...'). Many firms now adopt a more modern approach, setting out the instructions as if writing a letter. It is a matter for each firm to decide which approach they prefer. Nevertheless, the instructions should still be in a formal document, accompanied by a covering letter to counsel's clerk.

3.7 PRE-ACTION PROTOCOLS

Pre-action protocols are intended to be an important aspect of the CPR 1998. However, there are still only protocols for personal injury, clinical negligence, construction and defamation claims. (The details of these protocols are outside the scope of this book.) It is expected that protocols for other types of work will be introduced in due course. In addition, there is a Practice Direction on protocols.

The aims of pre-action protocols are:

(1) more pre-action contact between the parties;
(2) better and earlier exchange of information;
(3) better pre-action investigation by both sides;
(4) to put the parties in a position where they may be able to settle cases fairly and early without litigation;
(5) to enable proceedings to run to the court's timetable and efficiently, if litigation does become necessary.

Protocols deal with matters such as notification to the defendant of a possible claim as soon as possible, the form of the letter of claim, disclosure of documents, and the instruction of experts, if relevant.

Compliance with a protocol should help the parties involved make an informed decision on the merits of the case and lead to a greater number of settlements without the need for court proceedings.

Paragraph 2 of the Practice Direction states that the court will expect the parties to have complied with the substance of any protocol that applies to their dispute. Where non-compliance has led to proceedings that might otherwise not have been commenced or has led to unnecessary costs being incurred, the court may impose sanctions. These can include an order:

(i) that the party at fault pay some or all of his opponent's costs (perhaps on an indemnity basis – see **13.3.3**);
(ii) depriving a claimant who is at fault of some or all of the interest he may subsequently be awarded on any damages he recovers; or
(iii) requiring a defendant who is at fault to pay interest on some or all of any damages that are subsequently awarded to the claimant at a rate of up to 10 per cent per annum above base rate.

In exercising these powers the court should aim to place the innocent party in no worse a position than he would have been in had the protocol been complied with.

Paragraph 4 of the Practice Direction makes it clear that in cases not covered by a protocol the court will nonetheless expect the parties, in accordance with the overriding objective, to act reasonably in exchanging information and documents and in trying to avoid the need for proceedings.

3.8 SENDING THE LETTER OF CLAIM

When the solicitor is satisfied that the client has a valid claim, he should write a letter setting out full details of the claim to the prospective defendant. If the claim is of a type which is governed by a pre-action protocol, then the letter should contain all the information required by the protocol.

The letter is normally addressed to the defendant in person, but if the solicitor is already aware that the defendant has solicitors acting for him, it should be addressed to the solicitors, as it is a breach of the rules of professional conduct to write directly to a defendant in those circumstances. If the defendant is likely to be insured in respect of the claim, the solicitor should ask that the letter be passed on to the insurers.

The letter should normally require a response within a specified period of time, failing which the solicitor should warn the defendant that proceedings will be issued without further notice. The Practice Direction – Protocols says that, in the absence of any other published protocol, the parties and their advisers should follow the spirit of the existing protocols which suggest that the proceedings should not be issued without allowing the potential defendant 21 days to respond to the letter of claim. In the case of debt actions, the letter may have a fairly aggressive tone as usually in such cases that debtor will already have been given several opportunities to pay by way of reminder letters from the client. The claim letter in such a case will usually also state that, if proceedings are commenced, such proceedings will include a claim for interest and costs in addition to the debt.

If the potential defendant does not respond to the letter of claim, or responds denying liability, the next step will be to issue proceedings. Sometimes, however, the intended defendant will reply asking for further time to investigate the matter. If such a request is made, the existing protocols indicate that no proceedings should be issued for a further 3 months. Hopefully, in that period the parties will be able to negotiate a settlement, but if that has not happened it will usually be necessary to issue proceedings after all.

3.9 PRE-ACTION DISCLOSURE

In some cases, a party may wish to see documents held by the opponent in order to decide whether or not to take proceedings. An application for disclosure of documents prior to the start of proceedings is permitted under s 33 of the Supreme Court Act 1981 or s 52 of the County Courts Act 1984. The application must be supported by evidence and the procedure is dealt with in r 31.16(3) of the CPR 1998. The court may make an order for disclosure only where:

'(a) the respondent is likely to be a party to subsequent proceedings;
(b) the applicant is also likely to be a party to the proceedings;
(c) if proceedings had started, the respondent's duty by way of standard disclosure set out in rule 31.6, would extend to the documents or classes of documents of which the applicant seeks disclosure; and
(d) disclosure before proceedings have started is desirable in order to –
   (i) dispose fairly of the anticipated proceedings;
   (ii) assist the dispute to be resolved without proceedings; or
   (iii) save costs.'

An order under this Rule must specify the documents or class of documents which the respondent must disclose and require him, when making such disclosure, to specify any of those documents which he no longer has or which he claims the right or duty to withhold from inspection. The order may also specify the time and place for disclosure and inspection to take place.

Disclosure and inspection of documents is dealt with fully in Chapter 10.

3.10 SETTLEMENT

3.10.1 Negotiations

A solicitor may soon find that he is in a position to commence negotiations with his opposite number or the opponent directly (provided he is not represented) or with an insurance company (eg in a professional negligence case). The opportunity to negotiate will continue throughout the proceedings and even during the trial itself.

Further detail about the solicitor's authority to negotiate and the importance of conducting negotiations on a 'without prejudice' basis are to be found at **12.1**.

3.10.2 Pre-action offers under Part 36

It may be advantageous for a party who wishes to put forward an offer to settle to do so by way of a pre-action offer under r 36.10. This is dealt with at **12.4.1**.

3.11 RESEARCHING THE LAW

Researching the law will often not be necessary. The solicitor will be familiar with the relevant law in the areas in which he practises. Nevertheless, from time to time, unfamiliar points arise which need to be researched.

On a point of law, reference should be made to the recognised practitioner works in the relevant subject, but as textbooks rapidly become out of date, it is essential to check a current authority.

If the point to be researched is procedural then the only authorities the solicitor needs to refer to are the CPR 1998 and Practice Directions themselves, together with any relevant case-law on the interpretation of the Rules and Practice Directions.

Chapter 4

COMMENCING PROCEEDINGS

4.1 CHOICE OF COURT

Although the CPR 1998 apply to both the High Court and county courts, in some cases a solicitor will have a choice as to which court to start proceedings in. The general rule is that county courts have unlimited jurisdiction to hear all tort and contract cases. If the value of the case is £15,000 or below, it must be started in a county court. If the value of the case exceeds £15,000 then it can, if the solicitor so wishes, be started in the High Court. (A special rule applies to cases which include a claim for damages for personal injury. These must be commenced in a county court unless the value of the action is £50,000 or more.) In some cases, the High Court has exclusive jurisdiction, but these types of cases are beyond the scope of this book.

Where a claimant has the choice of issuing in the High Court or county court then, by para 2.4 of the Practice Direction to Part 7 of the CPR 1998, a claim should be started in the High Court if by reason of:

'(1) the financial value of the claim and the amount in dispute, and/or
(2) the complexity of the facts, legal issues, remedies or procedures involved, and/or
(3) the importance of the outcome of the claim to the public in general,

the claimant believes that the claim ought to be dealt with by a High Court judge.'

A claim should therefore be commenced in the High Court if that is where the case should be tried. Unless the case is complex or important to the general public (not just the parties themselves), it is unlikely to be tried in the High Court if the claim is less than £50,000 (see PD29, para 2.2). As a rough rule of thumb, therefore, you should issue in the county court for claims below £50,000 and in the High Court for claims for £50,000 or above.

There are approximately 230 county courts situated throughout England and Wales and, in most cases, the claimant can issue proceedings in any court he chooses. Similarly, if the claimant is issuing proceedings in the High Court, he has the choice of issuing in any of the District Registries of the High Court, which are usually situated in the same building as the county court, or the Central Office of the High Court in London. The High Court has three divisions, namely:

(a) the Queen's Bench Division, which includes the Admiralty Court and the Commercial Court;
(b) the Chancery Division, which includes the Companies Court and the Patents Court; and
(c) the Family Division.

If the claimant is claiming damages for breach of contract or tort, the action should be commenced in the Queen's Bench Division. The Queen's Bench Division produces a *Guide to Litigation* which is particularly aimed at those litigating in the Central Office.

Chapter 4 contents
Choice of court
Court personnel
Issuing proceedings
Parties to the action
Service
Time for service of claim form

The Commercial Court is part of the Queen's Bench Division. The Commercial Court sits in London and there are separate mercantile lists in Bristol, Birmingham, Cardiff, Chester, Leeds, Manchester, Liverpool and Newcastle for cases relating to commercial transactions. The Commercial Court produces a 'Guide to Commercial Court Practice', which gives guidance on the day-to-day practice in that court.

The Chancery Division of the High Court deals with such matters as trusts, contentious probate business, partnership actions, disputes about land, and landlord and tenant disputes. An action should be commenced in the Chancery Division if the claimant is claiming an equitable remedy such as specific performance, or if it is an intellectual property action, such as a copyright or passing-off action. As with Queen's Bench actions, a Chancery action can be commenced either in the Central Office in London or in a District Registry. Chancery matters can also be commenced in a county court.

The Family Division deals with High Court family matters which are outside the scope of this book.

Part 30 of the CPR 1998 deals with the powers of the High Court and county court to transfer matters from one court to another. Such a transfer could be:

(1) from a county court to the High Court;
(2) from the High Court to a county court;
(3) from one county court to another county court;
(4) from a District Registry to Central Office or from Central Office to a District Registry;
(5) from one Division of the High Court to another Division;
(6) to or from a specialist list (eg the Commercial Court).

In deciding whether to make a transfer order, the matters to which the court must have regard under r 30.3(2) include:

'(a) the financial value of the claim and the amount in dispute, if different;
(b) whether it should be more convenient or fair for hearings (including the trial) to be held in some other court;
(c) the availability of a judge specialising in the type of claim in question;
(d) whether the facts, legal issues, remedies or procedures involved are simple or complex;
(e) the importance of the outcome of the claim to the public in general;
(f) the facilities available at the court where the claim is being dealt with and whether they may be inadequate because of any disabilities of a party or potential witness;
(g) whether the making of a declaration of incompatibility under section 4 of the Human Rights Act 1998 has arisen or may arise.'

There are also provisions for automatic transfer to the defendant's home court in certain circumstances (see **8.5**), and provisions for transfer from Central Office to a county court if the claim is worth less than £50,000.

4.2 COURT PERSONNEL

The great bulk of both county court and High Court work is dealt with by district judges and, for matters proceeding in the Central Office in London, masters. These deal with the great majority of interim applications (see Chapter 9) and also have jurisdiction to hear trials where the amount involved does not exceed £15,000. Trials for amounts in excess of that figure are, in a county court, heard by circuit judges and, in the High Court, by High Court judges. Under Part 3 of the CPR 1998, the judges have extensive case management powers (see Chapter 8).

4.3 ISSUING PROCEEDINGS

A party who wishes to start proceedings must complete a claim form, which should either be handed in or sent to the court office. Proceedings are commenced when the court 'issues' the claim form by sealing it with the court seal (although for limitation purposes, the relevant date is the date when the court receives the claim form: see PD7, para 5.1). A copy of a claim form appears in Appendix A.

4.3.1 Completing the claim form

In addition to the points set out here, the Court Service provides detailed guidance notes on the completion of the claim form.

Claimant and defendant details

The person who makes the claim is described as the claimant and the person against whom it is made is the defendant.

The claim form must include an address at which the claimant resides or carries on business.

Where the defendant is an individual, the claimant should (if he is able to do so) include in the claim form an address at which the defendant resides or carries on business. This applies even if the defendant's solicitors have agreed to accept service of the claim form on the defendant's behalf.

Where one of the parties is not an individual over the age of 18 or is not suing or being sued in his personal capacity, special considerations may apply (see **4.4**). The Court Service guidance notes set out how these should be reflected in the claim form.

Brief details of claim

The claim form must contain a concise statement of the nature of the claim and specify the remedy that the claimant is seeking (see r 16.2(1) and the notes on completing the claim form).

The amount claimed/value

PD 7 at para 3 requires that if the claim is for money, the claim form must either state the amount claimed or, if the claim is for an unspecified amount of money (including a claim for damages), whether or not the claimant expects to recover:

(a) not more than £5,000; or
(b) more than £5,000 but not more than £15,000; or
(c) more than £15,000; or
(d) that the claimant cannot say how much he expects to recover.

In personal injury cases, the form must also state whether or not the claimant expects to recover more than £1,000 general damages for pain, suffering and loss of amenity.

This information assists the court in appropriately allocating the claim to the multi, fast or small claims track. Allocation of cases is dealt with in detail in Chapter 8.

The court fee

The claimant is obliged to pay a fee on issue of the claim form, based on the value of the claim. The amount of the fee should be stated on the front of the form. Details of court fees are contained in the Guide to Supreme Court Fees and the Guide to county court fees (which are available on the Court Service website).

Solicitor's costs

If the claim is for a specified amount of money, and was issued by a solicitor, the form should also include a figure for solicitor's costs. These are the fixed costs payable by the defendant, in addition to the court fee, should he admit the claim. Fixed costs are dealt with in Part 45 of the CPR 1998.

Issues under the Human Rights Act 1998

The claimant is obliged to state whether the claim does or will include any issues under the Human Rights Act 1998.

The particulars of claim

The details of the claimant's action, known as the particulars of claim, must either be set out in the claim form itself or in a separate document served within 14 days of the claim form. Care is needed in the drafting of the particulars of claim and this issue is considered in Chapter 6.

The statement of truth

The CPR 1998 requires that various documents, including the claim form, are verified by a statement of truth (see CPR 1998, Part 22). If the particulars of claim are served separately they must also be so verified.

The statement of truth may be signed either by the claimant, by his legal representative or by his litigation friend (see below at **4.4.1**). Where signed by the legal representative, the statement of truth will refer to 'the claimant's belief', whereas a client who is an individual should refer to his own belief. A legal representative who signs must do so in his own name, rather than in the name of his firm (PD 22 at para 3.10).

Where a legal representative signs a statement of truth, para 3.8 of PD 22 states that this will be taken as his statement:

'(1) that the client on whose behalf he has signed had authorised him to do so,
(2) that before signing he had explained to the client that in signing the statement of truth he would be confirming the client's belief that the facts stated in the document were true, and
(3) that before signing he had informed the client of the possible consequences to the client if it should subsequently appear that the client did not have an honest belief in the truth of those facts.' (The consequences are that

proceedings for contempt of court may be brought against the client: see r 32.14).

If a statement of case (which includes a claim form) is not verified by a statement of truth, it remains effective unless the court strikes it out, which the court may do on its own initiative or on the application of another party. If the statement of case is not struck out, the claimant will not, however, be allowed to rely on its contents as evidence (for example on an interim application: see Chapter 8).

4.4 PARTIES TO THE ACTION

If the claimant and defendant are both individuals of full age suing or being sued in their personal capacity, then there are no special considerations. In other cases, there may be special considerations because of the nature of the party concerned, for example, in cases where the claimant or defendant is a child, a patient, a partnership or a limited company. These special rules are considered below.

4.4.1 Children and patients

A child is a person aged under 18 and a patient is a person who is incapable of managing and administering his own affairs because of a mental disorder, as defined by the Mental Health Act 1983. Part 21 of the CPR 1998 contains special provisions relating to these types of litigant.

(1) The requirement for a 'litigation friend'

The Rules require a patient to have a litigation friend to conduct proceedings, whether as claimant or defendant, on his behalf. A child must also have a litigation friend to conduct proceedings on his behalf unless the court orders otherwise. In the case of patients, the litigation friend will usually be a person authorised under Part VII of the Mental Health Act 1983 to conduct legal proceedings in the name of a patient, and, in the case of a child, the litigation friend will normally be a parent or guardian.

By para 2.1 of the Practice Direction relating to Part 21: Children and Patients:

> 'It is the duty of a litigation friend fairly and competently to conduct proceedings on behalf of a child or patient. He must have no interest in the proceedings adverse to that of the child or patient and all steps and decisions he takes in the proceedings must be taken for the benefit of the child or patient.'

In relation to proceedings against a child or patient, a person may not, without permission of the court, make an application against a child or patient before proceedings have started or take any step in proceedings except:

- issuing and serving a claim form; or
- applying for the appointment of a litigation friend under r 21.6.

(2) Steps to be taken by a litigation friend

A person authorised under Part VII of the Mental Health Act 1983 to act as a litigation friend on behalf of a patient must file an official copy of the document which is his authority to act. Otherwise, a litigation friend acting on behalf of a patient or child must file a certificate of suitability. If acting on behalf of a claimant, this must be done when making the claim and, if acting on behalf of a defendant, when first taking a step in the proceedings. The certificate of suitability must state that the proposed litigation friend:

- consents to act;
- believes the party to be a child or patient (with reasons and medical evidence);
- can fairly and competently conduct proceedings on behalf of the party;
- has no adverse interest;
- if acting as a litigation friend for a claimant, undertakes to pay any costs which the claimant may be ordered to pay in the proceedings. (A counterclaim – see Chapter 7 – is treated like a claim for the purposes of the costs undertakings.)

The litigation friend must serve the certificate of suitability on every person on whom the claim form should be served and must then file a certificate of service when filing the certificate of suitability.

(3) Cessation of appointment of a litigation friend

In relation to a child, the appointment of a litigation friend ceases when the child becomes 18. The appointment of a litigation friend for a patient does not cease when the party ceases to be a patient. It continues until the appointment is ended by a court order sought by the former patient, the litigation friend, or any party.

(4) Settlement of cases brought by or against a child or patient

Special provisions apply where a case involving a child or patient is settled. Such a settlement is not valid unless it has been approved by the court. Before the court approves a settlement, it will need to know:

(a) whether and to what extent the defendant admits liability;
(b) the age and occupation (if any) of the child or patient;
(c) that the litigation friend approves of the proposed settlement.

Additional information is required in personal injury claims (see PD 21 at para 6.2).

The application to the court must, in most cases, be supported by a legal opinion on the merits of the settlement and the instructions on which it was based. Although the application will be heard in private, the formal approval of the settlement will usually be given publicly in open court – see *Beathem v Carlisle Hospitals NHS Trust* (1999) *The Times*, May 20.

If a claim by or against a child or patient is settled before proceedings are begun and proceedings are issued solely to obtain the court's approval of the settlement, the claim must include a request to the court for approval of the settlement and must be made under Part 8 of the CPR 1998 (see **7.3**).

If money is recovered by or on behalf of or for the benefit of a child or patient, or money paid into court is accepted by or on behalf of a child or patient, the money should be dealt with in accordance with the directions of the court. The court will usually direct that the money be paid into the High Court for investment. In relation to a child, the money must be paid out when the child becomes 18.

4.4.2 Partnerships

(1) Where a partnership is the claimant

Partnerships may sue in the name of the firm or by naming individual partners. It will often be simpler to use the firm name.

(2) Where a partnership is the defendant

Partnerships may be sued in the name of the firm or in the names of the individual partners. The names of the partners may be discovered by checking the firm's notepaper or the list of partners kept at the firm's principal place of business.

It is generally felt that one advantage of suing a partnership in the name of the firm is that service on the firm can be effected by serving any one of the partners or by serving the firm at its principal place of business. One disadvantage, however, of using the firm name is that if the claimant obtains judgment against the firm then the court's permission will be required before enforcing any judgment against persons not identified in the proceedings as partners who have not acknowledged service of the particulars of claim.

4.4.3 Sole traders

(1) Where a sole trader is the claimant

Sole traders are not allowed to sue in their business name; they must use their own name for the proceedings.

(2) Where a sole trader is the defendant

Sole traders carrying on business with a name other than their own can be sued in that name. In that case, the proceedings can be served on the sole trader either at his residence or at his place of business. If the trader is sued under his trade name, he will be referred to in the heading to the action as, for example, 'Anthony Tucker T/A Marble Designs' (T/A is an acceptable abbreviation of 'trading as').

4.4.4 Limited companies

(1) Where a limited company is the claimant

A company can sue under its corporate name.

(2) Where a limited company is the defendant

A company can be sued under its corporate name.

Before commencing proceedings against a company, the claimant should carry out a company search to confirm the corporate status and continued existence of the proposed defendant company, to confirm the correct name of the company and to ascertain the registered address of the company if it is intended to serve the company at its registered office.

4.4.5 Addition and substitution of parties (Part 19 of the CPR 1998)

On occasions, it will be necessary for another party to be added to an action or for a party to be replaced by another. For example, A may take proceedings against B for damages for negligence, and subsequently may discover that C was also negligent. A may then want to add C to the proceedings as a second defendant.

Or, A may sue B (an individual) for a debt, but A then discovers that his contract was not with B trading on his own account but with a company controlled by B. A will want to substitute the company for B as defendant.

As stated in r 19.4(2), an application for permission to remove, add or substitute a party may be made by:

'(a) an existing party; or
(b) a person who wished to become a party.'

The application may be made without notice and must be supported by evidence.

Nobody may be added or substituted as a claimant unless he has given his consent in writing and that consent has been filed with the court.

Rule 19.2 states:

'(2) The court may order a person to be added as a new party if –
  (a) it is desirable to add the new party so that the court can resolve all the matters in dispute in the proceedings; or
  (b) there is an issue involving the new party and an existing party which is connected to the matters in dispute in the proceedings, and it is desirable to add the new party so that the court can resolve that issue.
(3) The court may order any person to cease to be a party if it is not desirable for that person to be a party to the proceedings.
(4) The court may order a new party to be substituted for an existing one if –
  (a) the existing party's interest or liability has passed to the new party; and
  (b) it is desirable to substitute the new party so that the court can resolve the matters in dispute in the proceedings.'

Special provisions apply where parties are to be added or substituted after the end of the relevant limitation period.

Rule 19.5 states:

'(2) The court may add or substitute a party only if –
  (a) the relevant limitation period was current when the proceedings were started; and
  (b) the addition or substitution is necessary.
(3) The addition or substitution of a party is necessary only if the court is satisfied that –
  (a) the new party is to be substituted for a party who was named in the claim form in mistake for the new party;
  (b) the claim cannot properly be carried on by or against the original party unless the new party is added or substituted as claimant or defendant; or
  (c) the original party has died or had a bankruptcy order made against him and his interest or liability has passed to the new party.'

Part 19 also contains provisions enabling the Crown to be joined as a party to proceedings in which the court may wish to make a declaration of incompatibility in accordance with s 4 of the Human Rights Act 1998.

4.5 SERVICE

Once a claim form has been issued by the court, then it must be served on the other parties.

The rules governing service are set out in Part 6 of the CPR 1998.

4.5.1 Methods of service generally available

(1) Personal service

This is effected by leaving the document with the party (if an individual), a person holding a senior position (if the party is a company or other corporation), or a partner or person having control or management of the partnership business at its principal place of business (if the partners have been sued in the name of their firm). If the document is served after 5 pm on a business day or at any time on a bank holiday, Christmas Day or Good Friday, it will be treated as being served on the next business day.

(2) First-class post

This is deemed effective the second day after the document was posted to the address for service of the person to be served.

(3) Leaving the document

This is deemed effective on the day after the document was left at the address for service of the person to be served.

(4) Through a document exchange

This is deemed effective on the second day after it was left at the document exchange. The address for service of the party to be served must include a document exchange box number on his writing paper or that of his solicitor. This method of service cannot be used if the party has indicated in writing that he is unwilling to be served by DX.

(5) By fax

This is deemed effective on the day of transmission if transmitted before 4 pm on a business day or the next business day if transmitted otherwise. The party to be served or his legal representative must have indicated in writing to the party serving a willingness to accept service by fax and the fax number to which the document should be sent. A fax number set out on a statement of case or a response to a claim filed at the court is assumed so to indicate, but the mere presence of a fax number in a party's standard business letterhead is not (*Molins plc v GDSA* (2000) *The Times*, March 1). It is advisable also to send a hard copy in case the fax was not received.

(6) By other electronic means (eg e-mail)

This is permitted only when both the party serving and the party to be served are legally represented and the latter's solicitors have agreed in writing to the method of service and have provided an e-mail address or other electronic identification. It is effective on the second day after the day on which it was transmitted. Again, it is advisable to send a hard copy.

4.5.2 Calculating the deemed date of service

In calculating the date on which a document is deemed to be served, it should be noted that r 2.8 excludes a Saturday, Sunday, bank holiday, Christmas Day or Good Friday from calculations of periods of 5 days or less (see **5.2**).

4.5.3 Service by the court

Documents will usually be served by the court and the court will choose the appropriate method of service which will normally be by first-class post. A party who prepares a document which will be served by the court must provide the court with enough copies for the court to serve it on all other parties, together with a copy for the court's files.

Rule 6.3(1) provides that the court will not effect service where:

(a) a Rule or Practice Direction provides otherwise; or
(b) the court orders otherwise; or
(c) the party on whose behalf the document is to be served notifies the court that he wishes to serve it himself;
(d) the court has failed to serve the document and has sent a notice of non-service to the party on whose behalf the document was to be served.

Where the court has been unable to effect a service, it will notify the party who requested service. The notice will state the method of service attempted and service then becomes the responsibility of that party.

4.5.4 Addresses for service (r 6.5)

All parties must give an address for service within England and Wales and, if the party is legally represented, the address for service is his solicitor's address. This does not apply to service of the claim form (see **4.5.5**).

Where no solicitor is acting, and the party has not given an address for service, then service must be effected at the place shown in the following table:

NATURE OF PARTY TO BE SERVED	PLACE OF SERVICE
Individual	• Usual or last known residence
Proprietor of business	• Usual or last known residence or • Place of business or last known place of business.
Individual who is suing or being sued in the name of a firm	• Usual or last known residence or • Principal or last known place of business of the firm
Corporation incorporated in England and Wales other than a company	• Principal office of the corporation or • Any place within the jurisdiction where the corporation carries on its activities and which has a real connection with the claim
Company registered in England and Wales	• Principal office of the company or • Any place of business of the company within the jurisdiction which has a real connection with the claim
Any other company or corporation	• Any place within the jurisdiction where the corporation carries on its activities or • Any place of business of the company within the jurisdiction

NB 1: If a solicitor is authorised to accept service on behalf of a party and has so notified the other party, the document must be served on the solicitor.

NB 2: A company registered in England and Wales may also be served at its registered office.

4.5.5 Special rules relating to service of the claim form

The claim form should be served in one of the ways set out above, but rr 6.13–6.16 contain some special provisions.

Where the defendant is legally represented, the claim form may only be served on the defendant's solicitor if he is authorised to accept service. Where he has been nominated to accept service, however, this is the only address at which the claim form can be properly served (*Nanglegan v Royal Free Hampstead NHS Trust* (2001) *The Times*, February 14, CA).

If the claim form is served by the court, the court must send the claimant a notice which will include the date when the claim form is deemed to be served.

Where the claim form is served by the claimant, he must file a certificate of service within 7 days of service of the claim form, and may not obtain judgment in default (see **5.6**) unless he has filed the certificate of service (r 6.14).

The other special provisions concern service of the claim form by a contractually agreed method (r 6.15) and service of a claim form on the agent of an overseas principal (r 6.16).

4.5.6 Service out of the jurisdiction

(1) EU countries

No special permission is required to serve a defendant based in Scotland, Northern Ireland or any other EU country, provided the English courts have jurisdiction under the Brussels Convention (see Chapter 2).

The claim form must, however, contain a statement on the grounds on which the claimant is entitled to serve it outside the jurisdiction (r 6.19).

The usual form of words (set out in PD 6B) is:

> **I state that the High Court of England and Wales has power under the Civil Jurisdiction and Judgments Act 1982 to hear this claim and that no proceedings are pending between the parties in Scotland, Northern Ireland or another Convention territory of any contracting State as defined in section 1(3) of the Act.**

The time for responding to the claim form will usually be extended to 21 days.

There are special provisions as to the methods of service that are acceptable where the claim form is to be served outside the jurisdiction (see rr 6.24–6.26).

(2) Non-EU countries

The claimant must obtain permission to serve proceedings on a defendant outside the EU, for example an American company (but note that if such a company has an office in England and Wales, it could be served there just as if it were an English company).

The grounds for obtaining permission are set out in r 6.20 of the CPR 1998. Examples of the grounds set out in r 6.20 are where the claim is brought to enforce a contract which is governed by English law, or where the breach of contract occurred in England and Wales.

The application must be supported by evidence and is made without notice.

If an order permitting service outside the jurisdiction is made, the time-limit for responding to the claim will again be extended.

Service is usually effected through the judicial authorities of the State in question or the British Consul.

4.6 TIME FOR SERVICE OF CLAIM FORM

The claim form should be served within 4 months of being issued (r 7.5), although the court has a discretion to extend this period. It is preferable to apply for an extension before the 4-month period expires, since if the claimant does not apply for an extension until after that date, r 7.6(3) provides that the court may only extend time for service if:

(i) the court has been unable to serve the claim form; or

(ii) the claimant has taken all reasonable steps to serve the claim form but has been unable to do so; and

(iii) in either case, the claimant has acted promptly in making the application.

In *Vinos v Marks & Spencer plc* (2000) Lawtel, 8 June, the claim form was served 9 days after the expiry of the 4-month period. The claimant's solicitors had no explanation for this other than that it was an oversight and their application for an extension was dismissed. The Court of Appeal upheld the decision, holding that the wording of r 7.6(3) was such that an extension could not be granted in these circumstances as neither grounds (i) nor (ii) applied.

This decision has been followed in other cases. For example, extensions have been refused where the claimant's solicitor was mistaken as to the date on which the claim form was issued (*Satwinder Kaur v CTP Coil Ltd* (2000) unreported, 10 July); where the claimant's solicitor mistakenly served the defendant when he should have served the claim form on the defendant's solicitors who were nominated to accept service (*Nanglegan v Royal Free Hampstead NHS Trust* (2001) *The Times*, February 14, CA) and where the defendant's solicitors were served in the mistaken belief that they were authorised to accept service (*Smith v Probyn* (2000) *The Times*, March 29).

Chapter 5

RESPONDING TO PROCEEDINGS AND JUDGMENT IN DEFAULT

5.1 INTRODUCTION

When either the court or the claimant serves the Particulars of Claim on the defendant, they must also send the defendant Form N1C (Notes for Defendants) and Form N9 (the Response Pack). Copies of these forms appear in Appendix A. The Notes and the Response Pack explain to defendants how they should respond to the proceedings and the time-limits for doing so. There are three ways in which a defendant may respond, namely:

(a) by filing an acknowledgement of service;
(b) by filing a defence;
(c) by filing an admission.

It is important to note that the defendant need only respond once he has been served with the particulars of claim. Where he is served with a claim form, with particulars of claim 'to follow' he need do nothing.

Before considering these steps in turn, it is important to be clear about the rules relating to the calculation of the time for doing any act, such as filing an acknowledgement of service. As we shall see later in this chapter, if the defendant does not respond within the appropriate time period, the claimant may enter judgment in default against the defendant. It is essential that a party and his legal adviser are clear about the meaning of the various time periods prescribed in the rules.

Chapter 5 contents
Introduction
Computation of time
Acknowledgement of service
The defence
Admissions
Default judgments
Human rights

5.2 COMPUTATION OF TIME

Rule 2.8 sets out how to calculate any period of time for doing an act which is specified in the Rules, a Practice Direction or by a judgment or order of the court.

Any period of time expressed as a number of days will be a period of clear days as defined by r 2.8.

> *Example 1*
> On 1 October, the defendant is served with the particulars of claim. The defendant has 14 days (not including the day of service of the particulars of the claim) within which to either acknowledge service or file a defence. The deadline for doing so is 15 October.
>
> However, it should be noted that in computing a period of 5 days or less, any weekend or bank holiday must be ignored.

Example 2

An application to the court has been fixed for hearing on a Monday. Generally, the notice of the application must be served on the other party at least 3 days prior to the hearing. The notice must be served on the preceding Tuesday (ie where notice of a hearing is being given, both the day on which notice is served and the day of the hearing are excluded in calculating the clear days.)

If the time for doing an act ends on a day when the court office is closed, the time does not actually expire until the end of the first day on which the court office is next open.

Any order imposing a time-limit should, wherever practicable, give a calendar date (eg Monday, 19 October) and a time of day (eg 4 pm) for compliance.

Example 3

Month means a calendar month. So if a claim form is issued on 12 October, it must be served no later than 11 February.

5.3 ACKNOWLEDGEMENT OF SERVICE

When served with the particulars of claim, the defendant usually has a choice of what to do: he may either simply acknowledge service or file a defence. The defendant may acknowledge service if he is unable to file a defence in time or if he wishes to contest the court's jurisdiction. The time for acknowledging service is 14 days from service of the particulars of claim (which may have been set out on the claim form, served with it, or served subsequently).

The acknowledgement of service form is part of the response pack (Form N9). On the form, the defendant should set out his name in full and, if his name has been incorrectly set out in the claim form, it should be correctly set out on the acknowledgement of service form, followed by the words 'described as' and the incorrect name (eg John Patrick Smith described as Pat Smith). The defendant's address for service, which must be within England or Wales, must be stated. This will either be the defendant's residence or business address or, if the acknowledgement of service form is signed by his solicitor, his solicitor's address. The defendant must state on the form whether he intends to defend all of the claim, part of the claim, or wishes to contest jurisdiction. The form must be signed by the defendant or his solicitor. The defendant must file the completed acknowledgement of service form at court. The court will then forward a copy to the claimant.

If a defendant does wish to dispute the jurisdiction of the court, then he does not submit to the court's jurisdiction by filing an acknowledgement of service but, after filing the acknowledgement of service, he must then challenge the jurisdiction within the time-limit for filing a defence (see **5.4**) or he will be treated as having submitted to the jurisdiction. The application to the court to dispute the court's jurisdiction must be supported by evidence as to why England and Wales is not the proper forum for the case. If the court grants the defendant's application and finds that the claim should not have been brought in England and Wales, then the claim form will usually be set aside. In effect, that brings the proceedings to an end.

If the court refuses the defendant's application, then the original acknowledgement of service ceases to have effect and the defendant must file a further acknowledgement within 14 days or such other period as the court may direct.

5.4 THE DEFENCE

The defendant, if he wishes to defend the claim, must file a defence within 14 days of service of the particulars of claim or, if the defendant has acknowledged service, within 28 days of service of the particulars of claim. There are forms which the defendant can use which will have been served as part of the Response Pack. In the case of a claim for a specified amount, the appropriate form is Form N9B and, in the case of a claim for an unspecified amount or a non-money claim, the appropriate form is Form N9C. In practice, these forms will usually be used by defendants who are acting in person, but where solicitors are acting for a defendant, then the defence will usually be prepared as a separate document (see Chapter 6).

The time for filing a defence may be extended by agreement between the parties for a period of up to 28 days. If the parties do reach such an agreement, the defendant must give the court written notice of the agreement.

Any further extension can be authorised only by the court. The court will usually grant an extension but, if the claimant has complied with the pre-action protocols, such extension will be likely to be for a short period of time and will be granted at the defendant's expense. If, however, the claimant did not comply with the pre-action protocols, the court is likely to conclude that the defendant should be granted a significant extension of time. If the claimant has unreasonably refused to grant a voluntary extension of time and/or has opposed the defendant's application to the court unreasonably, the court may well order the claimant to pay the defendant's costs of seeking the extension.

When the defence is filed, a copy must be served on all other parties. The court will effect service, unless the defendant's solicitor has told the court that he will do so.

The contents of a defence, as required by the CPR 1998, are dealt with in Chapter 6.

5.5 ADMISSIONS (PART 14)

If a defendant wishes to admit either the whole or part of the claim, then the defendant should complete the appropriate sections of the Response Pack. The way in which the defendant should complete the forms and the consequences of doing so vary depending on the nature of the claim and whether the admission is in full or only in part.

5.5.1 Admissions in full of a claim for a specified amount

If a defendant admits the whole of a claim for a specified amount, he should serve the appropriate form of admission (Form N9A) on the claimant. This should be done within 14 days of service of the particulars of claim. On Form N9A, the defendant has to give certain personal details, together with details of his income and expenditure and he should also make an offer of payment, which can either be an offer to pay in full by a certain date, or an offer to pay by monthly instalments.

Upon receipt of the form, the claimant may then file a request for judgment. If the claimant accepts the defendant's offer to pay either by a certain date or by monthly instalments, then the claimant simply accepts the defendant's offer and files a request for judgment.

If the claimant rejects the defendant's offer to pay by a certain date or to pay by instalments, then the court will decide the appropriate order. If the claim is for not more than £50,000, a court officer may decide the rate of payment without any court hearing or, alternatively, the rate of payment will be decided by a judge. Where the rate of payment is to be decided by a judge, then the proceedings must be automatically transferred to the defendant's home court, if the defendant is an individual. The judge may make the decision without any hearing but, if there is to be a hearing, the parties must be given at least 7 days' notice. In deciding the time and rate of payment the court will take into account:

(a) the defendant's statement of means;
(b) the claimant's objections to the defendant's request; and
(c) any other relevant factors.

5.5.2 Part admission of a claim for a specified amount

If a defendant admits only part of a claim for a specified amount, he must do so by filing Form N9A at the court within 14 days of service of the particulars of claim. The court will then give notice of the admission to the claimant who must say whether he:

(a) accepts the offer in full satisfaction of his claim; or
(b) accepts the offer but not the defendant's proposals for payment; or
(c) rejects the offer and wishes to proceed with his claim.

The claimant has 14 days in which to file his notice and serve it on the defendant. If he does not do so, the claim will be stayed until he does file his notice.

If the claimant accepts the offer he will request judgment.

If the defendant has not requested time to pay, the claimant's request can stipulate the time for payment and the court will enter judgment accordingly.

If the defendant has requested time to pay, the procedure in **5.5.1** applies.

If the claimant rejects the offer, the case continues as a defended action.

5.5.3 Admissions of a claim for an unspecified amount (no offer made)

Where the defendant admits liability for a claim for an unspecified amount and makes no offer of payment, he must do so within the usual time for making an admission. The court will serve a copy of the admission on the claimant who may then apply for judgment.

The court will then enter judgment for the damages to be assessed. The hearing at which the damages are assessed is often called a 'disposal hearing'. Where needed, the court will give directions to the parties as to the steps to be taken to prepare for the disposal hearing and may also allocate the case to a track if that is appropriate (see Chapter 8).

5.5.4 Admissions of a claim for an unspecified amount (offer made)

Where the defendant admits liability for a claim for an unspecified amount and offers a sum of money in satisfaction of the claim, he must do so in the usual time for making an admission.

The court will serve a notice on the claimant requiring him to return the notice stating whether or not he accepts the amount in satisfaction of the claim. If he does not file the notice within 14 days, his claim will be stayed until he does file the notice.

If the claimant does not accept the amount offered, he will enter judgment for damages to be assessed at a disposal hearing.

If the claimant accepts the offer and the defendant has not asked for time to pay, the claimant may enter judgment for the amount offered and will stipulate when payment should be made.

If the defendant has asked for time to pay the usual procedure applies (see **5.5.1**).

5.5.5 Challenging the court's decision

Where the court has decided the time and rate of payment and the decision was made either:

(a) by a court officer; or
(b) by a judge without any hearing,

either party may apply for a redetermination by a judge. Such application must be made within 14 days of service of the determination on the applicant.

The case must be transferred to the defendant's home court if the claim is for a specified amount and the defendant is an individual (unless the case was started in a specialist list).

If the original decision was made by a court officer, the redetermination will be made by a judge without a hearing unless the application notice requests a hearing.

If the original decision was made by a judge, the redetermination must be at a hearing unless the parties agree otherwise.

5.5.6 Interest

Judgment where the defendant admits liability for the whole amount of a claim for a specified amount will include interest at the date of judgment if:

(a) interest has been properly claimed in the particulars of claim; and
(b) where the claim is for statutory interest it does not exceed 8 per cent per annum; and
(c) the claimant's request for judgment includes a calculation of interest from issue to judgment.

If the above conditions are not satisfied, the judgment will be for an amount of interest to be decided by the court and the court will give directions as to how this should be achieved.

5.5.7 Varying the rate of payment

By para 6.1 of the Practice Direction to Part 14, either party may apply to vary the time and rates of payment of a judgment on admissions if there has been a change of circumstances.

5.6 DEFAULT JUDGMENTS

5.6.1 Introduction

Once the proceedings have been served upon the defendant, it may be that the defendant takes no action. The defendant may fail to return the acknowledgement of service or file a defence. In those circumstances, the claimant can obtain judgment in default against the defendant. This means that the claimant obtains judgment without there being a trial of the issues involved in the case.

Cases where default judgment is not available

The claimant may not enter a default judgment in the following types of cases:

(a) if the claim is for delivery of goods under an agreement regulated by the Consumer Credit Act 1974;
(b) if it is a Part 8 claim (see Chapter 7);
(c) if it is a mortgage claim;
(d) if it is a claim for provisional damages;
(e) if it is in a specialist court.

5.6.2 Procedure

The claimant applies for default judgment by filing a request using the relevant form if he is claiming money (whether or not it is a claim for a specified amount) or goods (if the claim form gives the defendant the option of returning the goods). There are different forms, depending on whether the claim is for a specified or an unspecified amount. (See Forms N205A, N225A and N226.)

The claimant must satisfy the court that:

(a) the particulars of claim have been served on the defendant;
(b) the defendant has not acknowledged service/filed a defence and the relevant time period has expired;
(c) the defendant has not satisfied the claim;
(d) the defendant has not admitted liability for the full amount of the claim.

5.6.3 Claims for specified amounts

A request for default judgment for a specified amount may indicate the date for full payment or the times and rate at which it is to be paid by instalments. If it does not, the court will normally give judgment for immediate payment. Additional fixed costs are payable by the defendant (see CPR 1998, Part 45).

5.6.4 Claims for unspecified amounts

A request for default judgment for a claim for an unspecified amount is a request for the court to decide the amount of the claim and costs. This will involve a full hearing before a trial judge to decide the amount of the claim (again often called a disposal hearing), and it may, therefore, be necessary to allocate the claim to a track and give directions (see Chapter 8).

5.6.5 Interest

The default judgment may, in the case of a claim for a specified amount, include interest from the date of judgment if:

(a) the particulars of claim include the necessary details;
(b) any claim for statutory interest does not exceed 8 per cent per annum;
(c) the request for judgment includes a calculation of the amount of interest from the date from which it was calculated in the claim form to the date of request.

Otherwise the court will decide the amount of interest and will give directions for this.

5.6.6 Co-defendants

Where there are co-defendants, the claimant may enter a default judgment against one or more of the co-defendants whilst proceeding with his claim against the other defendants, provided the claim can be dealt with separately from the other defendants. Otherwise, the court will not deal with the default judgment until it deals with the claim against the other defendants.

5.6.7 Setting aside a default judgment

A defendant against whom a default judgment has been entered may apply to have it set aside. Such applications are considered in Chapter 9.

5.7 HUMAN RIGHTS

There is potential for an argument that the fact that a claimant can get a default judgment and thereby bring the case to an end deprives the defendant of his right to 'a fair and public hearing'. The counter argument is that the defendant still has the power to apply to set aside that judgment if he has a defence with real prospects of success. English default judgments have been recognised and enforced by the courts of other European Union States under the Brussels Convention on Jurisdiction and Enforcement of Judgments. That said, however, in most other European jurisdictions a claimant cannot obtain judgment merely because the defendant has failed to respond to the court proceedings. Instead, the claimant has to prove his claim judicially by presenting evidence to the court, and so there is a possibility that the default judgment procedure could be held to be a breach of the European Convention for the Protection of Human Rights and Fundamental Freedoms.

Chapter 6

STATEMENTS OF CASE

6.1 INTRODUCTION

Statements of case are the formal documents in which the parties set out their respective cases. They are served between the parties (as well as being filed at court) so that each party knows the case he will have to meet at the hearing. The statements of case are central to the litigation, since at trial the court will only decide those issues which are raised in the statements of case. They therefore require to be carefully drafted.

The claimant's first statement of case after the claim form is called the particulars of claim. As has been seen in Chapter 4, this may be contained within the claim form itself or be set out in a separate document served either with the claimant's claim form or within 14 days thereafter.

The defendant's statement of case is called a defence. Frequently, the only statements of case in an action will be the particulars of claim and the defence. In some cases, however, a claimant may wish to serve a reply to the defence and in other cases a defendant may wish to make his own claim against the claimant by way of the counterclaim (see Chapter 7).

The rules relating to statements of case are contained in Part 16 of the CPR 1998 and the accompanying Practice Directions. Part 16 does not apply if the claimant has used the Part 8 procedure (see Chapter 7).

Chapter 6 contents
Introduction
Contents of the particulars of claim
The defence
Reply to defence
Amendments to statements of case
Requests for further information

6.2 CONTENTS OF THE PARTICULARS OF CLAIM

6.2.1 What must be included?

Rule 16.4(1) states that the particulars of claim must include:

'(a) a concise statement of the facts on which the claimant relies;

(b) if the claimant is seeking interest, a statement to that effect and the details set out in paragraph (2) (see below);

(c) if the claimant is seeking aggravated damages or exemplary damages, a statement to that effect and his grounds for claiming them;

(d) if the claimant is seeking provisional damages, a statement to that effect and his grounds for claiming them; and

(e) such other matters as may be set out in a practice direction.'

The primary function of the particulars of claim is to state concisely the facts upon which the claimant relies. The claimant should state all facts necessary for the purpose of showing that he has a complete cause of action.

The Practice Direction to Part 16 goes into more detail as to what must be, or may be, included in the particulars of claim. There are particular requirements for the following types of cases:

- personal injury claims;
- fatal accident claims;
- recovery of land;
- hire purchase claims.

More generally, where a claim is based upon a written agreement, then by para 8.3 of the Practice Direction:

> '(1) a copy of the contract or documents constituting the agreement should be attached to or served with the particulars of claim and the original(s) should be available at the hearing, and
>
> (2) any general conditions of sale incorporated in the contract should also be attached (but where the contract is, or the documents constituting the agreement are bulky this practice direction is complied with by attaching or serving only the relevant parts of the contract or documents)'.

Therefore, where the claim arises out of a breach of a written contract, a copy of the relevant contract should be attached to, or served with, the particulars of claim.

By para 8.4:

> 'Where a claim is based upon an oral agreement, the particulars of claim should set out the contractual words used and state by whom, to whom, when and where they were spoken',

and by para 8.5:

> 'Where a claim is based upon an agreement by conduct, the particulars of claim must specify the conduct relied on and state by whom, when and where the acts constituting the conduct were done.'

Paragraphs 9.1–9.2 of the Practice Direction to Part 16 sets out further matters which *must* be specifically set out in the particulars of claim. For example, by para 9.2:

> 'The claimant must specifically set out the following matters in his particulars of claim where he wishes to rely on them in support of his claim:
>
> (1) any allegation of fraud,
> (2) the fact of any illegality,
> (3) details of any misrepresentation,
> (4) details of all breaches of trust,
> (5) notice or knowledge of a fact,
> (6) details of unsoundness of mind or undue influence,
> (7) details of wilful default, and
> (8) any facts relating to mitigation of loss or damage.'

Rule 16.4(2) sets out the details which must be supplied where, as will usually be the case, the claimant is seeking interest. In such cases, the claimant must:

> '(a) state whether he is doing so –
>
> (i) under the terms of a contract;
> (ii) under an enactment and if so which; or
> (iii) on some other basis and if so what that basis is; and

(b) if the claim is for a specified amount of money, state –
  (i) the percentage rate at which interest is claimed;
  (ii) the date from which it is claimed;
  (iii) the date to which it is calculated, which must not be later than the date on which the claim form is issued;
  (iv) the total amount of interest claimed to the date of calculation; and
  (v) the daily rate at which interest accrues after that date.'

If the claimant is claiming interest pursuant to statute, then in the High Court this would be under s 35A of the Supreme Court Act 1981 and, in the county court, under s 69 of the County Courts Act 1984. Alternatively, a claimant may be entitled to claim interest pursuant to a particular clause in a contract. A claimant would normally seek to do this where the contractual interest rate is higher than the current statutory interest rate of 8 per cent. Where the contract does not provide for payment of interest, the claimant may nevertheless be entitled to claim a higher rate of interest than the statutory rate if the Late Payment of Commercial Debts (Interest) Act 1998 applies (see **2.4.3**). A claimant who claims for interest under contract or the 1998 Act may well seek statutory interest under s 35A of the Supreme Court Act 1981 or s 69 of the County Courts Act 1984 in the alternative, just in case the court refuses to award interest under the contract or the 1998 Act.

Example of particulars of claim in a High Court debt action (particulars of claim endorsed on claim form)

Claim Form

In the	High Court of Justice Queen's Bench Division, Reading District Registry.
Claim No.	RD - 01 - 397

Claimant

Brewsters Limited,
Unit 12 Brownside Industrial Estate,
Reading,
Berkshire,
RG2 6DS.
Tel: 0118 5983990.

Defendant(s)

Gates Launderettes Limited,
73 Cider Street,
Slough,
Berkshire,
SL1 1PP.
Tel: 01753 547790.

SEAL

Brief details of claim

The claim is for an unpaid debt of £63,450 in respect of 3 industrial drycleaners and 6 industrial washing machines supplied by the Claimant to the Defendant.

Value

The Claimant expects to recover more than £15,000.

Defendant's name and address	Gates Launderettes Limited, 73 Cider Street, Slough, Berkshire, SL1 1PP.		£
		Amount claimed	63,450.00
		Court fee	500.00
		Solicitor's costs	100.00
		Total amount	64,050.00
		Issue date	02.10.01

The court office at Reading District Registry, 161-163 Friar Street, reading, RG1 1HE.
is open between 10 am and 4 pm Monday to Friday. When corresponding with the court, please address forms or letters to the Court Manager and quote the claim number.
N1 Claim form (CPR Part 7) (10.00)   *Printed on behalf of The Court Service*

	Claim No.	RD-01-397

Does, or will, your claim include any issues under the Human Rights Act 1998? ☐ Yes ☑ No

Particulars of Claim (attached)(to follow)

1. By clause 1 of a written agreement (the "Agreement") dated 16 May 2001 the Claimant agreed to sell to the Defendant machinery, namely 3 Chloridal 131 dry cleaning machines and 6 Isadal washing machines for an agreed price of £63,450.00. A copy of the Agreement is attached.

2. In pursuance of clause 6 of the Agreement the machinery was delivered to the Defendant's premises at 6, Station Road, Reading on 16 August 2001.

3. By clause 4 of the Agreement payment of the agreed price was due on the day of delivery.

4. In breach of the Agreement the Defendant has failed to pay the agreed price or any part thereof.

5. The claimant claims the sum of £63,450.00 and interest under s 35A of the Supreme Court Act 1981.

AND THE CLAIMANT CLAIMS:

1. The sum of £63,450.00.

2. Interest pursuant to s 35A of the Supreme Court Act 1981 at the rate of 8% per annum from 17 August 2001 (the day after delivery) to 2 October 2001 (47 days) amounting to £653.30 and continuing at the daily rate of £13.90 from 3 October 2001 until judgment or sooner payment.

Statement of Truth
*(I believe)(The Claimant believes) that the facts stated in these particulars of claim are true.
* I am duly authorised by the claimant to sign this statement

Full name   Brian Charlton.

Name of claimant's solicitor's firm   Collaws.

signed *Brian Charlton*   position or office held   Managing Director.
*(Claimant)(Litigation friend)(Claimant's solicitor)   (if signing on behalf of firm or company)

*delete as appropriate

Collaws,
14 Ship Street,
Weyford,
Guildshire, WE1 8HQ.
Ref: BM/ABC/Brewsters.
DX 1599 Weyford.
Fax: 01904 876554.

Claimant's or claimant's solicitor's address to which documents or payments should be sent if different from overleaf including (if appropriate) details of DX, fax or e-mail.

Example of particulars of claim in a county court action for breach of contract

IN THE WEYFORD COUNTY COURT   WF 01 No 876

BETWEEN

                      INDUSTRIAL MANUFACTURING LIMITED   Claimants

                      and

                      HEATECHS LIMITED   Defendants

PARTICULARS OF CLAIM

1. By a written contract made on 20 April 2001 between the Claimants and Defendants, the Defendants agreed to sell to the Claimants a central heating gas boiler and integrated water pump described as a Heatechs Powerheat Unit Model 312K ("the Unit") for the sum of £6,000 plus £1,050 VAT. A copy of the contract is attached.

2. At all material times the Defendants carried on business as manufacturers and suppliers of central heating boilers and systems.

3. The Claimants bought the Unit from the Defendants who sold it in the course of their business. It was an implied condition of the contract that the Unit should be of satisfactory quality.

4. Further or in the alternative, on 19 April 2001, the Claimants by their contracts manager, Ian Jones, expressly or by implication made known to the Defendants (represented by their sales manager, Polly Rees) the particular purpose for which they required the Unit, namely for the purpose of installation in the Claimants' factory as part of a heating system required to be in continuous use for six days per week. It was an express and/or implied condition of the contract that the Unit to be delivered by the Defendants should be reasonably fit for that purpose.

5. In purported performance of the contract the Defendants delivered the Unit on 29 June 2001 and it was installed by the Claimants on or about 2 July 2001.

6. In breach of the implied conditions the Unit delivered by the Defendants was not of satisfactory quality and was not reasonably fit for its purpose.

PARTICULARS OF BREACH

    (a) The integrated water pump failed to operate.
    (b) The impeller retaining nut on the integrated water pump was insufficiently secure owing to a defective thread.

7. As a consequence of the breaches of conditions the boiler in the Unit became or had become drained of water on 2 August 2001 and overheated as a result. When the pump effectively re-engaged cold water flowed into the boiler causing it to explode and rupture on 2 August 2001 and the pipe connections to distort.

8. By reason of the above the Claimants have suffered loss and damage.

PARTICULARS OF LOSS AND DAMAGE

Cost of replacement boiler	£12,000	+	£2,100 VAT
Installation of new boiler	£900	+	£157.50 VAT
Cost of pumping out boiler house and repairing damaged premises	£5,750	+	£1,006.25 VAT
Consequential losses as the result of production losses	£16,000	+	£2,800 VAT

9. In respect of damages awarded the Claimants are entitled to interest pursuant to s 69 of the County Courts Act 1984 at such rates and for such period as the Court thinks just.

AND THE CLAIMANTS CLAIM:

(1) Damages.
(2) Interest pursuant to s 69 of the County Courts Act 1984.

Dated 17th August 2001.   *Singleton Trumper & Co*

STATEMENT OF TRUTH

I believe that the facts stated in these Particulars of Claim are true.

Signed: *D Smith*
                 DAVID SMITH
                 Director

The Claimants' Solicitors are Singleton Trumper & Co of Bank Chambers, Streatham, London SW16 5PA where they will accept service of proceedings on behalf of the Claimants.

To the Defendants

To the Court Manager.

6.2.2 Particulars in statements of case

It is the practice to include detailed particulars of some aspects of the claim. For example, particulars of the breach of contract must always be stated so that the defendant knows exactly the manner in which he is alleged to have been in breach of contract. An example of this is paragraphs 6 and 8 of the particulars of claim in 'Industrial Manufacturing Ltd v Heatechs Ltd', set out above. Similarly, the detail of the claim for damages is often most conveniently set out in 'particulars of loss and damage'.

The prayer or claim for relief

The relief or remedy claimed must be specifically stated in the particulars of claim. Traditionally, it is also often repeated in summary form in a prayer or claim for relief. This appears towards the end of the particulars of claim, immediately before the date and will vary depending upon the subject matter of the claim.

In a debt action, the prayer or claim for relief will include the claim for the amount of the debt, the exact amount of interest claimed up to the date of issue of the proceedings and the daily rate of interest claimed thereafter. In a damages claim, it will include the claim for damages plus interest.

6.2.3 The statement of truth

If the particulars of claim are not part of the claim form itself, then they must be verified by a statement of truth (see **4.3**).

6.3 THE DEFENCE

As seen in Chapter 5, the defendant has a limited amount of time in which to file a defence with the court, depending upon whether or not an acknowledgement of service has been filed.

Rule 16.5 sets out what must be contained in the defence:

'(1) In his defence, the defendant must state –

    (a) which of the allegations in the particulars of claim he denies;

    (b) which allegations he is unable to admit or deny, but which he requires the claimant to prove; and

    (c) which allegations he admits.

(2) Where the defendant denies an allegation –

    (a) he must state his reasons for doing so; and

    (b) if he intends to put forward a different version of events from that given by the claimant, he must state his own version.

(3) A defendant who –

    (a) fails to deal with an allegation; but

    (b) has set out in his defence the nature of his case in relation to the issue to which that allegation is relevant,

    shall be taken to require that allegation be proved.

(4) Where the claim includes a money claim, a defendant shall be taken to require that any allegation relating to the amount of money claimed be proved unless he expressly admits the allegation.

(5) Subject to paragraphs (3) and (4), a defendant who fails to deal with an allegation shall be taken to admit that allegation.

(6) If the defendant disputes the claimant's statement of value under rule 16.3 he must –

   (a) state why he disputes it; and
   (b) if he is able, give his own statement of the value of the claim.

(7) If the defendant is defending in a representative capacity, he must state what that capacity is.

(8) If the defendant has not filed an acknowledgement of service under Part 10, he must give an address for service.

(Part 22 requires a defence to be verified by a statement of truth)

(Rule 6.5 provides that an address for service must be within the jurisdiction)'

As with any statement of case, the defence must be verified by statement of truth.

The defence must provide a comprehensive response to the particulars of claim and, therefore, in respect of each allegation in the particulars of claim, there should be an admission, a denial, or (where the defendant has no knowledge of the matter stated) a requirement that the claimant prove the point. Any denial must be explicit and a defendant must state his reasons for denying the allegation in the particulars of claim. If the defendant wishes to put forward a different version of events from that given by the claimant, the defendant must state his own version.

In order to ensure that every allegation in the particulars of claim is dealt with and nothing is admitted through omission (see r 16.5(5)), the defence usually answers each paragraph of the claim in turn. This is the approach adopted in the defence to the breach of contract claim between Industrial Manufacturing Limited and Heatechs Limited in the example set out below.

Example of a defence in a county court action for breach of contract

IN THE WEYFORD COUNTY COURT WF 01 No 876

BETWEEN

      INDUSTRIAL MANUFACTURING LIMITED Claimants

      and

      HEATECHS LIMITED Defendants

DEFENCE

1. The Defendants admit paragraphs 1 to 4 of the Particulars of Claim.

2. The delivery and installation of the Unit referred to in paragraph 5 of the Particulars of Claim was wholly in accordance with the terms of the contract and constituted full and complete performance thereof by the Defendants.

3. The Defendants deny that they were in breach of contract as alleged in paragraph 6 of the Particulars of Claim, or at all. The Defendants state that the Unit supplied was of satisfactory quality and fit for its purpose. In particular, the impeller retaining nut on the water pump was sufficiently secure and did not have a defective thread.

4. The Defendants make no admissions as to the loss and damage alleged in paragraphs 7 and 8 of the Particulars of Claim.

5. Further or alternatively, if (which is not admitted) the Claimants have suffered the loss and damage alleged in paragraphs 7 and 8 of the Particulars of Claim, the Defendants deny that the loss and damage occurred as a result of the alleged or any breach of condition by the Defendants. Any such loss or damage was caused by the Claimants' installation or subsequent use of the unit.

Dated the 27th August 2001.   *Haughton & Co*

STATEMENT OF TRUTH

The Defendants believe that the facts stated in the defence are true.

      Signed: *D Bennett*
           D. BENNETT
           Partner
           Houghton & Co,
           19 High Pavement,
           Lucreville,
           Wandleside.
           Solicitors for the Defendants,
           whose address is the Defendants'
           address for service.

To the Court Manager

To the Claimants.

When answering each paragraph of the claim, the defendant should clearly deny any allegations which are disputed and make clear admissions in respect of the factual issues which are not in dispute (eg paragraphs 1 and 2 in the example above). Any allegations of loss or damage which are disputed should be 'not admitted' in the defence, such as in paragraph 4 of the example. The defendant should also include any additional facts in the defence which make his side of the story clearer.

The consequence of making admissions in the defence is that the claimant does not have to prove the point at trial. Such admissions are most often made in respect of facts which came into existence prior to the breach of contract or negligent act, such as the date, the parties and the terms of the contract, or the date, location and vehicles involved in a road traffic accident.

If a defendant wishes to make a counterclaim against a claimant, the counterclaim should form part of the same document. Counterclaims are a form of Part 20 claim and are considered in more detail in the following chapter.

If a defendant wishes to rely upon the expiry of a limitation period, he must give details in his defence (Practice Direction to Part 16, para 14.1).

In relation to either the particulars of claim or the defence, by para 14.3 of the Practice Direction to Part 16, a party may:

'(1) refer in his statement of case to any point of law on which his claim or defence, as the case may be, is based,
(2) give in his statement of case the name of any witness he proposes to call, and
(3) attach to or serve with this statement of case a copy of any document which he considers is necessary to his claim or defence, as the case may be (including any expert's report to be filed in accordance with Part 35).'

A party may, therefore, for example, refer in a statement of case to any witnesses they intend to rely upon and may attach a copy of a witness statement to the statement of case. The Rules relating to the use of evidence are considered in Chapter 10.

6.4 REPLY TO DEFENCE

A claimant may wish to file a reply to the defence but is under no obligation to do so. He should do so if he needs to allege facts in answer to the defence which were not included in the particulars of claim. By r 16.7(1), a claimant who does not file a reply to the defence shall not be taken to admit the matters raised in the defence. There is therefore no corresponding rule of implied admission which we saw when looking at the defence itself. In practice, replies to defences are most common where the defendant has made a counterclaim in which case the claimant has to file a defence to the counterclaim and then will often incorporate a reply as well.

6.5 AMENDMENTS TO STATEMENTS OF CASE

In a perfect world, nobody would ever have to amend their statements of case. However, sometimes mistakes are made and on other occasions fresh information comes to light after the statement of case has been served. Part 17 of the CPR 1998 provides the ways in which statements of case can be amended.

6.5.1 Amendments before service

A party may amend his statement of case at any time before it has been served.

6.5.2 Amendments with permission

After a party has served his statement of case he can only amend it with either:

(a) the written consent of all of the parties; or
(b) the permission of the court.

On making an application for permission to amend the statement of case, the applicant should file a copy of the statement of case with the proposed amendments along with the application notice (see Chapter 9).

If the court grants permission for the amendment, the applicant must file the amended statement of case and serve the order and the amended statement of case on all other parties.

The statement of case will be endorsed with the words:

> **Amended [describe the type of statement of case] by Order of [name of master/district judge] dated [ ].**

The amended statement of case need not show the original text unless the court directs otherwise.

6.5.3 Directions following amendment

If the court gives permission to amend the statement of case, it may give directions regarding amendments to any other statement of case and service of the amended statements of case. It is common, for example, for a defendant to be allowed to amend his defence if the court has given the claimant permission to amend his particulars of claim.

6.5.4 Application to amend the statement of case outside the limitation period

If a claim is made after the relevant limitation period has expired, the defendant has an absolute defence. So if the amendment will add or substitute a new claim, the new claim must arise out of the same facts or substantially the same facts as the claim which the applicant has already made in the proceedings.

If the amendment is to correct a mistake as to the name of a party, the mistake must be genuine and one which would not have caused reasonable doubt as to the identity of the party in question.

If the amendment alters the capacity in which a party brings his claim, the new capacity must be one which that party had when the proceedings commenced or has since acquired.

6.5.5 Statements of truth

By r 22.1(2), amendments to the statement of case have to be verified by a statement of truth unless the court orders otherwise.

6.5.6 Costs

A party applying for an amendment will usually be responsible for the costs of and arising from the amendment.

6.5.7 Amendments without permission

Where a party has amended his statement of case without requiring the court's permission (ie in the case of an amendment by consent or before service), the court may disallow the amendment (r 17.2). A party may apply to the court asking it to exercise its discretion to disallow within 14 days of service of the amended statement of case.

6.6 REQUESTS FOR FURTHER INFORMATION (Part 18)

6.6.1 The request

A party to the action, or the court itself, may wish another party to give further information about its case. By r 18.1(1), the court may at any time order a party to:

'(a) clarify any matter which is in dispute in the proceedings; or
(b) give additional information in relation to any such matter, whether or not the matter is contained or referred to in a statement of case.'

If one of the parties requires further information then, before applying to the court for an order, that party should first serve a written request on the other party stating a date for the response, which must allow a reasonable time for the response.

A request should be concise and strictly confined to matters which are reasonably necessary and proportionate to enable the applicant to prepare his own case or to understand the case he has to meet.

Requests must be made as far as possible in a single comprehensive document and not piecemeal.

If the text of the request is brief and the reply is likely to be brief, then the request may be made by letter. If so, the letter must state that it contains a request made under Part 18 and must not deal with any other matter. Otherwise, the request should be made in a separate document.

Any request must:

(a) be headed with the name of the court and the title and number of the claim;
(b) state in its heading that it is a Part 18 request, identify the applicant and the respondent, and state the date on which it is made;
(c) set out each request in a separate numbered paragraph;
(d) identify any document and (if relevant) any paragraph or words in that document to which the request relates;
(e) state the date for a response.

If the request is not in the form of a letter, the applicant may, if this is convenient, put the request on the left-hand side of the document so that the response may appear on the right-hand side. If so, the applicant should serve two copies of the request on the respondent.

6.6.2 Response to the request

The response must be in writing, dated and signed by the respondent or his solicitor. If the original request was made in a letter, the response can also be in the form of a letter or a formal reply. If in a letter, it should state that it is a response to the request and should not deal with any other matters. The response should set out the same information as the request and then give details of the response itself. The respondent must file at court and serve on all parties a copy of the request and his response.

The response must be verified by a statement of truth.

6.6.3 Cases where the respondent does not respond to the initial request

If the respondent objects to all or part of the request or cannot comply with the request, he should inform the applicant, giving reasons and, where relevant, giving a date by which he will be able to comply with the request. He may do so by letter or by formal response. If the respondent considers that a response will involve disproportionate expense, he should explain briefly in his reply why he takes this view.

6.6.4 Applications for court orders

If no response is received or the response is considered to be inadequate, then the applicant can apply for an order from the court (see Chapter 9). The court will only grant an order if it is satisfied that the request is confined to matters which are reasonably necessary and proportionate to enable the applicant to prepare his case or understand the case he has to meet.

Chapter 7

PART 20 PROCEEDINGS AND PART 8 CLAIMS

7.1 INTRODUCTION

We have looked at the Rules relating to a claimant bringing a claim against a defendant. Part 20 of the CPR 1998 deals with other types of claim which may be brought in the proceedings. The types of claim covered by Part 20 are set out in r 20.2:

'(1) A Part 20 claim is any claim other than a claim by a claimant against a defendant and includes –

   (a) a counterclaim by a defendant against the claimant or against the claimant and some other person;
   (b) a claim by a defendant against any person (whether or not already a party) for contribution or indemnity or some other remedy; and
   (c) where a Part 20 claim has been made against a person who is not already a party, any claim made by that person against any other person (whether or not already a party).

(2) In this Part "Part 20 claimant" means a person who makes a Part 20 claim.'

Frequently, a defendant who has been sued by a claimant wants to make a claim against that person.

Example 1
A supplies goods to B.

B has paid 50% of the price, but the other 50% is unpaid.

B sues A for damages for breach of contract based on the allegation that the goods were not of satisfactory quality.

A defends the claim (on the basis that the goods were of satisfactory quality) and also counterclaims for the balance of 50% which is still outstanding.

This counterclaim is a Part 20 claim.

Another common scenario is where the defendant wishes to pass the blame, either in whole or in part, on to a third party. The defendant may be seeking a full indemnity from the third party, or a contribution towards any damages he has to pay the claimant. A claim for an indemnity often arises where there is a contractual relationship between the defendant and the third party, and the defendant alleges that the third party is obliged by the terms of the contract to indemnify him if he is found liable in respect of the claimant's action against him. Sometimes a right to an indemnity may arise from statute or by implication of law. An example of a claim for an indemnity is where a consumer sues a retailer in respect of goods which he alleges are not of satisfactory quality and the retailer alleges that there was an inherent defect in the goods and attempts to pass on liability to the manufacturer. The retailer will

Chapter 7 contents
Introduction
Procedure
Part 8 claims

claim an indemnity from the manufacturer in respect of any sums that he is ordered to pay to the consumer.

A claim for a contribution often arises where there are joint wrong-doers, and the defendant claims that the third party is partly responsible for the harm that the claimant has suffered. An example of a claim for a contribution is where the claimant claims damages from the defendant as a result of a road traffic accident, and the defendant alleges that another driver was partly to blame for the accident. A defendant will then claim a contribution from the other driver towards the damages which he is ordered to pay to the claimant.

These types of claims are further examples of Part 20 claims.

7.2 PROCEDURE

7.2.1 Counterclaims (Rule 20.4)

If a defendant wishes to make a counterclaim against a claimant, he should file particulars of the counterclaim with his defence. This should form one document, with the counterclaim following on from the defence. An example of a defence and counterclaim to a debt action appears below.

If a defendant does this, he does not need permission from the court to make the counterclaim. However, if a defendant decides to make a counterclaim after he has already filed his defence, he will need the court's permission. The application for permission should be made on notice.

If he wishes to dispute the counterclaim, the claimant (who does not have the option of acknowledging service) has to file a defence (known as a reply and defence to counterclaim) within the usual 14-day period. If the claimant fails to do so, the defendant may enter judgment in default on the counterclaim. Therefore, if the claimant requires more time to file a defence to the counterclaim, he should request an extension of time from the defendant. As already seen (see **5.4**), the parties can agree an extension of up to 28 days in addition to the initial 14-day period.

IN THE SOUTHCLIFFE COUNTY COURT SF-01-5525

BETWEEN

MR PETER PATTON   Claimant/Part 20 Defendant

and

MR DAVID DEMPSTER   Defendant/Part 20 Defendant

DEFENCE AND PART 20 COUNTERCLAIM

DEFENCE

1. At all material times the Claimant was in business as a furniture manufacturer.

2. Paragraph 1 of the Particulars of Claim is admitted.*

3. The Claimant sold the Furniture in the course of his business. It was an implied condition of the contract that the Furniture should be of satisfactory quality.

4. Further, at the time of making the contract, the Defendant expressly or by implication made known to the Claimant the particular purpose for which he required the Furniture, namely for use as boardroom tables with matching chairs and bookcases. Therefore, it was an implied condition of the contract that the Furniture should be reasonably fit for that purpose.

5. In purported performance of the contract the Claimant delivered the goods to the Defendant on 4 September 2001.

6. In breach of the implied conditions the tables were not of satisfactory quality and were not reasonably or at all fit for the Defendant's purpose.

PARTICULARS OF BREACH

The planks of wood making up the table tops were not fully seasoned and were clamped down too tightly.

7. As a consequence of the breach within 3 weeks of delivery a very deep crack running the entire length of one table and part of the length of the other table formed on the surface of the table tops.

8. Therefore the Defendant was entitled to reject the Furniture and did so in conversation with the Claimant in early October 2001 at the Claimant's premises and by telephoning the Claimant on 15 November 2001.

9. In the circumstances the Claimant is not entitled to the relief claimed or any relief.

PART 20 COUNTERCLAIM

10. The Defendant repeats the Defence.

11. On 3 September 2001 the Defendant paid to the Claimant £3,050 on account of the purchase price of the goods.

12. In the circumstances the Defendant is entitled to the return of this sum as money paid for a consideration which has wholly failed and to the payment of interest under section 69 of the County Courts Act 1984.

AND THE DEFENDANT COUNTERCLAIMS:

(1) £3,050.00.

(2) Interest pursuant to s 69 of the County Courts Act 1984 at the rate of 8% per annum equivalent to £53.60 for the period from and including 4 September 2001 to 22 November 2001 (80 days).

(3) Interest as above from 23 November 2001 at the rate of 67p daily until judgment or sooner payment.

Dated 22nd November 2001   *Collaws*

STATEMENT OF TRUTH

I believe that the facts stated in this Defence and Part 20 Counterclaim are true.

Signed: *D Dempster*
             DAVID DEMPSTER

The Defendant's solicitors are Collaws of Bishop Hall Road, Christlethorpe, Guildshire CH2 1DC where they will accept service of proceedings on behalf of the Defendant.

To: The Claimant/ Part 20 Claimant

       The Court Manager.

Note: Paragraph 1 of the Particulars of Claim states that by an oral contract made on 3 September 2001 at the Claimant's showroom in Southcliffe High Street the Claimant sold the Defendant 2 boardroom tables with 16 matching chairs ('the Furniture') for a total price of £15,250.

7.2.2 Contribution or indemnity between co-defendants (r 20.6)

If one defendant wishes to seek a contribution or indemnity from another defendant, after filing his acknowledgement of service or defence, he may proceed with his claim against his fellow defendant by:

(a) filing a notice containing a statement of the nature and grounds of his claim; and
(b) serving the notice on the co-defendant.

7.2.3 Other Part 20 claims (r 20.7)

In other Part 20 claims, such as a claim against a third party, the defendant may make a Part 20 claim without the court's permission by issuing a Part 20 claim form before or at the same time as he files a defence. A copy of a Part 20 claim form appears in Appendix A. Particulars of the Part 20 claim must be contained in or served with the claim form.

If a Part 20 claim is not issued at that time, the court's permission will be required. The application for permission can be made without notice, unless the court directs otherwise.

7.2.4 Applications for permission to make a Part 20 claim

When the court's permission is required, because the counterclaim or other type of Part 20 claim was not made at the time of filing the defence, then the application notice should be filed with a copy of the proposed Part 20 claim. The application for permission must be supported by evidence stating:

(a) the stage which the action has reached;
(b) the nature of the claim to be made by the Part 20 claimant, or details of the question or issue which needs to be decided;
(c) a summary of the facts on which the Part 20 claim is based; and
(d) the name and address of the proposed Part 20 defendant.

If there has been any delay in making the application, the evidence must also explain the delay. Where possible, the applicant should provide a timetable of the action to date.

Rule 20.9(2) sets out the matters the court takes into account in deciding whether to grant permission, and these include:

> '(a) the connection between the Part 20 claim and the claim made by the claimant against the defendant;
> (b) whether the Part 20 claimant is seeking substantially the same remedy which some other party is claiming from him; and
> (c) whether the Part 20 claimant wants the court to decide any question connected with the subject matter of the proceedings –
>   (i) not only between existing parties but also between existing parties and a person not already a party; or
>   (ii) against an existing party not only in a capacity in which he is already a party but also in some further capacity.'

The court may permit the Part 20 claim to be made, dismiss it, or require it to be dealt with separately from the claim by the claimant against the defendant.

7.2.5 Service

If the defendant did not need permission in order to make the Part 20 claim, then:

(a) in the case of a counterclaim he must serve it on every other party when he serves his defence;
(b) except for claims for contributions or indemnities from co-defendants, he must serve the Part 20 claim on the new party within 14 days of filing his defence.

If a defendant had to make an application for permission to issue a Part 20 claim, the court will give directions as to service when granting permission to make the claim.

If a defendant serves a Part 20 claim form on a person who is not already a party (such as a third party) he must also serve:

(a) forms for defending or admitting or acknowledging service of the claim;
(b) copies of every statement of case which has already been served; and
(c) such other documents as the court may direct.

The defendant must also serve copies of the Part 20 claim form on all existing parties to the action.

7.2.6 Judgment in default on Part 20 claims

Special rules apply where the Part 20 claim is not a counterclaim or a claim by a defendant for an indemnity or contribution against a co-defendant. In other Part 20 cases, if the party against whom a Part 20 claim is made fails to acknowledge service or file a defence, then:

(a) he is deemed to admit the Part 20 claim and will be bound by any decision in the proceedings between the claimant and the defendant which affects the Part 20 claim; and
(b) if a default judgment is entered against the Part 20 claimant, he may also enter judgment in respect of the Part 20 claim by filing a request in the relevant practice forms.

The Part 20 claimant will need permission to enter default judgment (which can be obtained without notice unless the court directs otherwise) if:

(a) he has not satisfied any default judgment obtained against him; or
(b) he is seeking any remedy other than a contribution or an indemnity.

7.2.7 Directions

If a defence is filed to a Part 20 claim (other than a counterclaim) the court will arrange a hearing to give directions as to the future conduct of the case. In giving directions, the court must ensure that, as far as practicable, the Part 20 claim and the main claim are managed together. At the directions hearing, the court may (see para 5.3 of the Practice Direction to Part 20):

'(1) treat the hearing as a summary judgment hearing,
(2) order that the Part 20 proceedings be dismissed,
(3) give directions about the way any claim, question or issue set out in or arising from the Part 20 claim should be dealt with,
(4) give directions as to the part, if any, the Part 20 defendant will take at the trial of the claim,

(5) give directions about the extent to which the Part 20 defendant is to be bound by any judgment or decision to be made in the claim.'

7.2.8 Title of the proceedings

Paragraphs 7.1–7.6 of the Practice Direction to Part 20 give information as to how parties to Part 20 claims should be described in the title of the action. The title of every Part 20 claim should include both the full name of each party and his status in the proceedings – ie claimant, defendant, Part 20 claimant, Part 20 defendant. For example, if a counterclaim is made against a claimant, then the claimant will thereafter be described as claimant/Part 20 defendant and the defendant will be described as defendant/Part 20 claimant. If there is more than one Part 20 claim, then the parties should be described, for example, as Part 20 claimant (first claim) or Part 20 claimant (second claim).

7.3 PART 8 CLAIMS

7.3.1 Introduction

The Part 8 claim procedure may be used by claimants where the claimant is seeking the court's decision on a question which is unlikely to involve a substantial dispute of fact or if a Rule or Practice Direction requires or permits the use of the Part 8 procedure.

The Practice Direction to Part 8 lists various types of claim for which the procedure may be used, which include:

(a) a claim by or against a child or patient which has been settled before the commencement of proceedings and the sole purpose of the proceedings is to obtain the approval of the court to the settlement; and
(b) a claim for a summary order for possession against named or unnamed defendants, occupying land or premises without the licence or consent of the person claiming possession.

7.3.2 Procedure

The claimant issues a Part 8 claim form (Form N208) which must state:

(a) the question the court is to decide or the remedy the claimant is seeking;
(b) any enactment under which the claim is being made;
(c) the representative capacity (eg litigation friend) of any of the parties.

Instead of serving particulars of claim, the claimant must file and serve any written evidence, usually in the form of witness statements, with the claim form.

The defendant must then file and serve an acknowledgement of service not more than 14 days after service of the claim form. Again, instead of serving a defence, the defendant has to file and serve his written evidence with the acknowledgement of service.

If the defendant fails to file an acknowledgement of service, the claimant is unable to obtain a default judgment, and the defendant may still attend the hearing of the claim. However, the defendant may not take part in the hearing unless the court gives permission.

The court may give directions, including a hearing date, when the claim form is issued, or otherwise as soon as practicable after the defendant has acknowledged service or the time for acknowledging service has expired.

All Part 8 claims will be allocated to the multi-track.

Chapter 8

CASE MANAGEMENT AND ALLOCATION OF CASES

8.1 INTRODUCTION

One of the key elements of the CPR 1998 is the notion of case management. As we saw in Chapter 1, r 1.4 imposes a duty on the court to manage cases actively.

Part 3 of the Civil Procedure Rules gives the court a wide range of case management powers. It should be noted that these powers are in addition to any powers given to the court by any other Rule or Practice Direction, or by any other enactment or any powers it may otherwise have.

8.2 THE COURT'S POWERS

Rule 3.1(2) sets out a non-exclusive list of the court's powers, which include:

(a) the power to extend or reduce the time for compliance with any Rule, Practice Direction or court order;
(b) the power to adjourn or bring forward a hearing date;
(c) the power to require a party or a party's legal representative to attend the court;
(d) the power to hold a hearing and receive evidence by telephone;
(e) the power to exclude an issue from consideration;
(f) the power to dismiss or give judgment on a claim after a decision on a preliminary issue;
(g) the power to take any other step or make any other order for the purpose of managing the case and furthering the overriding objective.

The court may make any order subject to conditions and can specify the consequence of non-compliance. Such conditions can include a requirement to pay a sum of money into court. In particular, by r 3.1(5), the court may order a party to pay a sum of money into court if that party has, without good reason, failed to comply with a Rule, Practice Direction or a relevant pre-action protocol. In exercising its power under r 3.1(5), however, the court must have regard to both the amount in dispute and the costs which the parties have incurred or which they may incur.

The court can normally exercise any of its powers of case management on its own initiative. However, before doing so, it must give any person likely to be affected by the order an opportunity to make representations within a specified time and in a specified manner.

If the court proposes to hold a hearing before making an order on its own initiative, it must give the parties at least 3 days' notice of the hearing.

The court may make a provisional order without notice to the parties. However, any party may then apply to set aside, vary or stay the order within 7 days of service of the

Chapter 8 contents
Introduction
The court's powers
Striking out
Relief from sanctions
Allocation
Allocation to a track
Human rights

order on that party (or such other period as the court may specify). The order must notify the parties of this right.

8.3 STRIKING OUT

Rule 3.4(2) gives the court a specific power to strike out all or part of a statement of case. The court can exercise this power if it appears to the court:

'(a) that the statement of case discloses no reasonable grounds for bringing or defending the claim;

(b) that the statement of case is an abuse of the court's process or is otherwise likely to obstruct the just disposal of the proceedings; or

(c) that there has been a failure to comply with a rule, practice direction or court order.'

8.3.1 Inadequate statements of case

The Practice Direction to Part 3 gives examples of the types of statement of case which may fall to be struck out within (a) above. These include particulars of claim which set out no facts indicating what the claim is about, for example, 'money owed £5,000' and particulars of claim which contain a coherent set of facts but those facts, even if true, do not disclose any legally recognisable claim against the defendant. As far as defences are concerned, it gives examples of a defence which consists of a bare denial or otherwise sets out no coherent statement of facts, or a defence which, whilst coherent, would not, even if true, amount in law to a defence to the claim.

The following is an example of how a judge might use this power.

Example
A claimant issues proceedings for the recovery of a debt. A defence is filed which simply consists of a bare denial that the money is due. The defence has therefore failed to comply with r 16.5 of the CPR 1998 (see Chapter 6). The judge, when looking at the case, may, as part of his case management powers under Part 3, make an order that unless the defendant files a full defence setting out his reasons for denying that the debt is owed within 7 days of service of the order, the defence will be struck out.

Note that the court may, as in the example given, make such an order of its own volition or, alternatively, the claimant in such a case may make an application to the court for an order in similar terms.

If, in the example given above, the defendant did not comply with the order, then the claimant would be able to obtain judgment simply by filing a request for judgment. As this was a debt claim, the claimant would be able to obtain judgment for the amount of the debt, together with interest and costs.

Continuing with the above example, if judgment is entered in these circumstances against the defendant then the defendant can apply to the court under r 3.6 for the judgment to be set aside. Such an application must be made not more than 14 days after the judgment has been served. If the judgment had been entered incorrectly (eg prematurely) then the court must set aside the judgment. However, if the judgment was entered correctly, then r 3.9 (relief from sanctions) applies.

8.3.2 Non-compliance with a Rule, Practice Direction or court order

The striking-out sanction is not confined to cases where the statement of case is defective. As stated in **8.3** above, the court can also strike out a party's statement of case and enter judgment against him for 'failure to comply with a rule, practice direction or court order'.

Striking out is, however, only one of a number of sanctions that the court can apply. How does the court decide what is appropriate? The starting point for decisions on sanctions for default is *Biguzzi v Rank Leisure plc* [1999] 1 WLR 1926. This was an early post-CPR case where the Court of Appeal emphasised the importance of compliance with the CPR 1998 and court orders, but recognised that, whilst it would, on occasions, be appropriate to deal with non-compliance by striking out, there were less drastic, but equally effective ways of dealing with default. In many cases, the use of these other powers would produce a more just result.

Sanctions other than striking out

COSTS

A common sanction is to require the party in default to pay the other party's costs occasioned by the delay on an indemnity basis. The court will make a summary assessment of those costs at the time of the hearing and may order those costs to be paid immediately. The solicitor handling the case would then have to explain to his client why he had been ordered to pay those costs.

Where the court forms the view that the fault lies not with the party himself but with his legal representative, the court may make a wasted costs order. This obliges the legal representative to pay costs incurred by a party as a result of any improper, unreasonable or negligent act or omission on the part of the legal representative (Supreme Court Act 1981, s 51). Before making such an order, the court must allow the legal representative a reasonable opportunity to attend a hearing and give reasons why the order should not be granted.

INTEREST

Alternatively, the court may make orders affecting the interest payable on any damages subsequently awarded to the claimant. If the party at fault is the claimant, the court will reduce the amount of interest payable on his damages. If the party in default is the defendant, the interest payable on the claimant's damages at the end of the case will be increased.

LIMITING THE ISSUES

The appropriate sanction may be to limit the issues that are allowed to proceed to trial. In *AXA v Swire Fraser* (2000) *The Times*, January 19, the defendant applied to strike out the claim on the basis of significant delay on the part of the claimant. One result of this delay had been that the trial had not taken place at the same time as another trial on similar issues. The Court of Appeal allowed the claim to continue, but confined the claimant to pursuing those issues that had not been raised at the earlier related trial.

THE UNLESS ORDER

The 'unless order' is not, strictly speaking, a sanction, but rather a suspended sanction. The court makes an order that unless a party complies with a particular court order or rule within a specified time, his claim or defence will be struck out.

Example
Although an order of the court required the defendant, D, to serve his witness statements on his opponent, C, by 8 November 2001, D did not do so. In order to force D to comply, C applies for and obtains an unless order requiring D to serve the witness statements by a new deadline (usually 7 or 14 days from the date of the unless order), failing which his defence will be struck out.

Given that there is a range of sanctions that the court can apply, when will it apply the ultimate sanction of striking out? In each case, the court will have to consider all the circumstances, and in particular the factors set out in r 3.9 (relief from sanctions). However, the case-law emphasises that the overriding objective of dealing with cases justly and the duty to ensure fairness will be a central consideration in the exercise of the court's discretion (see, eg, *Necati v Metropolitan Police Commissioner* (2001) LTL 19 January). The court should also bear in mind the observations of the Court of Appeal in *Arrow Nominees Inc v Blackledge* (1999) *The Times*, December 8 that striking out a case purely on the basis of a breach of the rules or an order of the court may infringe Article 6(1) of the European Convention on Human Rights unless the breach itself meant that it may no longer be possible to have a fair trial.

None of the above should, however, be read as a reluctance on the part of the courts to strike out a party's statement of case in appropriate circumstances. Where delay or non-compliance means that it is no longer possible to have a fair trial (see *Habib Bank Ltd v Abbeypearl Ltd & Others* [2001] 1 All ER 185) or where the default is so bad that it amounts to an abuse of the court (see *UCB Corporate Services Ltd v Halifax* [1999] 1 Lloyd's Rep 154) strike out may be the appropriate response.

8.4 RELIEF FROM SANCTIONS

A party's ability to obtain relief from the sanctions imposed by the court is dealt with by rr 3.8 and 3.9.

Where a party applies for relief from any sanction for failure to comply with any Rule, Practice Direction or court order, the court will consider all the circumstances including the following (r 3.9(1)):

'(a) the interests of the administration of justice;
(b) whether the application for relief has been made promptly;
(c) whether the failure to comply was intentional;
(d) whether there is a good explanation for the failure;
(e) the extent to which the party in default has complied with other rules, practice directions, court orders and any relevant pre-action protocol;
(f) whether the failure to comply was caused by the party or his legal representative;
(g) whether the trial date or the likely trial date can still be met if relief is granted;
(h) the effect which the failure to comply had on each party; and
(i) the effect which the granting of relief would have on each party.'

Although it is a relevant consideration on an application for relief whether the failure to comply is the failure of the party or his legal representative (r 3.9(1)(f)), the court will generally not be keen to spend time considering separately the conduct of the legal representatives from that which the party himself must be treated as knowing, encouraging or permitting (*Daryanani v Kumar & Co and Another* (2000) Lawtel,

15 March, CA). After all, the other side will be equally affected whether the shortcomings are those of the party or his representatives. On the other hand, the issue of where the fault lies will be very relevant to the question of whether a wasted costs order is appropriate.

An application for relief from sanctions must be supported by evidence.

Sanctions may also be imposed by the court for non-payment of any court fees. Where a party fails to pay a fee on filing an allocation questionnaire (see **8.5**), or a listing questionnaire (see **8.6.2(6)**), the court will serve notice requiring payment of the fee by a specified date. If the claimant does not pay the fee, or make an application for exemption from or remission of the fee within the specified time period, the claim will be struck out with costs.

8.5 ALLOCATION

Part 26 of the CPR 1998 deals with the preliminary stage of case management when cases are allocated to a particular track. This stage of case management arises where a defence has been filed.

Rule 26.2 provides for the automatic transfer of certain types of cases which are defended. If the claim is for a specified amount of money and the defendant is an individual, then, if the claim was not commenced in the defendant's 'home court', the court will transfer the proceedings to the defendant's home court when a defence is filed. The defendant's home court means the county court or High Court District Registry (or if appropriate, the Royal Courts of Justice) for the district in which the defendant resides or carries on business (see r 2.3(1)). This Rule also applies where the defendant admits part of the claim and the claimant wishes to continue with the remainder. The Rule does not apply if the claim was commenced in a High Court specialist list.

In most cases, the crucial preliminary case management issue is that of allocation.

Where the claim is defended then, on receipt of the defence, the court will serve each party with an allocation questionnaire. This is in Form N150 and a copy of this form appears in Appendix A. The court does have the power to dispense with the need for a questionnaire.

The questionnaire must be returned by the parties by the date stipulated in the questionnaire, which must be at least 14 days after service of the questionnaire. The claimant must pay a fee when filing his allocation questionnaire. Where there are two or more defendants, the questionnaire will be sent when all the defendants have filed their defence or when the period for filing the last defence has expired, whichever is the sooner. If the matter is going to be automatically transferred to the defendant's home court, then the court at which the proceedings had been commenced will serve an allocation questionnaire before the proceedings are transferred.

8.5.1 Completing the allocation questionnaire

The allocation questionnaire (Form N150) is a key document in the progress of a case and must be completed carefully by each party. The parties should consult one another and co-operate in completing the allocation questionnaire, although this must not delay its filing.

The first question on the form (paragraph (a)) asks the parties if they wish there to be a 1-month stay of proceedings so that they can attempt to settle the case. One of the key elements of the CPR 1998 is that parties should be given encouragement to settle their disputes without having to go to trial. If all the parties request a stay, the court will order a stay of 1 month. Alternatively, the court, of its own initiative, may order a stay if it considers it appropriate. If a stay is granted and the parties feel they require more time than the initial 4 weeks to try to reach a settlement, then any of the parties may, by letter to the court, request an extension of time. This will usually be for a maximum of 4 weeks, although more than one extension of the stay may be granted. If a settlement is reached, the claimant must tell the court. If a settlement is not reached, the court will allocate the case and give directions in the usual way.

Paragraph (b) asks the parties whether there is any reason why the case needs to be heard at a particular court. If the claim has been issued in the Central Office of the Royal Courts of Justice (RCJ), then each party should state whether he considers the claim should be managed and tried at the RCJ and, if so, why.

As set out in para 2.6 of the Practice Direction to Part 29, claims suitable for trial in the RCJ include:

'(1) professional negligence claims,
(2) Fatal Accident Act claims,
(3) fraud or undue influence claims,
(4) defamation claims,
(5) claims for malicious prosecution or false imprisonment,
(6) claims against the police,
(7) contentious probate claims.'

If a claim does not fall within one of the above categories and has an estimated value of less than £50,000, then it will generally be transferred from the RCJ to a county court. If it has a value of more than £50,000, it will be transferred to a District Registry.

Paragraph (c) of the allocation questionnaire asks the parties to state whether they have complied with any relevant pre-action protocols and, if not, to explain the reasons why.

Paragraph (d) asks the parties if they have made an application to the court, including an application for summary judgment (see Chapter 9) or to join another party into the action. Any such application should be made as soon as possible.

Paragraph (d) then asks the parties to name the witnesses of fact they will be calling and what facts they are witnesses to.

This paragraph also deals with expert evidence and asks the parties various questions about whether and, if so, how they wish to use expert evidence at the trial.

Lastly, paragraph (d) asks the parties which track they consider is most suitable for their case. As already seen in Chapter 1, there are three tracks:

- small claims;
- fast track;
- multi-track.

The basic criteria for allocation to a particular track is the value of the claim which is in dispute, disregarding interest, costs and any question of contributory negligence. If there is a counterclaim or other Part 20 claim, in assessing the value the court will not aggregate the claims but generally will regard the largest of the claims as determining the financial value of the claim. So, for example, if the original claim was for £10,000, but there is a counterclaim valued at £25,000, the latter figure will be the relevant one for allocation purposes.

The parties should indicate at paragraph (e) any dates on which their expert witnesses or any other essential witness will be unavailable to give evidence. It is advisable also to state why the experts are unavailable on those dates (*Matthews v Tarmac Bricks and Tiles Ltd* [1999] CPLR 463).

Paragraph (e) asks the parties to state how long they estimate the trial or final hearing will take.

Paragraph (g) asks the parties to provide an estimate of costs incurred to date and the overall costs of the case.

Paragraph (h) asks the parties whether they have attached documents to the questionnaire and whether they intend to make any applications in the immediate future. The parties are also asked whether there is any other information which could assist the judge in managing the case.

8.5.2 Failure to file an allocation questionnaire

If none of the parties has filed an allocation questionnaire within 14 days, the matter will be referred to a judge for directions and the judge will usually order that all claims, defences and counterclaims should be struck out unless an allocation questionnaire is filed within 3 days of service of the order.

If some, but not all, of the parties have filed an allocation questionnaire, the court will allocate the case on the basis of the information available or, if it does not have enough information, it will list an allocation hearing. Otherwise, the court will only hold an allocation hearing on its own initiative if it considers that it is necessary to do so. Where the court does order an allocation hearing to take place, the parties must be given at least 7 days' notice of the hearing. Where an allocation hearing does take place then, by para 6.5 of the Practice Direction to Part 26, the legal representative who attends should, if possible, be the person responsible for the case and must, in any event, be familiar with the case, be able to provide the court with the information it is likely to need to take its decisions about allocation and case management, and have sufficient authority to deal with any issues that are likely to arise.

Paragraph 6.6 of the Practice Direction to Part 26 sets out the sanctions which the court will usually impose where a party has been in default in connection with the allocation procedure. In particular, where an allocation hearing takes place because a party has failed to file an allocation questionnaire or to provide further information which the court has ordered, the court will usually order that party to pay, on the indemnity basis (see Chapter 13), the costs of any other party who has attended the hearing, summarily assess the amount of those costs (see **9.3**), and order them to be paid forthwith or within a stated period. The court may order that if the party does not pay those costs within the time stated, that party's statement of case will be struck out.

These are very severe sanctions and emphasise the fact that the allocation stage is extremely important in the overall case management of the proceedings. It is imperative that the parties return the allocation questionnaires, properly completed and within the requisite time period, as failure to do so can lead to the sanctions set out above.

By para 2.4 of the Practice Direction to Part 26, if a court hearing takes place (eg, on an application for summary judgment under Part 24 – see Chapter 9) before the claim is allocated to a track, the court may, at that hearing, either dispense with the need for the parties to file allocation questionnaires, treat the hearing as an allocation hearing, make an order for allocation and give directions for case management, or fix a date for allocation questionnaires to be filed and give other directions. This is an example of the general principle in the Rules that whenever a case comes for hearing before the court, the court should endeavour to carry out as much case management at that hearing as possible.

8.6 ALLOCATION TO A TRACK

After the filing of the allocation questionnaires, or after the allocation hearing, or after the end of any stay of proceedings, the court will allocate the case to one of the three tracks. Generally, the most important factor in allocation will be the financial value of the claim.

Claims not exceeding £5,000 will normally be allocated to the small claims track (unless it is a personal injury case where the general damages exceed £1,000, or a landlord and tenant repair case where the cost of the repairs and any other damages exceed £1,000).

Claims between £5,000 and £15,000 will normally be allocated to the fast track.

Claims exceeding £15,000 will normally be allocated to the multi-track.

However, r 26.8(1) sets out other factors to which the court shall have regard, including:

'(a) the financial value, if any, of the claim;
(b) the nature of the remedy sought;
(c) the likely complexity of the facts, law or evidence;
(d) the number of parties or likely parties;
(e) the value of any counterclaim or other Part 20 claim and the complexity of any matters relating to it;
(f) the amount of oral evidence which may be required;
(g) the importance of the claim to persons who are not parties to the proceedings;
(h) the views expressed by the parties; and
(i) the circumstances of the parties.'

Furthermore, the fast track is the normal track for claims with a value exceeding £5,000, but not £15,000, only if the trial is likely to last for no longer than one day; oral expert evidence at trial will be limited to no more than one expert per party in relation to any expert field and there will be expert evidence in no more than two expert fields. For example, if the court at the allocation stage considered that the trial was likely to last two days then the court will usually allocate it to the multi-track.

In assessing the financial value of a claim, the court will disregard any amount not in dispute, any claim for interest, costs and any allegation of contributory negligence.

The court will not allocate proceedings to a track if the financial value of any claim in those proceedings exceeds the limit for that track unless all the parties consent to the allocation of the claim to that track.

So, for example, in a straightforward debt case worth £20,000, if one party asked for it to be allocated to the fast track rather than the multi-track, the court could not do this unless the other party consented (r 26.7(3)).

When it has allocated a claim to a track, the court will serve notification on every party. The court may subsequently re-allocate a claim to a different track either on the application of any party or on its own initiative.

If a party is dissatisfied with the allocation to a particular track, PD 26, para 11 provides that he may:

(a) appeal, if the order was made at a hearing at which he was present or represented, or of which he was given due notice; or
(b) in any other case (eg the case was allocated without an allocation hearing), apply to the court to re-allocate the claim.

8.6.1 Allocation to the small claims track

Part 27 of the CPR 1998 deals with allocation to the small claims track. The small claims track is designed to provide a procedure whereby claims of not more than £5,000 in value can be dealt with quickly and at minimal cost to the parties.

In most small claims cases, after allocation, the court will simply give standard directions and fix a date for the final hearing. The court does have the power to hold a preliminary hearing, but this will happen only in a very limited number of cases. Certain parts of the CPR 1998 do not apply to small claims, including Part 18 (Further Information), Part 31 (Disclosure and Inspection), Part 32 (Evidence), most of Part 35 (Experts and Assessors) and Part 36 (Offers to Settle and Payments into Court). The intention is to make the procedure as simple as possible because, in most cases, solicitors will not be involved. The reason for this is that, under r 27.14, the costs which can be recovered by a successful party are extremely limited and therefore it is usually uneconomic for solicitors to represent the parties in a case proceeding on the small claims track.

The standard directions which the court gives in small claims cases are set out in various forms which are in Appendix A to the Practice Direction for Part 27 of the CPR 1998. The directions vary depending on the type of case so that there are particular directions for claims arising out of road accidents and particular directions for claims arising out of holidays or weddings. The most simple forms of direction are set out in Form A and are as follows:

'1 Each party shall deliver to every other party and to the court office copies of all documents (including any expert's report) on which he intends to rely at the hearing no later than [ ] [14 days before the hearing].
2 The original documents shall be brought to the hearing.
3 [Notice of hearing date and time allowed.]
4 The court must be informed immediately if the case is settled by agreement before the hearing date.'

The hearing itself will be informal and, if all parties agree, the court can deal with the claim without a hearing at all. In other words, a court could make a decision based on the statements of case and documents submitted rather than by hearing oral evidence.

As mentioned earlier, the costs which can be recovered in a small claims case are limited by r 27.14. Generally speaking, the only costs recoverable are the fixed costs attributable to issuing the claim, any court fees paid and sums to represent travelling expenses and loss of earnings. On those (rare) occasions where expert evidence is called, a limited amount may be recovered in respect of the expert's fees. The court does have power to award further costs if a party has behaved unreasonably.

It should be noted, however, that where a claim has been allocated to the small claims track but is subsequently reallocated to another track, after reallocation, the rules of either the fast track or the multi-track in relation to costs will apply from the date of reallocation.

8.6.2 Allocation to the fast track

When a case is allocated to the fast track, the court will give directions as to how the case is to proceed to trial.

(1) Timetable

Paragraph 3.12 of the Practice Direction to Part 28 (The Fast Track) sets out a typical timetable for case preparation of a case allocated to the fast track:

Disclosure [see Chapter 10]	4 weeks
Exchange of witness statements	10 weeks
Exchange of experts' reports	14 weeks
Court sends listing questionnaires	20 weeks
Parties file listing questionnaires	22 weeks
Trial	30 weeks

These periods will run from the date of the Notice of Allocation.

The trial date will either be a fixed date or a 'trial period', not exceeding 3 weeks, within which the trial will take place. At this stage, the court is more likely to fix a 'trial period' rather than a fixed date for trial.

The parties may agree directions between themselves, but, if they do so, the directions must be approved by the court (which will not necessarily accept them).

Fast track standard directions, dealing with disclosure, etc, are set out in the Appendix to the Practice Direction to Part 28.

(2) Varying directions (r 28.4)

Although the parties can vary certain directions by written agreement, for example for disclosure or exchange of witness statements, an application must be made to the court if a party wishes to vary the dates for:

(a) the return of a listing questionnaire;
(b) the trial;
(c) the trial period.

Furthermore, the parties cannot agree to vary any matter if the variation would lead to a variation of any of those dates. For example, it would not be possible to agree to defer the exchange of witness statements until after the date for the return of the listing questionnaire, since this would almost inevitably lead to the need to defer the trial.

The Practice Direction to Part 28 states that any party who wishes to have a direction varied should take steps to do so as soon as possible (para 4.2(1)). There is an assumption that if an application to vary directions is not made within 14 days of the service of the original order then the parties are content that the directions were correct in the circumstances then existing (para 4.2(2)).

A party dissatisfied with a direction or other order given by the court should either:

(a) appeal, if the direction was given or the order was made at a hearing at which he was present or represented or of which he had due notice; or
(b) in any other case, apply to the court to reconsider its decision. Such an application would be heard by the same judge or same level of judge who gave the original decision.

(3) Variation by consent

Where the agreement to vary relates to an act which does not need the court's consent or relates to agreements about disclosure, the parties need not file their written agreement to vary (which will usually be recorded in correspondence). In any other case, the party must apply to the court for an order by consent. The parties must file a draft of the order sought and an agreed statement of the reasons why the variation is sought. The court may make an order in the agreed terms, or in other terms, without a hearing, but it may direct that a hearing is to be listed.

(4) Failure to comply with directions

If a party fails to comply with a direction, any other party may apply for an order enforcing compliance and/or for a sanction to be imposed.

The application should be made without delay.

The Practice Direction to Part 28 is quite clear that a failure to comply with directions will not normally lead to a postponement of the trial date (see para 5.4(1)). This will not be allowed unless the circumstances of the case are exceptional.

If it is practical, the court will exercise its powers in a manner that enables the case to come up for trial on the date or within the period previously set.

In particular, the court will assess what steps each party should take to prepare the case for trial, direct that those steps be taken in the shortest possible time and impose a sanction for non-compliance. Such a sanction may, for example, deprive a party of the right to raise or contest an issue or to rely on evidence to which the direction relates.

Further, if the court is of the view that one or more issues can be made ready for trial within the time fixed, the court may direct that the trial will proceed on the issues which are, or will then be, ready. The court can also order that no costs will be allowed for any later trial of the remaining issues or that those costs will be paid by the party in default. If the court has no option but to postpone the trial, it will do so for the shortest possible time and will give directions for the taking of all outstanding necessary steps as rapidly as possible.

It is clear, therefore, that the trial date is virtually sacrosanct and the parties should ensure that they are ready for trial on the due date.

(5) Directions as to exchange of witness statements and exchange of expert reports

We shall look in detail at evidence in Chapter 11. However, the evidence of those witnesses on whom a party intends to rely at trial must be exchanged in the form of witness statements and experts' reports. The exchange should normally be simultaneous. So far as expert evidence is concerned, the direction in relation to the evidence will say whether it gives permission for oral evidence or written reports or both and will name the experts concerned. The court will not make a direction giving permission for an expert to give oral evidence unless it believes that it is necessary in the interests of justice to do so. In fast track cases, therefore, the usual provision will be for expert evidence to be given by means of written reports and experts will not be allowed to give oral evidence at the trial. Furthermore, the court may order that a single joint expert be appointed, rather than allowing each party to appoint their own.

(6) The listing questionnaire

The purpose of the listing questionnaire is to check that directions have been complied with so that the court can fix a date for the trial (or confirm the date if one has already been fixed).

The notice of allocation will specify a date by which the parties should return the listing questionnaire. This date will be not more than 8 weeks before the trial date or the trial period. The listing questionnaire will have been sent to the parties at least two weeks before it has to be filed at court. A copy of the listing questionnaire (Form N170) appears in Appendix A. Parties are encouraged to exchange copies of the questionnaires before filing them with the court. A cost estimate should also be filed and served.

If no party files a listing questionnaire, the court will normally direct that any claim, defence or counterclaim will be struck out unless a listing questionnaire is filed within 3 days. If some, but not all, parties have filed a listing questionnaire, the court will give its normal listing directions or may hold a hearing (see below).

(7) Listing directions

The court will confirm or fix the date, length and place of the trial. The court will normally give the parties at least 3 weeks' notice of the trial.

The parties should try to agree directions. The agreed directions should deal with, among other things:

(a) evidence;
(b) a trial timetable and time estimate;
(c) preparation of a trial bundle.

The court may fix a listing hearing on 3 days' notice if either:

(a) a party has failed to file the listing questionnaire; or
(b) a party has filed an incomplete listing questionnaire; or
(c) a hearing is needed to decide what directions for trial are appropriate.

Prior to the trial, the parties should try to agree the contents of the trial bundle (see **13.1.3**) which will contain all documents needed for use at the trial. The standard directions require that this bundle should be lodged with the court by the claimant not more than 7 days and not less than 3 days before the start of the trial. Included in the bundle should be a case summary, not exceeding 250 words, outlining the matters still in issue, and referring, where appropriate, to the relevant documents. This is designed to assist the judge in reading the papers before the trial. The case summary should be agreed by the parties if possible.

8.6.3 Allocation to the multi-track (Part 29 of the CPR 1998)

(1) Directions

Cases which have a value of more than £15,000 will, as we have seen, usually be allocated to the multi-track. The multi-track therefore includes an enormously wide range of cases, from the fairly straightforward to the most complex and weighty matters involving claims for millions of pounds and multi-party actions. Case management on the multi-track has to reflect this wide diversity of actions. In straightforward cases, the standard directions which we have already looked at in relation to the fast track may be perfectly adequate, but in more complex cases the court will need to adapt the directions to the particular needs of the case.

When the matter is allocated to the multi-track, the court will either:

(a) give directions for the management of the case and set a timetable for the steps to be taken between the giving of directions and the trial; or
(b) fix a case management conference or a pre-trial review or both and give such directions relating to the management of the case as it sees fit.

The court will fix the trial date or the period in which the trial is to take place as soon as practicable. There is no deadline, however, of 30 weeks as we saw in the fast track.

In a fairly straightforward case, the court may well give directions without holding a case management conference. If it does so, then, by para 4.10 of the Practice Direction to Part 29, its general approach will be:

> '(1) to give directions for the filing and service of any further information required to clarify either party's case,
> (2) to direct standard disclosure between the parties,
> (3) to direct the disclosure of witness statements by way of simultaneous exchange,
> (4) to give directions for a single joint expert on any appropriate issue unless there is a good reason not to do so,
> (5) ... to direct disclosure of experts' reports by way of simultaneous exchange on those issues where a single joint expert is not directed,
> (6) if experts' reports are not agreed, to direct a discussion between experts ...
> (7) to list a case management conference to take place after the date for compliance with the directions, and
> (8) to specify a trial period.'

Alternatively, the parties themselves may agree directions (subject to the approval of the court), but, if so, the directions should deal with the above matters.

(2) The case management conference

In many multi-track cases, the court will hold a case management conference where it feels that more of a 'hands on' approach is needed.

At any case management conference, the court will (para 5.1 to the Practice Direction):

> '(1) review the steps which the parties have taken in the preparation of the case, and in particular their compliance with any directions that the court may have given,

(2) decide and give directions about the steps which are to be taken to secure the progress of the claim in accordance with the overriding objective, and

(3) ensure as far as it can that all agreements that can be reached between the parties about the matters in issue and the conduct of the claim are made and recorded.'

(3) Topics the court will consider at the case management conference

These are likely to include:

(a) Whether each party has clearly stated their case, for example has the claimant made clear the claim he is bringing and the amount he is claiming, so that the other party can understand the case he has to meet? As we saw in Chapter 1, r 1.4(2)(b) requires the court to identify the issues in dispute at an early stage.

(b) Whether any amendments are required to the claim form, a statement of case or any other document.

(c) What disclosure of documents, if any, is necessary.

(d) What expert evidence is reasonably required and how and when that evidence should be obtained and disclosed.

(e) What factual evidence should be disclosed.

(f) What arrangements should be made about the giving or clarification of further information and the putting of questions to experts.

(g) Whether it will be just and will save costs to order a split trial (eg on liability and quantum) or the trial of one of more preliminary issues.

In all cases, the court will set a timetable for the steps it decides are necessary to be taken.

The case management conference is an extremely important hearing and it is essential that the parties are properly prepared for it. The person who attends the hearing on behalf of a party should be someone who is personally involved in the conduct of the case, and who has the authority and information to deal with any matter which may reasonably be expected to be dealt with at such a hearing, including the fixing of the timetable, the identification of issues and matters of evidence.

The consequences of failing to send a properly prepared legal representative to a directions hearing were considered by the Court of Appeal in *Baron v Lovell* [1999] CPLR 630. The court can make an order imposing a sanction (see **8.3.2**), for example, awarding costs against the party in default on an indemnity basis.

Where the inadequacy of the person attending or his instructions leads to the adjournment of the conference, the court will usually make a wasted costs order against the solicitor concerned personally.

The Practice Direction to Part 29 sets out, at para 5.6, guidelines as to how parties should prepare for the case management conference. They should:

'(1) ensure that all documents that the court is likely to ask to see (including witness statements and experts' reports) are brought to the hearing,

(2) consider whether the parties should attend,

(3) consider whether a case summary will be useful, and

(4) consider what orders each wishes to be made and give notice of them to the other parties.'

A case summary should set out a brief chronology of the claim, the issues of fact which are agreed or in dispute and the evidence needed to decide them. It should not normally exceed 500 words and should be prepared by the claimant and agreed with the other party, if possible. Its purpose is to assist the judge at the case management conference, in particular to determine what issues should be tried and what evidence will be required to do so.

Any party who wishes to apply for an order which is not usually made at a case management conference should issue and serve his application in plenty of time if he knows that the application will be opposed, and he should warn the court if the time allowed for the case management conference is likely to be insufficient for his application to be heard.

(4) Variation of directions

A party who wishes to vary a direction (eg because of a change of circumstances) must apply as soon as possible. There is an assumption that if an application to vary directions was not made within 14 days of service of the directions order, the parties were content that the directions ordered were correct in the circumstances then existing.

A party who is dissatisfied with the direction may appeal but, if he was not notified of the hearing or was not present when it was made, he must apply for the court to reconsider, and the court will give all parties 3 days' notice of the hearing.

(5) Non-compliance with directions

If a party fails to comply with a direction, any other party may apply for an order for compliance and/or the imposition of a sanction. Any delay in making the application will be taken into account by the court.

As we saw in the fast track, the trial date is virtually sacrosanct. The court will not allow failure to comply with directions to lead to the postponement of the trial unless the circumstances are exceptional.

(6) The listing questionnaire

The date for filing the completed listing questionnaire will be not later than 8 weeks before the trial date or the start of the trial period and the questionnaire will have been served on the parties at least 14 days before that date. Again, the parties will be encouraged to exchange copies of the questionnaires before they file them. If none of the parties file a questionnaire, the court will usually order that the claim, the defence and any counterclaim will be struck out unless any party files a questionnaire within 3 days of service of the order.

If only some of the parties have filed a questionnaire, the court will usually fix a listing hearing and give directions.

On receipt of the listing questionnaires, the court may decide that it is necessary to hold a pre-trial review (or may decide to cancel one already listed). The court must give the parties at least 7 days' notice of its decision.

As soon as practicable after:

(a) each party has filed a completed listing questionnaire,
(b) the court has held a listing hearing, or
(c) the court has held a pre-trial review,

the court will:

(a) set a timetable for the trial unless a timetable has already been fixed or the court considers that it will be inappropriate to do so; and
(b) fix the date for the trial or the week within which the trial is to begin (or, if it has already done so, confirm that date).

As with the fast track, the court will also order, on listing, that a trial bundle of documents be prepared.

8.7 HUMAN RIGHTS

It may be tempting for a litigant whose statement of case has been struck out either as disclosing no reasonable claim or defence (as the case may be) or for non-compliance with a Rule or order, to seek to quash the decision as being contrary to his right to a fair trial under Article 6. Clear judicial discouragement has, however, already been given by the Court of Appeal in *Daniels v Walker* (see **1.4**). The obligation on the court in the overriding objective to seek to deal with cases justly will make such challenges difficult to pursue successfully.

Chapter 9

APPLICATIONS TO THE COURT

9.1 INTRODUCTION

In this chapter, we shall consider the way in which a party to the case can make an application to the court. We are considering applications made after the issue of proceedings and before the trial. These are known as interim applications.

Part 23 of the CPR 1998 sets out the general rules governing applications to the court. These rules are subject to any express provisions which may apply to specific types of application.

Chapter 9 contents
Introduction
Applications generally
Costs
Appeals against an interim order
Particular types of application
Interim remedies
Interim payments
Security for costs
Human rights

9.2 APPLICATIONS GENERALLY

An application to the court is made by an application notice. Form N244 (see Appendix A) may be used.

The party who is making the application is, not surprisingly, known as the applicant, and the person against whom the order is sought is known as the respondent.

9.2.1 Where to make the application

By r 23.2, the application must be made to the court where the action has been started or the court to where the action has been transferred. If the action has already been listed for trial, it must be made to the court where the trial is to take place. Most applications will be heard by the master (in the Royal Courts of Justice) or district judge.

9.2.2 Content of the application notice

By r 23.6, an application notice must state what order the applicant is seeking and, briefly, why the applicant is seeking the order.

If the applicant wishes to rely on matters set out in the application notice as evidence at the hearing, then it must be verified by a statement of truth.

9.2.3 Draft order

The Practice Direction to Part 23 states that, except in the most simple application, the applicant should bring to any hearing a draft of the order sought. If the case is proceeding in the Royal Courts of Justice and the order is unusually long or complex, it should also be supplied on disk for use by the court office.

9.2.4 Evidence in support of the application

As we shall see later in this chapter, certain of the rules set out a specific requirement for evidence in support of a particular application. Apart from that, the Practice Direction to Part 23 states that, where there is no specific requirement to provide evidence, it should be borne in mind that, as a practical matter, the court will often need to be satisfied by evidence of the facts that are relied on in support of or for opposing the application. The evidence will usually take the form of a witness statement, although a party may also rely on the contents of a statement of case or the application notice itself as evidence, provided it is verified by a statement of truth.

Affidavits (see **11.7**) may be used, but the extra cost of preparing an affidavit over and above that of a witness statement may be disallowed since affidavits are no longer required, except for a limited number of specific applications.

Any evidence relied upon must be filed at the court as well as served on the parties with the application notice. Any evidence in response must be served as soon as possible.

9.2.5 Service of the application notice

Unless the rules relating to a particular type of application specify another time-limit, the application notice must be served at least 3 clear days before the court is to deal with the application. The court may allow a shorter period of notice if this is appropriate in the circumstances. When served, the application notice must be accompanied by a copy of any supporting written evidence and a copy of any draft order.

9.2.6 Consent orders

If the parties have reached agreement on the order they wish the court to make, they can apply for an order to be made by consent without the need for attendance by the parties. The parties must ensure that they provide the court with any material it needs to be satisfied that it is appropriate to make the order, and usually a letter will suffice.

9.2.7 Orders made without notice

Most applications have to be made on notice so that the other party can respond and object to the application if it wishes to do so. However, in certain cases it is possible for an application to be made without notice being given to the other side. Paragraph 3 of the Practice Direction to Part 23 indicates that this may be done in the following circumstances:

(a) where there is exceptional urgency;
(b) where the overriding objective is best furthered by doing so;
(c) by consent of all parties;
(d) with the permission of court;
(e) where a date for a hearing has been fixed and the party wishes to make an application at that hearing but he does not have sufficient time to serve an application notice, he should inform the other party and the court of the intended application as soon as possible and make the application orally at the hearing;

(f) where a court order, Rule or Practice Direction permits.

When an order is made on an application without notice to the respondent, a copy of the order must be served on the respondent, together with a copy of the application notice and the supporting evidence. The order must contain a statement of the right of the respondent to make an application to set aside or vary the order. The respondent may then apply to set aside or vary the order within 7 days of service of the order on him.

If a party has been served with notice of an application but fails to attend, the court may make an order in that party's absence. However, in those circumstances the court may re-list the application of its own initiative or on the application of any party.

9.2.8 Telephone hearings

The Practice Direction to Part 23, para 6 sets out provisions which enable the court to deal with applications by way of a telephone hearing. This will normally be by way of a British Telecom conference call system, or some other comparable system, whereby all the parties can speak together at the same time. All parties must consent for the hearing to be dealt with in this way. This method of dealing with applications is most useful where one or more of the parties' solicitors are located a considerable distance from the court and it is not feasible to instruct local agents to attend on their behalf.

9.3 COSTS

The costs of the application are at the discretion of the master or district judge who hears the application.

The Practice Direction to Part 44 of the CPR 1998 sets out, at para 8.5, the different orders which are usually made and the effect of those orders. They are as follows:

Term	Effect
Costs Costs in any event	The party in whose favour the order is made is entitled to the costs in respect of the part of the proceedings to which the order relates, whatever other costs orders are made in the proceedings
Costs in the case Costs in the application	The party in whose favour the court makes an order for costs at the end of the proceedings is entitled to his costs of the part of the proceedings to which the order relates.
Costs reserved	The decision about costs is deferred to a later occasion, but if no later order is made the costs will be costs in the case.
Claimant's/Defendant's costs in the case/application	If the party in whose favour the costs order is made is awarded costs at the end of the proceedings, that party is entitled to his costs of the part of the proceedings to which the order relates. If any other party is awarded costs at the end of the proceedings, the party in whose favour the final costs order is made is not liable to pay the costs of any other party in respect of the part of the proceedings to which the order relates.
Costs thrown away	Where, for example, a judgment or order is set aside, the party in whose favour the costs order is made is entitled to the costs which have been incurred as a consequence. This includes the costs of – (a) preparing for and attending any hearing at which the judgment or order which has been set aside was made; (b) preparing for and attending any hearing to set aside the judgment or order in question; (c) preparing for and attending any hearing at which the court orders the proceedings or the part in question to be adjourned; (d) any steps taken to enforce a judgment or order which has subsequently been set aside.
Costs of and caused by	Where, for example, the court makes this order on an application to amend a statement of case, the party in whose favour the costs order is made is entitled to the costs of preparing for and attending the application and the costs of any consequential amendment to his own statement of case.

Term	Effect
Costs here and below	The party in whose favour the costs order is made is entitled not only to his costs in respect of the proceedings in which the court makes the order but also to his costs of the proceedings in any lower court.
No order as to costs Each party to pay his own costs	Each party is to bear his own costs of the part of the proceedings to which the order relates whatever costs order the court makes at the end of the proceedings.

If the order made at the hearing makes no mention of costs, none are payable in respect of that application.

If the court makes an order for costs in favour of one of the parties to the application (usually the successful party, but not necessarily so) then the court will make a summary assessment of costs there and then. Any such costs are payable within 14 days, unless the court orders otherwise (r 44.8).

In order for the court to be able to assess the costs at the end of the application, the parties are required, not less than 24 hours prior to the hearing, to file and serve a statement of costs. This provides a breakdown of the costs incurred in relation to the application. A model form of the statement of costs (Form N260) appears in Appendix A. If a party fails to comply with this requirement without reasonable excuse, this will be taken into account by the court in deciding what costs order to make.

On a few occasions, the court may award fixed costs rather than making one of the orders set out above (see, eg, **9.5.2** below). Part 45 sets out the occasions on which fixed costs may be granted and specifies the amount awarded to the paying party. Where fixed costs are granted there is, of course, no need for a summary assessment.

9.3.1 Conditional fee agreements and the summary assessment of interim application costs

This is dealt with at para 14 of PD 44. The fact that one (or even both) of the parties has entered into a conditional fee agreement (a 'CFA') will not prevent the costs of the interim application from being summarily assessed.

Receiving party CFA funded

Where the receiving party (the party whose costs are to be paid) is CFA funded, the court cannot order payment to be made unless satisfied that the receiving party is immediately liable to his solicitor for the costs of the application under the terms of the CFA. To order otherwise would be contrary to the indemnity principle (see **13.3**). Where the CFA is drafted in such a way that the receiving party is not currently liable for the costs of the interim application, the court may direct the paying party to pay the costs into court to await the outcome of the case.

It should be noted that where the receiving party is on a CFA, the court's summary assessment can deal only with the base costs. The question of whether the paying party should be responsible for the success fee on those costs (and if so to what extent) will not be considered by the court until the conclusion of the case.

Paying party CFA funded

A party who is CFA funded may not be in a position to pay interim costs if ordered to do so. Although many CFA clients have the benefit of after-the-event insurance, it is common for such policies not to cover the payment of interim costs awarded to the other side. The court may, therefore, decide to defer the payment of the interim costs until the end of the action. In considering whether to do so, the court should take into account the unfairness of this on the receiving party.

9.4 APPEALS AGAINST AN INTERIM ORDER

The procedure for appeals is set out in Part 52. An appeal from a decision of a district judge in a county court is made to a circuit judge and from a master or district judge in the High Court to a High Court judge.

Permission to appeal is required and will only be granted if the appeal has a real prospect of success or there is some other compelling reason for the appeal to be heard (r 52.3(6)). Permission may be sought either at the original hearing or from the appeal court within 14 days of the original decision. If permission is sought at the original hearing but refused, a further application for permission may be made to the appeal judge.

The appeal hearing will usually be limited to a review of the district judge or master's original decision and no new evidence will be admitted unless the court orders otherwise (r 52.11). The appeal will be allowed if the original decision was either wrong or unjust because of a serious procedural or other irregularity. If the appeal is allowed, the appeal judge may make a variety of orders (eg setting aside or varying the original order and ordering a re-hearing).

9.5 PARTICULAR TYPES OF APPLICATION

9.5.1 Applications to set aside a default judgment (Part 13 of the CPR 1998)

The mandatory grounds

Under r 13.2, the court is obliged to set aside a default judgment that was wrongly entered before the defendant's deadline for filing acknowledgement of service or defence (whichever is applicable) expired. The court is also obliged to set aside a default judgment entered after the claim was paid in full.

The discretionary grounds

Rule 13.3(1) gives the court the power to set aside or vary a default judgment where:

'(a) the defendant has a real prospect of successfully defending the claim; or
(b) it appears to the court that there is some other good reason why –
    (i) the judgment should be set aside or varied; or
    (ii) the defendant should be allowed to defend the claim.'

The court will take account of the promptness of the defendant's application and it is therefore essential that the defendant should issue the application as soon as he becomes aware of the default judgment. The application to the court must be on notice and must be supported by evidence.

Example

A issues a claim form (endorsed with particulars of claim) against B, claiming the price of goods sold and delivered to B. B receives the claim form but forgets to deal with it and A is able to enter default judgment.

B then instructs solicitors. They immediately apply to set the default judgment aside. The evidence in support of the application is a witness statement from B in which he states the goods were not of satisfactory quality.

If B can show that he has a real prospect of successfully defending the claim, the default judgment will be set aside. He may, however, have to pay the costs of the application, which will be summarily assessed, as he was to blame for the default judgment being entered. If the evidence in support of his application was very strong, he might argue that the claimant should have consented to the application as it was clear that the court would set aside the default judgment. In that situation, he may not have to pay the costs of the application.

If the original claim was for a specified amount of money and the defendant is an individual then, if the judgment was not entered in the defendant's home court, the application to set aside the default judgment will be transferred to the defendant's home court, unless the claim was commenced in a specialist list.

The claimant's duty

If the claimant discovers that the defendant did not receive the particulars of claim before the claimant entered judgment, then the claimant is under a duty to set aside the default judgment himself. This can normally be done by letter rather than making an on notice application to the court.

9.5.2 Summary judgment – Part 24 of the CPR 1998

We saw in the previous chapter that the court has the power, under its case management powers contained in Part 3 of the CPR 1998, to strike out a statement of case if it discloses no reasonable grounds for bringing or defending the claim. The court has similar powers under Part 24 of the CPR 1998, which deals with applications for summary judgment. The aim behind the Part 24 procedure is to enable a claimant or defendant to obtain judgment at an early stage without the time and expense involved in proceeding to a full trial.

Grounds for the application

Rule 24.2 states that:

'The court may give summary judgment against a claimant or defendant on the whole of the claim or on a particular issue if –

(a) it considers that –

 (i) that claimant has no real prospect of succeeding on the claim or issue; or

 (ii) that defendant has no real prospect of successfully defending the claim or issue; and

(b) there is no other compelling reason why the case or issue should be disposed of at trial.'

Therefore, either party can make an application for summary judgment (or indeed the court could list the case for a Part 24 hearing on its own initiative). According to para 1.3 of the Practice Direction to Part 24, the application may be based on:

'(1) a point of law (including a question of construction of a document),
(2) the evidence which can reasonably be expected to be available at trial or the lack of it, or
(3) a combination of these.'

The court can give summary judgment against a claimant in any type of proceedings and against the defendant in most types of proceedings, with some exceptions which are beyond the scope of this book.

Procedure

The claimant may not apply for summary judgment until the defendant has filed an acknowledgement of service or a defence, unless the court gives permission. The reason for this is that, if the defendant fails to file an acknowledgement of service or defence, the claimant can enter a default judgment without having to make an application for summary judgment. If the claimant applies for summary judgment before the defendant has filed a defence, then the defendant need not file a defence until the application for summary judgment has been heard.

The defendant can apply for summary judgment at any time. Irrespective of who makes the application, it should be made without delay and usually prior to, or at the time of, filing of allocation questionnaires.

The respondent to the application must be given at least 14 days' notice of the date fixed for the hearing and the issues which it is proposed that the court will decide at the hearing.

The application notice itself must state that it is an application for summary judgment and the application notice or the evidence contained or referred to in it, or served with it, must, as stated in para 2(3) of the Practice Direction to Part 24:

'(a) identify concisely any point of law or provision in a document on which the applicant relies, and/or
(b) state that it is made because the applicant believes that on the evidence the respondent has no real prospect of succeeding on the claim or issue, or (as the case may be) of successfully defending the claim or issue to which the application relates, and

and in either case state that the applicant knows of no other reason why the disposal of the claim or issue should await trial.'

If the application notice does not contain all the applicant's evidence, it should identify the written evidence (such as a witness statement or statement of case) the applicant intends to rely on. The application notice should also inform the respondent of his right to file and serve written evidence in reply.

A respondent who wishes to rely on written evidence must file and serve this at least 7 days before the hearing.

An applicant who wishes to rely on written evidence in reply to the respondent's submissions must file and serve it at least 3 days before the hearing.

These provisions as to evidence also apply in cases where the court has fixed a summary judgment hearing of its own initiative.

Orders the court may make on an application for summary judgment

On a Part 24 application the court may order:

'(1) judgment on the claim,
(2) the striking out or dismissal of the claim,
(3) the dismissal of the application,
(4) a conditional order.'

(para 5.1 of the Practice Direction to Part 24)

A conditional order is an order which requires a party:

'(1) to pay a sum of money into court, or
(2) to take a specified step in relation to his claim or defence, as the case may be,

and provides that that party's claim will be dismissed or his statement of case will be struck out if he does not comply.'

(para 5.2 of the Practice Direction to Part 24)

The court is likely to make a conditional order where it appears to the court possible that a claim or defence may succeed but improbable that it will do so. For example, where a claimant applies for summary judgment in a debt case, if the court is not satisfied that the defence has a 'real prospect' of success, but none the less considers that success is possible (although improbable) the court may allow the defendant to continue to defend the action on the condition that he pays the amount of the claim into court. The money would remain in court pending the final outcome of the case. If the defendant fails to make the payment into court, then the defence would be dismissed and the claimant would be entitled to enter judgment.

Directions

When the court determines a summary judgment application it may:

(a) give directions as to the filing and serving of a defence, if one has not already been filed; and
(b) give further directions.

So, where the court dismisses the application or makes an order that does not completely dispose of the claim, the court may well give case management directions as to the future conduct of the case.

Costs

The costs order made at the conclusion of the hearing will depend on the outcome of the application. Where the applicant is successful in obtaining summary judgment for a specified sum, the court will usually award fixed costs (see Part 45). The fixed costs are £175 if the judgment exceeds £25 but does not exceed £5,000 and £210 if the judgment exceeds £5,000. In fairly straightforward cases, it is likely that the court will award fixed costs. However, it is open to the successful applicant to ask for costs to be summarily assessed if these are going to be more than the fixed costs.

9.5.3 Application for further information (Part 18 of the CPR 1998)

As we saw in Chapter 6, a party may request further information from another party to clarify any matter which is in dispute or give additional information in relation to any such matter.

If the request is not met, the party can apply for an order from the court.

Provided that the request made complied with para 1 of the Practice Direction to Part 18 (see Chapter 6), and at least 14 days have elapsed, the application notice need not be served on the other party and the court may deal with the application without a hearing (Practice Direction to Part 18, para 5.5(1)). Otherwise, the application notice must be served on the other party.

9.6 INTERIM REMEDIES (Part 25)

The court has wide powers to grant parties to an action, or to a proposed action, various interim remedies. These are set out in r 25.1.

'(1) The court may grant the following interim remedies –

    (a) an interim injunction;

    (b) an interim declaration;

    (c) an order –

        (i) for the detention, custody or preservation of relevant property;

        (ii) for the inspection of relevant property;

        (iii) for the taking of a sample of relevant property;

        (iv) for the carrying out of an experiment on or with relevant property;

        (v) for the sale of relevant property which is of a perishable nature or which for any other good reason it is desirable to sell quickly; and

        (vi) for the payment of income from relevant property until a claim is decided;

    (d) an order authorising a person to enter any land or building in the possession of a party to the proceedings for the purposes of carrying out an order under sub-paragraph (c);

    (e) an order under section 4 of the Torts (Interference with Goods) Act 1977 to deliver up goods;

    (f) an order (referred to as a "freezing injunction") –

        (i) restraining a party from removing from the jurisdiction assets located there; or

        (ii) restraining a party from dealing with any assets whether located within the jurisdiction or not;

    (g) an order directing a party to provide information about the location of relevant property or assets or to provide information about relevant property or assets which are or may be the subject of an application for a freezing injunction;

    (h) an order (referred to as a "search order") under section 7 of the Civil Procedure Act 1997 (order requiring a party to admit another party to premises for the purpose of preserving evidence etc);

    (i) an order under section 33 of the Supreme Court Act 1981 or section 52 of the County Courts Act 1984 (order for disclosure of documents or inspection of property before a claim has been made);

    (j) an order under section 34 of the Supreme Court Act 1981 or section 53 of the County Courts Act 1984 (order in certain proceedings for disclosure of documents or inspection of property against a non-party);

(k) an order (referred to as an order for interim payment) under rule 25.6 for payment by a defendant on account of any damages, debt or other sum (except costs) which the court may hold the defendant liable to pay;

(l) an order for a specified fund to be paid into court or otherwise secured, where there is a dispute over a party's right to the fund;

(m) an order permitting a party seeking to recover personal property to pay money into court pending the outcome of the proceedings and directing that, if he does so, the property shall be given up to him; and

(n) an order directing a party to prepare and file accounts relating to the dispute.'

An interim remedy can be obtained before proceedings are issued (eg for pre-action disclosure of document – see **10.5**), during proceedings or even after judgment has been given. A court can grant a remedy before a claim is issued only if the matter is urgent or it is otherwise desirable to do so in the interests of justice. Unless the court orders otherwise, a defendant may not apply for one of the orders listed in r 25.1 until he has filed an acknowledgement of service or defence.

A court can grant an interim remedy on an application made without notice if it appears to the court that there are good reasons for not giving notice. Examples of applications which will, by their very nature, be made without notice, are freezing injunctions and search orders. A freezing injunction restrains a party from removing his assets from the jurisdiction (ie England and Wales). If notice was given to the respondent of such an application, the respondent could simply transfer his assets prior to the hearing of the application.

A search order is an order compelling the respondent to allow his premises to be searched by the applicant. It is obtained where the applicant believes that the respondent has documents which, it is usually alleged, belong to the applicant. Again, if notice was given to the respondent in advance, it would be a simple matter for the respondent to hide the documents somewhere else. Because freezing injunctions and search orders can be quite draconian in their impact upon the respondent, such applications must be made to a High Court judge and the evidence in support of these applications must be by way of affidavit. Evidence in support of other applications for interim remedies is by the usual methods:

(i) witness statements;
(ii) the application notice;
(iii) the statement(s) of case.

The contents of (ii) and (iii) can only be relied on as evidence where they contain a statement of truth.

9.7 INTERIM PAYMENTS

One particular type of interim remedy is an interim payment. An interim payment is an advance payment on account of any damages, debt or other sum (excluding costs) which a defendant may be held liable to pay. The interim payment procedure enables a claimant who has a strong case on liability to avoid the financial hardship and/or inconvenience which might otherwise be suffered because of any delay during the period between the start of the action and its final determination.

Before making an application to the court, the claimant should try to negotiate with the defendant or the defendant's insurance company to obtain a voluntary interim payment. If one is not forthcoming, and if the claimant feels he has good grounds for making the application, then the application should be made as soon as possible.

A claimant may not seek an interim payment until after the time for acknowledging service has expired. The claimant may make more than one application.

9.7.1 Procedure

An application notice for an interim payment must be supported by evidence and be served at least 14 days before the hearing date.

The evidence required in support of an interim payment application is set out in para 2.1 of PD 25B. The evidence must deal with:

(i) the amount of the interim payment being sought;
(ii) the items or matters in respect of which the interim payment is sought;
(iii) the likely amount of the final judgment;
(iv) the reasons for believing that the conditions for an interim payment are satisfied (see below);
(v) any other relevant matters;
(vi) (in personal injury cases) details of special damages and past and future loss;
(vii) (in fatal accident cases) details of the nature of the claim and the people on whose behalf it is being made.

Any documents in support of the application should be exhibited.

If the respondent wishes to rely on evidence then this should be served at least 7 days before the hearing. If the applicant wishes to use evidence in reply to the respondent's evidence, this should be served at least 3 days before the hearing.

9.7.2 Conditions for making the order

The conditions for the court making an interim payment are as follows:

(i) the defendant against whom the order is sought has admitted liability to pay damages or some other sum of money to the claimant;
(ii) the claimant has obtained judgment against that defendant for damages to be assessed or for a sum of money (other than costs) to be assessed;
(iii) the court is satisfied that if the claim went to trial the claimant would obtain judgment for a substantial amount of money (other than costs) against the defendant from whom he is seeking an order for an interim payment.

Special rules apply in personal injury cases whereby the defendant must be covered by insurance or be a public body.

The amount of the interim payment awarded by the court must not exceed a reasonable proportion of the likely amount of the final judgment after taking account of any allegations of contributory negligence and any set off or counterclaim.

If a defendant has made an interim payment, the court may order repayment or order one defendant to reimburse another defendant.

9.7.3 Consequences of an interim payment order

If a defendant has made an interim payment which exceeds his total liability under the final judgment, the court may award interest on the overpaid amount from the date of the interim payment.

The trial judge will not be told about any interim payment until after he has decided all issues of liability and quantum unless the defendant consents.

9.8 SECURITY FOR COSTS

A defendant may be confident that he can successfully defend the claimant's claim against him, but he may feel that if he does so and obtains an order for costs against the claimant, the claimant may not pay those costs. In this situation, the defendant may be able to obtain an order for security for costs against the claimant. The usual way in which security is provided is by the claimant paying a sum of money into court. The order will state the amount to be paid into court and the time-limit for making the payment. If the claimant fails to comply with the order the action can be dismissed.

The procedure for applying for an order for security for costs is dealt in Part 25 of the CPR 1998. The most common grounds for obtaining an order for security for costs are:

(i) that the claimant is ordinarily resident out of the EU; or
(ii) that the claimant is a company or other body (whether incorporated inside or outside Great Britain) and there is reason to believe that it may not be able to pay the defendant's costs if ordered to do so.

It should be noted that this procedure is available only for defendants (including a Part 20 defendant) to use against claimants.

9.9 HUMAN RIGHTS

Various aspects of the rules relating to interim applications to the court might have a human rights dimension, these being orders made without notice; summary judgment; security for costs; and public access.

9.9.1 Orders made without notice

The very fact that an order has been made against a party without telling him of the application and giving him the opportunity to be heard makes it seem that he has not had a fair hearing and his human rights have been infringed. However, there is always a procedure for the respondent to be heard at a later date on whether the order should have been made or whether it should now be set aside. Given that the courts do need to be able to act urgently to protect a litigant's rights where those rights are in danger, most orders made without notice should be able to withstand a human rights challenge.

9.9.2 Summary judgment

A litigant who has summary judgment entered against him has not been able to have a full trial of his case with oral evidence and cross-examination of witnesses. There has, however, been a hearing on the merits and the court will have read the evidence in the form of witness statements. This is not like a default judgment where the court has entered judgment for the claimant as a purely administrative act without considering any evidence at all. As a result, the summary judgment procedure should withstand any human rights challenge.

A conditional order made on an application for summary judgment might be more open to challenge under the Human Rights Act 1998. This is an order which requires the respondent to pay a sum of money into court as a condition of being allowed to continue to bring or defend the claim. If the money is not paid, the respondent will lose the case. There might be an argument that a litigant of limited means whose case is stifled in this way is not getting a fair trial because a wealthier litigant would still be able to continue with the litigation. It should be noted that the Court of Appeal has stated (albeit not in the context of a summary judgment application) that an order requiring an impecunious party to pay money into the court with which he clearly cannot comply, should not be made (*Chapple v Williams* [1999] CPLR 731). Where, however, the court has imposed a condition which the respondent can reasonably meet, because it has concluded that the respondent's prospects of success are improbable, is there any real injustice?

9.9.3 Security for costs

The objection raised in the previous paragraph that the claim may be unjustly stifled applies equally to an order for security for costs. Indeed, perhaps more so, since there will have been no explicit finding by the court that the claimant's prospects of success are improbable. The European Court considered an application for security for costs in *Tolstoy Miloslavsky v UK* (1995) 20 EHRR 442. The applicant had lost a libel case and been ordered to pay substantial damages. The Court of Appeal would only permit him to appeal if he paid into court a significant sum as security for his opponent's costs. He complained that, given his circumstances, the effect was to stifle his appeal. The European Court took the view that the Court of Appeal's order had been legitimate in principle and proportionate in the particular circumstances. However, the European Court gave weight to the fact that the appeal was thought to have no prospect of success and that there had been a lengthy trial at first instance. By implication, an order for security where the party cannot raise the sum ordered and there is a reasonable prospect of success could well be a breach of Article 6(1).

9.9.4 Public access

Article 6(1) of the Convention also states that:

> 'Judgment shall be pronounced publicly but the press and public may be excluded from all or part of the trial in the interests of morals, public order or national security in a democratic society, where the interests of juveniles or the protection of the private life of the parties so require, or to the extent strictly necessary in the opinion of the court in special circumstances whereby publicity would prejudice the interests of justice.'

Although this provision could be interpreted as being limited to the final trial of the action, the Rules Committee interpreted it as extending to interim applications. As a result, Part 39 of the CPR 1998 establishes a presumption that the public are entitled to access to any interim application subject to a list of well defined exceptions such as applications to approve a settlement of a claim brought by a child. In practice, most interim applications continue to be heard in the master or district judge's room, rather than in a courtroom, but requests from a non-party to sit in will usually be granted.

Chapter 10

DISCLOSURE AND INSPECTION OF DOCUMENTS – PART 31 OF THE CPR 1998

10.1 PURPOSE OF DISCLOSURE AND INSPECTION

The main purpose of this stage of the litigation process is to enable the parties to evaluate the strength of their case in advance of the trial. The parties have to reveal to each other the documents which have a bearing on the case. The process is intended to promote settlements and therefore a saving in costs. It ensures that the parties are not taken by surprise at the trial and that the court has all relevant information in order to do justice between the parties. Disclosure is governed by Part 31 of the CPR 1998, which applies to all claims save those allocated to the small claims track.

10.2 DEFINITION OF 'DISCLOSURE'

'Disclosure' is defined in r 31.2 which states:

> 'A party discloses a document by stating that the document exists or has existed.'

This is done by preparing and serving a list of documents on every other party (see **10.8**).

10.3 DEFINITION OF 'DOCUMENTS'

'Documents' are defined in r 31.4 as being anything in which information of any description is recorded. 'Documents' therefore include written documents, audio-tapes, video-tapes, computer disks and photographs.

10.4 STANDARD DISCLOSURE

When a court makes an order for a party to give disclosure of documents, the order is limited to standard disclosure unless the court directs otherwise. Standard disclosure is defined in r 31.6 and requires a party to disclose:

(a) the documents on which he relies; and
(b) the documents which:

   (i) adversely affect his own case;
   (ii) adversely affect another party's case; or
   (iii) support another party's case; and

Chapter 10 contents
Purpose of disclosure and inspection
Definition of 'disclosure'
Definition of 'documents'
Standard disclosure
Disclosure of copies
The duty to search
The right of inspection
Procedure for standard disclosure
The disclosure statement
Continuing obligation
Withholding inspection
Withholding other documents
Failure to disclose
Subsequent use of disclosed documents
Applying for specific disclosure
Pre-action disclosure
Non-party disclosure
Human rights

(c) the documents which he is required to disclose by a relevant Practice Direction.

The duty of disclosure is limited to documents which are or have been in a party's control (see r 31.8). This means that:

(a) the document is or was in his physical possession; or
(b) he has or has had a right to possession of it; or
(c) he has or has had a right to inspect or take copies of it.

Documents held by a party's agent would therefore be within that party's control.

Note that it is open to the parties to agree in writing to dispense with or limit standard disclosure.

10.5 DISCLOSURE OF COPIES

A party need not disclose more than one copy of a document unless the copy contains 'a modification, obliteration or other marking or feature' on which the party intends to rely, or which supports another party's case, or which could adversely affect his own or another party's case. In that case, the copy document is treated as a separate document.

10.6 THE DUTY TO SEARCH

During standard disclosure, a party must make a reasonable search for all documents which could adversely affect his own or another party's case or which support another party's case.

What is reasonable depends on:

(a) the number of documents involved;
(b) the nature and complexity of the proceedings;
(c) the ease and expense of retrieval of any particular document; and
(d) the significance of the document.

If a party has not searched for certain documents on the grounds of unreasonableness, he must state this in his disclosure statement (see **10.9**) and identify the category or class of document in question.

The party should also bear in mind the overriding principle of proportionality (see r 1.1(2)(c)). The Practice Direction to Part 31 suggests, at para 2, for example, that it may be reasonable to decide not to search for documents coming into existence before some particular date or to limit the search to documents in some particular place or places, or to documents falling into particular categories.

10.7 THE RIGHT OF INSPECTION

Rule 31.3 gives a party a right of inspection of a disclosed document, except where:

(a) the document is no longer in the control of the party who disclosed it;
(b) the party disclosing the document has a right or a duty to withhold inspection of it; or

(c) a party considers it would be disproportionate to the issues in the case to permit inspection of documents within a category and states in his disclosure statement (see **10.9**) that inspection of those documents will not be permitted on the grounds that to do so would be disproportionate.

Where a party has a right to inspect a document, that party wishing to inspect must give written notice of his wish to inspect and the party who disclosed the document must permit inspection not more than 7 days after the date on which he received the notice. Rather than going to inspect the documents personally, a party may also request a copy of the document, provided the party also undertakes to pay reasonable copying costs. In this case, the party who disclosed the document must supply him with a copy not more than 7 days after the date on which he received the request.

10.8 PROCEDURE FOR STANDARD DISCLOSURE

Where an order for standard disclosure has been made, each party must make and serve a list of documents using practice form N265 (a copy of which appears in Appendix A), which must identify the documents in a convenient order and manner and as concisely as possible. The Practice Direction to Part 31, at para 3.2, states that it will normally be necessary to list the documents in date order, to number them consecutively and to give each a concise description (eg letter, claimant to defendant). It also suggests that where there is a large number of documents all falling into a particular category, the disclosing party may list those documents as a category rather than individually, for example:

50 bank statements relating to account number at bank dated to .

The list is in three parts. The first part of the list sets out the documents within the party's control and which he does not object to the other party inspecting. The second part of the list sets out other documents of which the party has control but where the party objects to the other party inspecting them. The most common reason for objection to inspection is that the party claims privilege in relation to those documents (see **10.11**).

The third part of the list consists of documents which a party has had but which are no longer in his control. The list must indicate what has happened to these documents.

10.9 THE DISCLOSURE STATEMENT

It will have been seen from the definition of standard disclosure that a party is under an obligation to disclose documents which might adversely affect his own case or support another party's case. A party is therefore under an obligation to disclose documents which could be very detrimental to that party's chances of success, but which the other party does not know exist until disclosure. It is, therefore, essential that parties comply fully and honestly with the requirements of disclosure. Partly for that reason, the list of documents contains a disclosure statement (see r 31.10(5)). This is a statement made by the party disclosing the documents:

(a) setting out the extent of the search that has been made to locate documents of which disclosure is required;
(b) certifying that he understands the duty to disclose documents;
(c) certifying that, to the best of his knowledge, he has carried out that duty.

Where the party making the disclosure statement is a company, firm, association or other organisation, the statement must also identify the person making the statement, the office or position he holds, and explain why he is considered the appropriate person to make the statement.

Proceedings for contempt of court may be brought against a person if he makes, or causes to be made, a false disclosure statement without an honest belief in its truth. The proceedings require the permission of the court unless they are brought by the Attorney-General.

The Practice Direction also states that if the disclosing party has a legal representative acting for him, the legal representative must endeavour to ensure that the person making the disclosure statement understands the duty of disclosure.

A solicitor, therefore, is under a clear duty to advise his client as to the requirements of disclosure. The solicitor must ensure as far as possible that all documents which have to be disclosed are preserved and made available for inspection.

10.10 CONTINUING OBLIGATION

Disclosure is a continuing obligation and continues until the proceedings are concluded. If documents to which the duty of disclosure extends come to a party's notice at any time during the proceedings, even though the party has already supplied a list of documents, he must immediately notify every other party.

The process of disclosure does not therefore come to an end simply because a list has been supplied. If a document is created after that date then it too must be disclosed to the other party if it comes within the definition of standard disclosure.

10.11 WITHHOLDING INSPECTION

As we have already seen, a party can withhold the right to inspect a document which has been disclosed. The usual reason for this is that a party claims that the documents are privileged from inspection. These privileged documents fall into three classes:

(a) documents protected by legal professional privilege;
(b) documents tending to incriminate the party producing them;
(c) documents privileged on the grounds of public policy.

10.11.1 Legal professional privilege

(1) Communications passing between a party and his legal advisers or between a party's legal advisers ('advice privilege')

Letters and other communications passing between a party and his solicitor are privileged from production and inspection provided they are written by or to the solicitor in his professional capacity and for the purpose of obtaining legal advice or assistance for the client. 'Legal advice' is not confined to telling the client the law; it includes information passed by solicitor to client, or vice versa, so that advice may be sought and given, and it includes advice about what should prudently and sensibly be done in the relevant legal context.

Privilege, however, does not extend without limit to all solicitor/client communications. The range of assistance given by solicitors to their clients has greatly broadened in recent times; for example many solicitors now provide investment advice to clients. The scope of legal professional privilege has to be kept within reasonable bounds.

The privilege extends to communications between a party and his solicitor's employee or agent, and also to communications between a party and a solicitor in his service, for example a solicitor to a government department or in a legal department of a commercial enterprise. The privilege also covers instructions and briefs to counsel, counsel's opinions, and counsel's drafts and notes.

(2) Communications passing between the solicitor and a third party ('litigation privilege')

Communications passing between the solicitor and a third party are only privileged from production and inspection if:

(i) they come into existence after litigation is contemplated or commenced; and
(ii) they are made with a view to the litigation, either for the purpose of obtaining or giving advice in regard to it, or for obtaining evidence to be used in it.

Examples of documents which may come within this head of privilege are a report from an expert obtained by a solicitor with a view to advising his client about existing or contemplated litigation, or witness statements obtained by a solicitor for the purpose of existing or contemplated litigation.

(3) Communications between the party personally and a third party ('litigation privilege')

Documents which have passed between the party personally and a third party are privileged if the dominant purpose for which they were produced was to obtain legal advice in respect of existing or contemplated litigation or to conduct, or aid in the conduct, of such litigation. It must be the case that litigation was reasonably in prospect at the time when the document was brought into existence, and that the dominant reason for obtaining the document was to enable solicitors to advise as to whether a claim should be made or resisted, for example a report compiled following an accident may be prepared for the purpose of obtaining legal advice as to whether to resist a claim, or it may be prepared with a view to avoiding similar accidents in the future.

In order to determine whether the document is privileged, one must look at the dominant purpose at the time when it came into existence. If the document is subsequently used by solicitors for the purposes of litigation, that will not mean that it is privileged, if the original purpose of the document was something different.

Where a party is not an individual, this form of privilege is also applied to communications between individuals within that organisation. Thus, a memorandum sent by one partner of a firm to another would be privileged if it was prepared for the dominant purpose of obtaining legal advice in respect of existing or contemplated litigation or to aid the conduct of such litigation.

(4) Waiver of privilege

The privilege is the privilege of the client and not of the solicitor and therefore it may be waived by the client but not by the solicitor.

Once a copy of a privileged document is served on the other side, the privilege is waived. Subsequent to disclosure and inspection, each party is required by the court to serve on the other(s) copies of the witness statements and expert reports upon which he intends to rely at trial (see further Chapter 11). This waives the privilege in these documents.

Special considerations apply to the letter of instruction given by a solicitor to an expert whose report is relied upon at trial (see **11.13.3**).

10.11.2 Documents tending to incriminate the party who would produce them

A party is entitled to claim privilege for documents which will tend to incriminate either himself or his spouse. This rule applies to criminal liability or penal proceedings under the law of any part of the UK.

10.11.3 Documents privileged on the ground of public policy

If production of a document would be injurious to the public interest, it must be withheld on the ground of public policy.

This ground of privilege does not depend on the objection of a party to the production of the document. The judge should insist on the rule even if the question of privilege is not raised by the parties.

The judge has to consider whether the withholding of the documents is necessary for the proper functioning of the public service.

Examples of documents which have been withheld from production on this ground are documents dealing with matters of national defence, information as to ill treatment of children given to the NSPCC, local authority social work records, probation service records, and evidence which might reveal the identity of a police informant.

10.11.4 Challenging a claim to privilege

A party who wishes to challenge his opponent's claim to privilege can apply for the court to decide whether the claim to privilege should be upheld. In any case where there is a claim to privilege, the court may require the party claiming privilege to produce the document to the court and may invite any person, even if they are not a party, to make representation.

10.11.5 Inadvertent disclosure of privileged documents

If privileged documents are mistakenly listed in part 1 of a party's list (instead of part 2), no harm is done if the error is spotted before the other side inspects the document since the list may be amended and re-served.

Damage may, however, be done where inspection of privileged material is allowed inadvertently, for example where copies of privileged documents have been sent in error to the other side's solicitor. However, under r 31.20, the receiving party is not permitted to use the documents or their contents without the permission of the court.

Should he attempt to do so the disclosing party may be able to persuade the court to grant an injunction requiring the receiving party and his solicitor to return the documents, without retaining a photocopy and restraining the use of the privileged material in the litigation. The court has a discretion whether to grant an injunction and will only do so if satisfied that the mistake was evident to the solicitor receiving the documents, or, if not, that it would have been obvious to a hypothetical reasonable solicitor that disclosure had occurred as a result of an obvious mistake (*IBM Corporation & Anor v Phoenix International (Computers) Ltd* [1995] 1 All ER 413).

Where the mistake is less than obvious, there is no obligation on the solicitor receiving the documents to make enquiries of the sending party (*Norman Roger Breeze v John Stacy & Sons Ltd* (1999) *The Times*, July 8, CA).

The Guide to the Professional Conduct of Solicitors 8th edn (Law Society Publishing, 1999) makes it clear that as soon as a solicitor who receives privileged documents realises that the sender has made an obvious mistake, he should immediately stop reading the documents, inform the other side and return the documents. He may inform his client what has happened.

10.12 WITHHOLDING OTHER DOCUMENTS

10.12.1 Without prejudice correspondence

As mentioned in Chapter 3, attempts to settle a case should usually be conducted on a 'without prejudice' basis. Without prejudice correspondence is not privileged from inspection in the same way that solicitor–client correspondence is; both solicitors have seen the letter anyway. If, however, there are, for example, three parties involved in an action and the without prejudice correspondence has taken place between only two of the parties, such correspondence is privileged from inspection by the third party.

The importance of correspondence being without prejudice, however, is that it cannot be referred to at court. So, a concession made by a party when trying to settle a case cannot be used against him at the trial.

> *Example*
> A is suing B for a debt of £150,000. A's solicitor writes to B's solicitor on a without prejudice basis saying A will accept £120,000 if that sum is paid immediately. B rejects this compromise.
>
> B cannot refer to this letter at trial and A can still try to obtain judgment for the full amount of the claim.

This rule is to encourage litigants to reach a settlement, if possible. It means that all negotiations which are genuinely aimed at a settlement are excluded from being given in evidence. The rule applies whether the negotiations are oral or in writing and thus applies to an attendance note of a without prejudice conversation as well as to correspondence.

Although as a matter of good practice the words 'without prejudice' should appear on this type of correspondence, the presence or absence of the words is not conclusive. What is important is that the letter is a genuine attempt to settle the case. If there is a dispute as to whether or not a communication is privileged in this way, the court can examine the document (obviously in advance of the trial so that the trial judge does not see it) to see whether or not its purpose was to settle the dispute. If it was, it is privileged; if not, then even if it carries the words 'without prejudice', it is not.

Once a settlement is concluded, any 'without prejudice' correspondence can be produced in court to show the terms agreed between the parties. This might be necessary if, for example, a dispute arose as to enforcement of an agreed settlement.

10.13 FAILURE TO DISCLOSE

A party who fails to disclose a document or fails to allow inspection of a document may not rely on that document unless the court permits. However, the rule is likely to be of limited impact, since a party is far more likely to withhold a document that would assist his opponent at trial than one which he would wish to rely on. Note, importantly, however, that a party who fails to disclose a document which harms his case may find that his case is struck out as a result of failure to comply with an order for specific disclosure (see **10.15**).

10.14 SUBSEQUENT USE OF DISCLOSED DOCUMENTS

Where a document has been disclosed to a party, he may only use that document for the purposes of the case in which it has been disclosed unless:

(a) the document has been read or referred to during a public hearing (eg at trial); or
(b) the court grants permission; or
(c) the party who disclosed the document and the person to whom the document belongs consent.

Where (a) applies, the court may make an order restricting or prohibiting the use of the document.

10.15 APPLYING FOR SPECIFIC DISCLOSURE

If a party is dissatisfied with disclosure provided by the other party and believes it is inadequate, then he may make an application for an order for specific disclosure. The application notice must specify the order the applicant wants the court to make and the grounds of the application must be set out in the application notice or in the supporting evidence. For example, in a claim arising out of the supply of allegedly defective goods sold by the defendant to the claimant, the claimant may suspect that the defendant should have quality control records. If these have not been disclosed, then an application for specific disclosure may be justified.

Before making such an application, a party should write to the other side explaining why they believe the documents are disclosable and asking the other party to comply properly with the order for disclosure. If a satisfactory response is not forthcoming, then it would be appropriate to issue the application.

An order for specific disclosure can require a party to:

(i) disclose specified documents or classes of documents;
(ii) carry out a search as specified by the order and disclose any documents located as a result of that search.

When deciding whether to make an order for specific disclosure, the court will take into account all the circumstances of the case and, in particular, the overriding objective in r 1.1. If the court concludes that the party from whom specific disclosure is sought has failed adequately to comply with the obligation imposed by the order for disclosure, the court will usually make such order as is necessary to ensure that those obligations are properly complied with. For example, the order will often be made in the form of an unless order.

A party can also apply for an order for specific inspection which would require a party to permit inspection of documents which he omitted from his disclosure statement on the grounds that inspection would be disproportionate.

10.16 PRE-ACTION DISCLOSURE

As we saw in Chapter 3, a party may make an application for pre-action disclosure.

This procedure will normally be used where a party is unsure whether he has a good case against another party and, therefore, does not know whether to issue proceedings. The party could, therefore, apply for pre-action disclosure against the intended defendant so that he can then make an informed decision as to whether or not to issue proceedings against that person.

10.17 NON-PARTY DISCLOSURE

Where proceedings are already in existence, then a party to the proceedings can apply for disclosure against a non-party.

The application must be supported by evidence.

The court may order non-party disclosure only if:

(a) the documents in question are likely to support the applicant's case or adversely affect the case of another party; and
(b) disclosure is necessary to dispose fairly of the case or to save costs.

The order must:

(a) specify the documents or classes of documents to be disclosed; and
(b) require the non-party to specify which documents are no longer in his control and which are privileged.

The order may specify a time and place for disclosure and inspection and may require the non-party to indicate what has happened to the documents which are no longer in his control.

This procedure enables a party to proceedings which are already in existence to obtain disclosure of documents from a non-party if it is going to help resolve the issues in the case.

The most common application of this procedure would be where a party indicates in his list of documents that he no longer has a document in his possession. He also indicates that X now has possession of that document.

The other party may then write to X asking for a copy of the document. If X refuses to supply that copy voluntarily, the other party could then apply for an order for non-party disclosure against X.

10.18 HUMAN RIGHTS

Article 6(1) requires the disclosure of relevant documents to all parties in civil proceedings (see, eg, *McGinley and Egan v UK* (1998) 27 EHRR 1). Is it therefore possible that some of the rules relating to privilege could be open to attack as interfering with the right to a fair hearing under Article 6(1)? It is almost inconceivable that the rules on legal professional privilege or without prejudice correspondence could be successfully attacked on this basis, and the privilege against self-incrimination is such a well recognised bastion of human rights that it is bound to be supported (it has already featured in one important Scottish decision on human rights).

However, withholding documents on the grounds that they are covered by public interest immunity has always been a controversial part of the common law and is virtually certain to be the subject of human rights litigation sooner rather than later.

Chapter 11

EVIDENCE

11.1 INTRODUCTION

The rules on evidence are contained primarily within Parts 32 and 33 of the CPR 1998. These Rules do not change the law on the admissibility of evidence save for the fact that the court, as might be expected through its court management powers, can control the evidence brought before the court.

Rule 32.1 states:

'(1) The court may control the evidence by giving directions as to –
   (a) the issues on which it requires evidence;
   (b) the nature of the evidence which it requires to decide those issues; and
   (c) the way in which the evidence is to be placed before the court.
(2) The court may use its power under this rule to exclude evidence that would otherwise be admissible.
(3) The court may limit cross-examination.'

In exercising its powers under this Rule, the court will bear in mind the overriding objective in r 1.1 and will attempt to define and identify the issues between the parties. For example, the court may decide, prior to the trial, that a particular issue which has been raised is no longer important and make an order excluding any evidence which the parties intended to use in relation to that particular issue.

11.2 WITNESS EVIDENCE

Under r 32.2(1), the general rule is that any fact which needs to be proved is to be proved at trial by oral evidence given in public and at any other hearing by evidence in writing. The Rules also provide that the court may allow a witness to give evidence by any means, including a video link.

As already seen in Chapter 8, when giving directions for trial, the court will usually order witness statements to be exchanged. Rule 32.4(2) states that the court will order a party to serve on the other parties any witness statement of the oral evidence which the party serving the statement intends to rely upon in relation to any issue of fact to be decided at the trial. As outlined at **11.6**, where a witness statement is not served, the witness will only be allowed to give evidence at trial with the court's permission.

The court can give directions as to the order in which witness statements are to be served. Usually the court will order simultaneous exchange, but may order one party (usually the claimant) to serve first (sequential exchange). Once a witness statement is served, it ceases to be privileged (see further **10.11.1(4)**).

Chapter 11 contents
Introduction
Witness evidence
Form of witness statements
Use of witness statements at trial
Witness summaries
Sanctions for non-service of witness statements
Affidavits
Opinion evidence
Hearsay evidence
Use of plans, photographs and models as evidence
Notice to admit facts
Notice to admit or prove documents
Expert evidence
Assessors
Human rights

11.3 FORM OF WITNESS STATEMENTS

Rules relating to the form of witness statements are set out in paras 17–20 of the Practice Direction to Part 32.

The witness statement should be headed in the same way as any other court document and the top right-hand corner should state:

(a) the party on whose behalf the statement is filed;
(b) the initials and surname of the witness;
(c) the number of the statement in relation to that witness;
(d) the identifying initials and number of each exhibit referred to; and
(e) the date the statement was made.

The statement should be in the witness's own words as far as practicable. It should be in the first person and state:

(a) the full name of the witness;
(b) where he lives or, if the statement is made as part of his employment or business, where he works, his position in the business and the name of the business;
(c) his occupation or description; and
(d) (if so) that he is a party or an employee of a party.

The statement must indicate which of the statements are based on the witness's own knowledge and which are matters of information or belief, and the source of his information and belief. The statement is required to be set out in numbered paragraphs and will generally outline the relevant events chronologically. Dates and any other numbers should be expressed in figures, not words.

Any exhibit used in connection with a witness statement should be verified and identified by the witness and remain separate from the statement. Exhibits should be numbered and, where a witness makes more than one statement in which there are exhibits in the same proceedings, the numbering of the exhibits should run consecutively throughout and not start again with each witness statement.

The witness statement must contain a statement of truth in the following words:

I believe that the facts stated in this witness statement are true.

The statement of truth must be signed by the witness himself. Proceedings for contempt of court may be brought against a person who makes a false statement in a witness statement without an honest belief in its truth.

11.4 USE OF WITNESS STATEMENTS AT TRIAL

Having served a witness statement on the other side, the witness will usually be called to give oral evidence at trial, unless the court orders otherwise or the party uses the statement as hearsay evidence (see **11.9**).

The witness statement will stand as the evidence-in-chief of the witness unless the court orders otherwise. When preparing a witness statement to be used at trial, it is, therefore, essential to ensure that the statement is comprehensive. A witness may amplify his statement or give evidence of matters which have arisen since he served his witness statement but only if the court gives permission. The court will do so only if it considers that there is good reason not to confine the evidence of the witness to the contents of his witness statement. Further, the statement should only contain evidence that the witness could give orally at trial, ie evidence that is admissible and relevant to the issues.

If a party who has served a witness statement does not call the witness or use the statement as hearsay evidence, any other party may use the witness statement as hearsay evidence.

As the witness statement will usually stand as the evidence-in-chief, the witness will normally simply be asked to confirm that it is true and will then be subject to cross-examination by the other side. It is because it is subject to cross-examination that oral evidence from witnesses is considered to be the 'best' form of evidence as it has been tested in court.

11.5 WITNESS SUMMARIES

Sometimes it will be very difficult to persuade a witness to give a witness statement. As we shall see in the next chapter, the means exist to compel a witness to come to court but it is obviously risky to do that if you do not know what the witness is going to say and, of course, as no witness statement will have been exchanged, permission of the court will be necessary anyway before the witness can give oral evidence.

> *Example*
> Fred is suing his former employers for damages arising out of an accident he suffered at work. His former colleague, Mark, could give evidence about poor safety practices within the firm, but has refused to give a witness statement to Fred's solicitors as he is worried that if he does he might be dismissed.

Rule 32.9 now provides that a party can apply to court without notice for an order to serve a 'witness summary'. This provision applies where a party is required to serve a witness statement for trial but cannot obtain one. The witness summary contains:

(a) the evidence which would otherwise go in a witness statement; or
(b) if the party serving the summary does not know what evidence will be given, the areas about which they propose to question the witness;
(c) the witness's name and address.

Unless the court orders otherwise, the summary must be served on the other side at the same time as the witness statements.

11.6 SANCTIONS FOR NON-SERVICE OF WITNESS STATEMENTS

If a party does not serve a witness statement or witness summary within the proper time-limit, the witness cannot give oral evidence unless the court gives permission.

Delay in exchanging witness statements was considered by Buckley J in *Mealey Horgan plc v Horgan* (1999) *The Times*, July 6. Although the CPR 1998 clearly give the court power to prevent a party from relying on evidence which he has failed to disclose on time, the judge took the view that this would be an exceptional step which could be justified only if the party seeking to rely on the evidence had deliberately broken earlier court orders or the delay was so inexcusable that allowing the evidence to be used would necessitate an adjournment of the trial to give the other party the opportunity to deal with the new evidence.

In that case, Buckley J also considered whether it would be appropriate to penalise the party who had failed to serve his witness statement in time by requiring him to pay money into court as security for the other party's claim or costs. Again, he thought that this was an inappropriate method of dealing with an isolated incident involving a relatively short delay which had not prejudiced the other party. A payment into court would normally be ordered only if there had been a history of repeated failure to comply with court orders.

The normal penalty for delay in serving witness statements, therefore, is that the party in default will have to apply, at his own expense, for permission to use the evidence. Apart from the cost and the inconvenience of having to do this, there will be no other penalty and the party at fault will still be able to use the evidence.

11.7 AFFIDAVITS

Affidavits are sworn statements of evidence, ie the maker of the affidavit has to swear before a solicitor (not his own), or other authorised person, that the contents of the affidavit are true. Prior to the CPR 1998 coming into force, affidavits were the usual means of submitting evidence at interim applications. As we have seen, however, evidence at such applications is now given by witness statements, the statement of case itself or the application notice – provided it contains a statement of truth.

In the great majority of cases, therefore, there is no need to go to the extra expense (an oath fee) of using sworn affidavits as evidence. Indeed, if you do, it is very unlikely that the court would allow you to recoup the extra cost from the other side.

On some occasions, however, it is still necessary to use affidavits. The Rules provide that if you are applying for a freezing injunction or search order (see **9.6**), the evidence in support of such an application must be by way of affidavit rather than a witness statement.

11.8 OPINION EVIDENCE

The general rule is that opinion evidence is not admissible. The function of a witness is to relate the facts to the court so that the court can draw its own conclusions. There are some situations in which it may be difficult for a witness to separate fact and opinion. A typical example is speed. If a witness gives evidence that a vehicle was being driven at 'about 60 mph', that is only the witness's opinion. Nevertheless, it is difficult to see how else the witness could express what he saw unless he restricted himself to describing the speed as 'fast'. Accordingly, whilst the cogency of the witness's assessment of the speed might be challenged, it would usually be admissible. Similarly, a witness may be permitted to express a view that 'John was drunk'. Properly, the witness should relate the physical characteristics which led to that conclusion, presumably slurred speech, glazed eyes, an unsteadiness of gait, and breath smelling of alcohol. However, the witness's opinion, whilst it might be challenged, will be admissible. This is confirmed by s 3(2) of the Civil Evidence Act 1972 which states that:

'... where a person is called as a witness in any civil proceedings, a statement of opinion by him on any relevant matter on which he is not qualified to give expert evidence, if made as a way of conveying relevant facts personally perceived by him, is admissible as evidence of what he perceived.'

As is indicated in the section, the other main exception to the inadmissibility of opinion evidence concerns expert evidence (see **11.13**).

11.9 HEARSAY EVIDENCE

Special considerations apply where hearsay evidence is to be used. Before looking at these, it is necessary to understand what is meant by 'hearsay'.

11.9.1 Definition

Hearsay evidence is defined in s 1(2)(a) of the Civil Evidence Act 1995 as 'a statement made otherwise than by a person while giving oral evidence in the proceedings which is tendered as evidence of the matters stated'.

Hearsay evidence may be an oral or written statement made outside the courtroom which is repeated to the court in order to prove the truth of the matter stated out of court.

Therefore, in considering whether evidence is hearsay, there are two questions to consider:

(a) Does the evidence consist of an oral or written statement made outside the courtroom?
(b) Is that statement being presented to the court in order to prove that it is true? If the previous statement is being related, for example to show a person's state of mind or simply to show that the statement was made, then it will not be hearsay.

Example 1
Richard is giving evidence. He says in his evidence, 'Dave told me that Peter had stolen a car'. Richard is repeating what someone else said outside the courtroom, so the first part of the definition of hearsay is satisfied. But, consider why Richard is giving this evidence. If it is as part of a case against Peter where it is relevant to show that Peter did, indeed, steal a car, then it will be hearsay. On the other hand, if Richard is giving evidence in a defamation claim brought by Peter against Dave, then it will not be hearsay. Here, Richard is not giving the evidence to show that Peter stole a car. (Indeed, this would be exactly what Peter does not want to show!) Here, Richard is relating the evidence simply to show that the statement was made.

Example 2
Michael booked a holiday with Fancy Tours Limited. When booking, the agent assured him that the hotel would be quiet and peaceful, close to the beach and with its own swimming pool. However, the hotel was noisy, some distance

away from the beach, and did not have a swimming pool. Michael is now suing for misrepresentation and wishes to repeat in evidence the statements made to him. This will not be hearsay because it is not being related to show the truth of those statements. It is being related to show the effect that the statements had on his state of mind, namely that he was misled by the misrepresentations.

Hearsay evidence may be either first-hand or multiple.

Example 1
Sara gives evidence of something that she was told by John (in order to prove the truth of John's statement). Sara's evidence is first-hand hearsay.

Example 2
Sara also gives evidence of something that John was told by Michelle (in order to prove the truth of what Michelle said). This evidence is multiple hearsay.

11.9.2 Using hearsay evidence

Section 1 of the Civil Evidence Act 1995 provides that, in civil proceedings, evidence shall not be excluded on the ground that it is hearsay. Therefore, hearsay evidence is admissible in civil proceedings. Section 2 of the Act provides that a party proposing to bring hearsay evidence must notify any other party of that fact and, on request, give particulars of/or relating to the evidence. This must be read in conjunction with Part 33 of the CPR 1998 which sets out the rules relating to how hearsay evidence can be used.

Rule 33.2 states:

'(1) Where a party intends to rely on hearsay evidence at trial and either –

(a) that evidence is to be given by a witness giving oral evidence; or
(b) that evidence is contained in a witness statement of a person who is not being called to give oral evidence;

that party complies with section 2(1)(a) of the Civil Evidence Act 1995 by serving a witness statement on the other parties in accordance with the court's order.

(2) Where paragraph (1)(b) applies, the party intending to rely on the hearsay evidence must, when he serves the witness statement –

(a) inform the other parties that the witness is not being called to give oral evidence; and
(b) give the reason why the witness will not be called.

(3) In all other cases where a party intends to rely on hearsay evidence at trial, that party complies with section 2(1)(a) of the Civil Evidence Act 1995 by serving a notice on the other parties which –

(a) identifies the hearsay evidence;
(b) states that the party serving the notice proposes to rely on the hearsay evidence at trial; and
(c) gives the reason why the witness will not be called.

(4) The party proposing to rely on the hearsay evidence must –

(a) serve the notice no later than the latest date for serving witness statements; and

(b) if the hearsay evidence is to be in a document, supply a copy to any party who requests him to do so.'

Therefore, if a party serves a witness statement which contains hearsay evidence, then simply serving the statement on the other party complies with the notice requirements of the Civil Evidence Act 1995. However, if a party does not intend to call a witness but instead intends to rely on the statement itself as hearsay evidence, then that party must inform the other side when he serves the witness statement that he is not calling the witness to give oral evidence and give the reason why the witness will not be called.

Notice of intention to rely on hearsay evidence is not required for evidence at hearings other than trials such as interim applications.

11.9.3 Other matters relating to the use of hearsay evidence

(1) Weight to be attached to hearsay evidence

Section 4 of the Civil Evidence Act 1995 provides guidelines for the courts to assist them in assessing the weight they should attach to hearsay evidence.

It provides that the court is to have regard to any circumstances from which any inference can reasonably be drawn as to the reliability or otherwise of the evidence, and, in particular, to:

(a) whether it would have been reasonable and practicable for the party adducing the evidence to have called the person who made the original statement as a witness;
(b) whether the original statement was made contemporaneously with the events in question;
(c) whether the evidence involves multiple hearsay;
(d) whether any person involved had any motive to conceal or misrepresent matters;
(e) whether the original statement was edited, or was made in collaboration with someone else or for a particular purpose;
(f) whether the circumstances suggest an attempt to prevent proper evaluation of the weight of the evidence.

(2) Right of the opposing party to cross-examine the person who originally made the statement

Section 3 of the Civil Evidence Act 1995 provides that where a party adduces hearsay evidence from a person whom he does not call as a witness, any other party may, with the permission of the court, call that person as a witness and cross-examine him. An application for such permission must be made not later than 14 days after service of the hearsay notice (CPR 1998, r 33.4).

(3) Competence (Civil Evidence Act 1995, s 5)

Hearsay evidence is not admissible if the original statement was made by a person who was not competent as a witness because of his mental or physical infirmity or lack of understanding.

(4) Credibility (Civil Evidence Act 1995, s 5)

Where hearsay evidence is adduced and the person who made the original statement is not called as a witness, evidence is still admissible to attack or support his credibility, or to show that he has made another inconsistent statement. The party wishing to call such evidence must give notice to the other party not later than 14 days after service of the hearsay evidence (CPR 1998, r 33.5).

(5) Previous inconsistent statements (Civil Evidence Act 1995, s 6)

A statement made previously by a person who is called as a witness in the proceedings is admissible in evidence, provided the requirements of the Civil Evidence Act 1995 regarding hearsay evidence are complied with. Thus, prior notice of the intention to adduce the statement in evidence must be given to the other party.

However, a party who calls a person as a witness may not adduce evidence of a previous statement by that person, except with permission of the court, or to rebut a suggestion of recent fabrication.

The effect of this provision is that, where a party calls a witness to give evidence at the trial, the opposing party may cross-examine the witness about a previous inconsistent statement provided that he has complied with the requirements of the Civil Evidence Act 1995 concerning the use of hearsay evidence.

The party calling the witness may adduce evidence of a previous statement by that person only in the circumstances mentioned above (ie with the court's permission or to rebut a suggestion of recent fabrication). Again, the requirements of the Civil Evidence Act 1995 regarding the use of hearsay evidence should have been complied with.

However, this does not prevent a person's witness statement being treated as his evidence-in-chief. The judge at the trial can, and usually will, still order that a witness statement which was served before the trial shall stand as the evidence-in-chief of that witness. The witness will, of course, be present at the trial, and will be subject to cross-examination. In these circumstances, his witness statement is not treated as hearsay evidence.

11.10 USE OF PLANS, PHOTOGRAPHS AND MODELS AS EVIDENCE (r 33.6)

Where evidence such as a plan, photograph, model or the records of a business or public authority is to be given in evidence and it is not:

(a) contained in a witness statement, affidavit, or expert's report;
(b) to be given orally at the trial; or
(c) the subject of a hearsay notice;

the evidence will not be admissible unless the party intending to use the evidence has disclosed his intention to use such evidence within the deadline for serving witness statements.

He must disclose his intention at least 21 days before the hearing, if:

(a) there are not to be witness statements; or
(b) he intends to use the evidence solely to disprove an allegation made in a witness statement.

If the evidence forms part of an expert's report, he must disclose his intention when he serves his expert's report.

Where a party has given notice of his intention to put in the evidence, he must give every other party an opportunity to inspect it and to agree to its admission without further proof.

11.11 NOTICE TO ADMIT FACTS (r 32.18)

In order to try to avoid the expense of proving a particular fact at trial, a party may serve on another party a notice requiring him to admit certain facts or a certain part of his case, as specified in the notice.

Such a notice must be served no later than 21 days before the trial.

If the party upon whom the notice is served refuses to admit the relevant fact(s), the other party will still be required to prove the fact(s) at trial. Where, however, he does so, the court may take this into account when considering the issue of costs. Effectively, this means that the party who served the notice will usually recover the cost of proving the facts in question (even if they lose the case).

11.12 NOTICE TO ADMIT OR PROVE DOCUMENTS (r 32.19)

A party is deemed to admit that any document disclosed in a list of documents served under Part 31 is genuine unless he serves notice that he wants the document to be proved at trial.

A notice to prove a document must be served by the later of the following:

(a) the latest date for serving witness statements; or
(b) within 7 days of disclosure of the document.

11.13 EXPERT EVIDENCE (Part 35)

As we saw in Chapter 3, in many cases a party may wish to instruct an expert and rely upon expert evidence. However, parties do not have an unfettered right to use expert evidence and, as part of its case management powers, the court will restrict expert evidence to that which is reasonably required to resolve the proceedings, bearing in mind the overriding objective and the issue of proportionality.

11.13.1 The duty of an expert

Although in many cases an expert is instructed by one particular party, r 35.3 makes it clear that the duty of an expert is to help the court on the matters within his expertise, and this duty overrides any obligation to the person from whom he has received instructions or by whom he is paid. If the expert is unsure of the nature of these obligations, he may file a request for directions from the court. Experts should, therefore, be completely objective and unbiased in the way in which they provide their opinion for the benefit of the court (see *Stevens v Gullis* [1999] BLR 394).

An expert is not disqualified by the fact of being employed by one of the parties, although the court will need to be satisfied that the expert was sufficiently aware of his responsibilities to the court (*Field v Leeds City Council* (2000) *The Times*,

January 18, CA). Given the risk of the appearance of bias, parties will generally prefer to instruct an expert who is independent.

11.13.2 The court's power to restrict expert evidence

Rule 35.4 provides that no party may call an expert or put in evidence an expert's report without the court's permission. Permission is usually granted at the directions stage, and the party applying for permission must identify both the field in which he wishes to rely on expert evidence and, where practicable, the expert in that field on whose evidence he wishes to rely. As we saw in Chapter 8, this information should normally be provided in the allocation questionnaire.

The options available to the court in giving directions on expert evidence include:

(a) directing that no expert evidence is to be adduced at all, or no expert evidence of a particular type or relating to a particular issue;
(b) limiting the number of expert witnesses which each party may call, either generally or in a given speciality;
(c) directing that evidence is to be given by one or more experts chosen by agreement between the parties or, where they cannot agree, chosen by such other manner as the court may direct.

The court will also decide whether it is necessary for experts to give oral evidence at trial. This is probably going to be the case on a multi-track case but, in fast track cases, the normal provision is that expert evidence be given in the form of a written report or reports rather than by way of oral evidence.

The court also has the power to limit the amount of the expert's fees and expenses that the party who wishes to rely on the expert may recover from any other party.

11.13.3 The letter of instruction to an expert witness

One would normally expect the letter of instruction from a solicitor to an expert witness to be a privileged document (see **10.11**). However, r 35.10(4) states:

> 'The instructions referred to in paragraph (3) [the letter of instructions to the expert] shall not be privileged against disclosure but the court will not, in relation to those instructions –
>
> (a) order disclosure of any specific document; or
> (b) permit any questioning in court other than by the party who instructed the expert,
>
> unless it is satisfied that there are reasonable grounds to consider the statement of instructions given under paragraph (3) to be inaccurate or incomplete.'

Care must be taken, therefore, in drafting the letter of instruction to the expert witness as it is possible that in due course it will have to be disclosed to the other party. As we shall see, in any event the report itself must contain the substance of all material instructions received.

11.13.4 Form of expert evidence

Expert evidence is to be given in a written report unless the court directs otherwise, and, if the party wishes to rely on the expert evidence at trial, the report must be disclosed to the other party in accordance with the directions given by the court. The usual order is for simultaneous mutual exchange on or before a set date.

When first obtained, an expert's report which has been prepared for the purpose of the litigation, is a privileged document. It need only be disclosed to the other party if the party who commissioned it wishes to rely on it at trial. If he decides not to rely on the report (perhaps because it is unfavourable) he does not have to allow the other side to inspect it. It is, however, discloseable in part 2 of the list of documents.

11.13.5 Contents of the report

Rule 35.10 and the Practice Direction to Part 35 give detailed instructions on the contents of an expert's report. The report must:

(a) be addressed to the court and not to the party from whom the expert has received his instructions;
(b) give details of the expert's qualifications;
(c) give details of any literature or other material which the expert has relied on in making the report;
(d) say who carried out any test or experiment which the expert has used for the report and whether or not the test or experiment has been carried out under the expert's supervision;
(e) give the qualifications of the person who carried out any such test or experiment;
(f) where there is a range of opinion on the matters dealt with in the report, summarise the range of opinion and give reasons for his own opinion;
(g) contain a summary of the conclusions reached;
(h) contain a statement that the expert understands his duty to the court and has complied with that duty;
(i) contain a statement setting out the substance of all material instructions. The statement should also summarise the facts and instructions given to the expert which are material to the opinions expressed in the report or upon which those opinions are based;
(j) comply with the requirements of any approved expert's protocol (no such protocol has yet been published).

The report must also be supported by a statement of truth that states:

I believe that the facts I have stated in this report are true and that the opinions I have expressed are correct.

11.13.6 Questions to the expert

After an expert's report has been disclosed, the party who did not instruct the expert may put written questions to the expert about his report.

Such written questions:

(a) may be put once only;
(b) must be put within 28 days of service of the report;
(c) must be to clarify the report unless the court permits or the other party agrees to allow questions for a different purpose.

The answers will be treated as part of the expert's report.

11.13.7 Discussion between experts (r 35.12)

The court may direct a discussion between experts to require the experts to:

(a) identify the issues in the proceedings; and
(b) where possible, reach agreement on an issue. (Any agreement is not binding on the parties unless they have already expressly agreed to be bound by any such agreement.)

The court may specify the issues which the experts must discuss.

The court may also direct that, after the discussion, the experts must prepare a statement for the court which:

(a) shows the issues on which they are agreed and on which they disagree; and
(b) summarises the reasons for disagreement.

The content of the discussion will not be referred to at the trial without the consent of the parties.

The purpose of this rule is to try to ensure that the issues on which the experts do disagree are narrowed down as far as possible. This will save both time and costs at the trial.

11.13.8 The joint expert

Whether it is appropriate for each party to call their own expert evidence depends on the issues raised in each particular case. However, in a fast track case the general approach of the court is to order a single joint expert unless there is good reason not to do so (see para 3.9 of PD 28). A joint expert is less likely to be ordered in a multi-track case. Even where the court is willing to allow the parties to call their own expert evidence on the issue of liability, it may order a joint expert on any quantum issues that require expert evidence.

Where the court orders a joint expert it will usually direct that:

(i) the parties should prepare joint instructions for the expert;
(ii) the expert's fees should be paid jointly by the parties; and
(iii) if the parties have been unable by a set date to agree on the identity of the expert, further directions should be obtained from the court.

It is less likely in the case of a joint expert that the court will think it appropriate to allow oral evidence at trial.

Where there is an order for a joint expert there is of course no need for a direction that reports be exchanged.

There is useful guidance from the Court of Appeal in relation to dealing with problems with a joint expert in the case of *Daniels v Walker* [2000] 1 WLR 1382:

(i) where the parties cannot agree joint instructions for the expert, it is perfectly proper for one party to give separate or supplemental instructions;
(ii) where a party is dissatisfied with the expert's report, then he should first submit questions to the expert;
(iii) if this does not resolve the problem, the dissatisfied party can apply to the court for permission to call another expert. This application will be granted if the court is satisfied that it would be unjust, having regard to the overriding objective, to refuse to allow the further evidence to be called;

(iv) where the dissatisfied party has already obtained its own expert's report, the court should not grant permission for that evidence to be used at trial until the experts have met to resolve their differences. Permission for oral evidence to be given at trial is a last resort.

11.14 ASSESSORS (r 35.15)

In some cases of a technical nature, the court may seek the assistance of someone with technical knowledge in the relevant field. Such a person is known as an assessor, and has a judicial role in that he is instructed to assist the court. He is not an expert witness and cannot be cross-examined by any of the parties. His function is to 'educate' the judge and to enable the judge to reach a properly informed decision.

By r 35.15, the assessor shall take such part in the proceedings as the court may direct. The court may direct the assessor to prepare a report and/or direct the assessor to attend the trial. Any report prepared by an assessor will be sent to the parties.

The use of assessors remains rare.

11.15 HUMAN RIGHTS

11.15.1 Hearsay evidence

In *R v Marylebone Magistrates Court ex parte Andrew Clingham* (2001) LTL 22 January, the provisions in the Civil Evidence Act 1995 permitting hearsay evidence to be adduced in civil proceedings were challenged as a breach of Article 6(1). The complaint being that since the evidence could not be challenged by cross-examination the trial was unfair. The Divisional Court held that the admission of hearsay evidence did not automatically result in an unfair trial under Article 6(1). It was of course important that the court should consider the weight to be attached to the evidence under s 4 of the Act.

11.15.2 Expert evidence

The ability of parties to challenge directions restricting the use of expert evidence has been dented by the case of *Daniels v Walker* (see above). The defendant complained that the refusal to allow him to call his own expert evidence, when dissatisfied with the conclusions reached by a joint expert, had amounted to a breach of his right to a fair trial under Article 6. The Court of Appeal decided that since permission to rely on the additional evidence would not have been refused had this been unjust pursuant to the overriding objective, there could be no question of a contravention of the right to a fair trial. Provided therefore that the court is careful to apply the overriding objective in reaching decisions about the use of expert evidence, it is likely to be difficult for parties to challenge successfully under Article 6. The same principle would apply to case management decisions about witnesses of fact.

Chapter 12

SETTLEMENT

Most disputes are resolved not by a judgment of the court but by the parties reaching a settlement. This can happen at any stage from before the issue of proceedings to during the trial. Settlement may be achieved as a result of negotiations, which will often involve the use of the procedures set out in Part 36, or (less commonly) the use of Alternative Dispute Resolution.

In this chapter, we consider negotiations, the provisions of Part 36 and various ways in which settlements are recorded in writing. Alternative Dispute Resolution is dealt with in Chapter 15.

Chapter 12 contents
Negotiations
Pre-action settlements
Settlements reached after the issue of proceedings
Part 36
Claims involving children and patients
Discontinuance

12.1 NEGOTIATIONS

12.1.1 Solicitor's authority

The scope of the solicitor's authority to negotiate on his client's behalf depends on whether or not proceedings have been issued. Prior to issue, the solicitor has no implied authority to settle the client's claim. Acceptance of any offer can, therefore, only be subject to the client's approval. Where the client wishes to accept, it is advisable for the solicitor to obtain written confirmation of this.

Once proceedings have been issued, the solicitor has implied authority to compromise a claim. However, in practice, it is always advisable to seek the client's express instructions.

12.1.2 Basis on which to conduct negotiations

Negotiations can be conducted either orally or in writing. Whichever method is adopted, care should be taken to ensure that the negotiations proceed on a 'without prejudice' basis. This ensures that the negotiations cannot be referred to in court at a later date except to prove the terms of any settlement reached.

It is arguably unnecessary to use the words 'without prejudice' because any negotiations which take place as a part of a genuine attempt to settle a claim are impliedly 'without prejudice'. However, it is preferable to mark any correspondence accordingly or to clarify at the start of a meeting/telephone negotiation that this is the basis on which you are proceeding.

Negotiation is dealt with further in the LPC Resource Book *Skills for Lawyers* (Jordans), Chapter 11.

12.2 PRE-ACTION SETTLEMENTS

12.2.1 Costs and interest

Where a settlement is reached prior to the issue of proceedings, the claimant will not be entitled to recover his legal costs unless this has been agreed. Nor will he be entitled to interest under s 69 of the County Courts Act 1984, s 35A of the Supreme Court Act 1981 or the Late Payment of Commercial Debts (Interest) Act 1998. There may, however, be an entitlement to interest under contract. Whatever the position, it is important that the parties are clear whether any amount for costs and/or interest is included in the terms being proposed.

12.2.2 Recording a pre-action settlement

It is equally important that once settlement terms have been agreed, they are clearly and accurately recorded in writing, so that the agreement can be enforced if one of the parties defaults.

It will often be sufficient for a settlement reached before the issue of proceedings to be recorded in an exchange of correspondence. Commonly, there will be a letter from the defendant setting out the terms being offered 'in full and final settlement' of all claims which the claimant may have and a reply from the claimant accepting these terms. More complicated settlements may be recorded in a formal settlement agreement.

12.3 SETTLEMENTS REACHED AFTER THE ISSUE OF PROCEEDINGS

It is preferable for the settlement to be recorded in a court order or judgment, since this will make enforcement easier if the agreement is not honoured. In particular, enforcement proceedings may be commenced to recover any money due under the settlement (including costs). The date by which payment of any debt or damages is due must, however, be specified in the judgment or order.

12.3.1 Consent orders or judgments

Where none of the parties is a litigant in person, it will often be possible to avoid an application to the court by drawing up a consent order or judgment for sealing by a court officer under r 40.6. Although in theory the court retains the power not to approve the proposed order, it will in practice only be referred to a judge if it appears to be incorrect or unclear. An example of a consent judgment appears in Appendix B.

12.3.2 *Tomlin* orders

A *Tomlin* order stays the action on agreed terms that are set out in a schedule to the order (an example of such an order appears in Appendix B). The parties may choose to use a *Tomlin* order if:

- they wish to keep some or all of the settlement terms confidential; or

- the terms agreed include provisions that go beyond the boundaries of the litigation or are beyond the power of the court to order.

The order should contain a 'liberty to apply' clause. This allows a party to enforce by reviving the action and seeking an order that the terms should be complied with.

It should be noted that where one party is to pay the other's costs, the court will not be able to assess the amount of those costs unless provision is made for this in the order (rather than the schedule). Similarly, any provision for the payment of money out of court needs to be contained in the order.

12.4 PART 36

The purpose of Part 36 is to encourage settlement by imposing pressure on the recipient of a settlement offer to accept it. The pressure lies in the fact that a failure to accept will usually result in a penalty in costs, and sometimes in interest. A Part 36 settlement can be put forward by either a claimant or a defendant (including a Part 20 claimant or defendant).

12.4.1 Pre-action offers (r 36.10)

Before proceedings are issued, it is open to both parties to offer to settle. The terms can include both monetary and other proposals. Any offer must be expressed to be open for at least 21 days from the date it is received. If it is not accepted, the court will take the offer into account when exercising its discretion as to costs. Once proceedings have been issued, the offer cannot be accepted without the permission of the court.

Differences between claimant's and defendant's pre-action offers

As mentioned in **12.2.1**, a claimant who settles before proceedings is not, as a general rule, entitled to recover costs or interest unless this is agreed to by the defendant. A claimant making a pre-action offer under r 36.10 will, therefore, need to make it clear whether he expects to receive interest and costs.

The position is different for the defendant. As an exception to the general rule, a defendant is required by r 36.10 to offer to pay the claimant's costs up to the expiry of the period for acceptance. He is not obliged to offer interest, but would be wise to make sure that his position on this is made clear.

It should also be noted that, once proceedings have been issued a defendant is obliged to back up his offer with a Part 36 payment (see **12.4.2** below). Unless the defendant pays into court at least as much his pre-action offer within 14 days of service of the claim form, the court will not take the pre-action offer into account in deciding costs.

Where a defendant refuses to accept a pre-action offer and is ordered at trial to pay the claimant more than that amount, the court may impose on the defendant the penalties in r 36.21 (set out at **12.4.4** below).

12.4.2 Defendant's Part 36 payment

Once proceedings have been issued, a defendant may make a Part 36 payment into court. This applies whether or not he has made a pre-action offer. The defendant is required to file a Part 36 payment notice (also known as a 'notice of payment in') which the court serves on the claimant (see Appendix A). Alternatively, the defendant can choose to serve the notice, in which case he must file a certificate of service with the court.

The payment notice must comply with the requirements of r 36.6 and para 5 of PD 36. Many of these requirements are aimed at ensuring that the terms on which the payment is offered are clear. Thus the notice must state:

- the amount of the payment in;
- whether the payment relates to the whole claim or to part of it or to any issue that arises in it and if so which part or issue;
- whether it takes into account any counterclaim;
- where an interim payment (see **9.7**) has been made, that the payment takes this into account; and
- where the payment is stated to be exclusive of interest, whether interest is being offered and, if so, the period(s) and rate(s) for which it is offered.

The payment notice must be signed by the defendant or his solicitor.

PD 36 at para 3.4 provides that a defendant who wishes to withdraw or reduce a Part 36 payment must obtain the court's permission to do so.

Acceptance

The claimant has 21 days from service of the notice to accept. If, within this time, the claimant serves the defendant with notice of acceptance, the claim is stayed and the claimant is entitled to the costs of the proceedings on the standard basis up until that date. The notice of acceptance (see Appendix A) must also be filed at court.

Provided the amount offered is reasonable, acceptance has a number of advantages for the claimant. The proceedings are brought to an end without the expense, uncertainty and stress of a trial. The claimant has an entitlement to costs and has the comfort of knowing that the settlement money is immediately available, subject to its being released by the court. In most circumstances, the court will do this on receipt of the notice of acceptance, without the need for a court order.

The position is slightly more complicated where the Part 36 payment only covers part of the proceedings. In such cases, acceptance will have the effect of staying only that part of the proceedings and, unless the parties have been able to reach agreement, the court will have to decide on costs.

Late acceptance

The claimant may only accept after the 21-day period with the consent of the defendant or the permission of the court. This may not be granted. For example, new evidence may have come to light which makes it more likely that the claimant will lose the case. Where the court grants permission, it will also decide what costs order it should make.

Non-acceptance

Where the claimant does not accept the Part 36 payment the proceedings will, of course, continue. If at trial the claimant fails to obtain a judgment exceeding the amount of the Part 36 payment, the court will, unless it considers it unjust, make a 'split costs order' (r 36.20). This means that the defendant is required to pay the claimant's costs of the action until the end of the 21-day period and the claimant is ordered to pay the defendant's costs from then on (in addition to his own costs). Since the run-up to trial and the trial itself are generally the most expensive periods in the litigation, the consequences for a claimant who fails to beat a Part 36 payment can be severe.

Further, if the defendant made a pre-action offer which he backed up by a Part 36 payment within 14 days of service of the claim form, the court may order an earlier split in the costs. The claimant may be ordered to pay his own and the defendant's costs after the last day for acceptance of the pre-action offer.

Where the claimant does better than the Part 36 payment, the court has a discretion as to costs, but will usually order the defendant to pay the claimant's costs of the action on a standard basis.

Example

In January 2000, C sues D for damages estimated at £12,000 plus interest and costs. D defends. On 3 September 2001, C is served with notice that D has made a Part 36 payment of £7,000 plus interest. C does not accept by 24 September 2001.

The table sets out the likely cost consequence of various outcomes at trial.

Result at trial	**Likely costs order (subject to the court's discretion)**
C awarded more than £7,000 plus interest (ie C 'beats' Part 36 payment).	C awarded his costs of the action to be paid by D on the standard basis
C awarded £7,000 or less plus interest (ie C fails to 'beat' Part 36 payment).	The court will make a split costs order: D ordered to pay C's costs on the standard basis up to and including 24 September 2001 C ordered to pay his own costs and D's costs on the standard basis from 25 September 2001 until judgment
C loses at trial.	C ordered to pay D's costs of defending the action on the standard basis

There is a flowchart summarising the consequences of acceptance and non-acceptance of a Part 36 payment in Appendix B.

Tactical considerations

From the point of view of a defendant who considers himself at risk on liability, a Part 36 payment can provide a useful mechanism for pressurising the claimant to accept a reasonable settlement and will often be used tactically as part of settlement discussions. Of course, the defendant has to make a careful assessment of how much to pay in. An over-generous payment will be snapped up by a claimant eager to receive more than the true value of the claim. An unrealistically low payment will impose no real pressure, since the claimant will feel confident of beating it at trial. The wise defendant will aim to pitch his payment at a level that is just high enough for the claimant to feel that it would be unsafe not to accept.

Also important is the stage in the proceedings at which a Part 36 payment is made. The earlier this is done, the greater the potential costs protection for the defendant and the greater the pressure placed on the claimant. Thus, the vulnerable defendant should make a payment in as soon as he has the information to judge its amount accurately.

12.4.3 Defendant's Part 36 offer

Once proceedings have started, the only way that a defendant faced with a monetary claim can generally obtain costs protection is by paying money into court. The court will not usually grant a split costs order against a claimant who has failed to beat an offer which could have been made in the form of a Part 36 payment. However, where the claim is non-monetary (eg a dispute over ownership of property), the defendant may put forward a Part 36 offer.

Requirements in relation to Part 36 offers

The offer must comply with various requirements set out at r 36.5 and PD 36, similar to those relating to a notice of payment in. It must:

- be in writing;
- state that it is a Part 36 offer;
- be expressed to be open for at least 21 days after the date it is received;
- state whether the offer relates to the whole claim and whether it takes into account any counterclaim;
- be signed by the defendant or his solicitor.

Where the offer is made by a company or other corporation, it may be signed by someone holding a senior position (such as a director, manager or other officer), provided their position is stated. The written offer must be served on the claimant's solicitor.

It should be noted that the fact that the offer must be expressed to be open for a period of 21 days does not prevent the defendant from withdrawing it within that period provided it has not been accepted. The Court of Appeal so confirmed in *Scammell and Others v Dicker* [2001] 1 WLR 631, concluding that the effect of Part 36 was not to exclude the general law of contract that an unaccepted offer could be withdrawn.

Acceptance or non-acceptance of defendant's Part 36 offer

Acceptance by the claimant of the offer has the same effect as acceptance of a Part 36 payment:

- the claimant must file and serve a notice of acceptance;
- the proceedings are stayed; and
- the claimant receives his costs on a standard basis up to the date of acceptance.

As with a Part 36 payment, late acceptance is possible with the consent of the defendant or the permission of the court. The consequences of non-acceptance are also the same. If the claimant fails to 'beat' the offer at trial, the court will, unless it considers it unjust, make a split costs order.

Mixed monetary and non-monetary claims

In the case of a claim that contains both monetary and non-monetary elements, the defendant must make a Part 36 payment in respect of any money being offered. In such circumstances, the claimant is not entitled to accept the payment but not the non-monetary terms. The defendant is obliged to warn the claimant in the payment notice that if the money is accepted, he is deemed also to have accepted the offer in its entirety.

12.4.4 Claimant's Part 36 offer

It is not appropriate for a claimant to make a Part 36 payment. Instead, once proceedings have started, he may make a Part 36 offer, setting out in writing the terms on which he would be prepared to settle. The offer must comply with the requirements in **12.4.3** above.

A claimant's Part 36 offer in respect of a monetary sum is deemed to be inclusive of interest unless stated otherwise. If interest is required on top, the amount and rate must be stated.

Acceptance

If the defendant accepts the Part 36 offer within the time set, the proceedings are stayed on the terms suggested by the claimant and the defendant pays the claimant's costs on the standard basis up until the date of acceptance.

Late acceptance is possible, provided the parties can agree the question of costs. If they cannot, the defendant may only accept with the permission of the court.

Non-acceptance

CLAIMANT'S FAILURE TO BEAT THE PART 36 OFFER

No specific penalty is imposed on the claimant if he fails at trial to do better than the proposals in his Part 36 offer although the making of the offer may be taken into account by the court in exercising its general discretion as to costs.

CLAIMANT SUCCEEDS IN BEATING HIS PART 36 OFFER

Where the claimant does better at trial than the proposals in his Part 36 offer, r 36.21 provides that the court will, unless it considers it unjust to do so, order that the claimant:

(1) be awarded interest on the whole or part of any sum awarded to him (excluding interest) at a rate not exceeding 10 per cent per annum above the Bank of England's base rate for some or all of the period from the expiry of the deadline for acceptance; and/or
(2) recover his costs on the indemnity basis from that date; and/or
(3) be awarded interest on those costs at up to 10 per cent per annum above base rate.

In addition, to the extent that the court does not impose interest on damages under (1), it may impose interest in the usual way. It should be noted that the maximum interest that can be awarded for any period of time is 10 per cent per annum above the base rate.

In considering whether it would be unjust to impose these penalties, the court will take into account all the circumstances of the case, including:

(1) the terms of the Part 36 offer;
(2) the stage in the proceedings when any Part 36 offer or payment was made;
(3) the information available to the parties at that time; and
(4) the conduct of the parties with regard to giving or refusing information for the purposes of enabling the offer or payment to be evaluated.

Example 1

C alleges a breach of contract by D, occurring in March 1999.

C issues proceedings in December 1999 claiming damages estimated at £75,000 plus interest. In March 2000, C makes a Part 36 offer of £60,000 plus interest. The deadline for acceptance is 27 March 2000. D does not accept and the case proceeds to trial.

(i) If C wins but fails to beat his Part 36 offer

If D loses at trial and is ordered to pay C damages of £60,000 plus interest or less, the court will usually award C his costs of the action on the standard basis plus statutory interest (at 8 per cent per annum).

(ii) If C wins and beats his Part 36 offer

If D loses at trial and is ordered to pay C damages of more than £60,000 plus interest, the court will unless it considers it unjust impose penalties under r 36.21. The court has a discretion but might order D to pay:

- the usual statutory interest (8 per cent per annum) on the damages awarded from March 1999 (when C's cause of action arose) until 27 March 2000 (when the deadline for acceptance of the Part 36 offer expired), plus
- interest on the damages awarded from 28 March 2000 to the date of judgment at 10 per cent per annum above the current Bank base rate, plus
- the costs incurred by C up to 27 March 2000 on the standard basis, plus
- the costs incurred by C thereafter on the indemnity basis, plus
- interest on the indemnity basis costs from the date of judgment until payment at 10 per cent above the current base rate.

(iii) If D wins

D will usually be awarded his costs of defending the action on the standard basis. C suffers no penalty for failing to recover more than his Part 36 offer.

Example 2

Where one party makes an offer or payment under Part 36, the other may well choose to counter with a Part 36 offer or payment of their own. What is the effect of this?

Settlement 139

Assume the same facts as in Example 1, save that having rejected C's Part 36 offer of 27 March 2000, D chooses to make a Part 36 payment of £40,000 plus interest. C does not accept the Part 36 payment and the action proceeds to trial.

The table sets out the likely cost consequences of various possible outcomes at trial:

Result at trial	Likely costs order (subject to the court's discretion)
C is awarded more than £60,000 plus interest at trial.	Penalties under r 36.21 imposed (as in (ii) of Example 1)
C is awarded more than £40,000 plus interest at trial but not more than £60,000 plus interest.	D pays C's costs of the action on the standard basis (as in (i) of Example 1 above)
C wins at trial but is awarded £40,000 plus interest or less.	D's Part 36 payment has been effective. The court is likely to make a split costs order under which: (a) D will have to pay C's costs of the action on the standard basis plus his own costs up until the last day that D's Part 36 payment could have been accepted by C without the court's permission; and (b) from that point onwards, C will have to pay D's costs on the standard basis plus his own costs.
C loses at trial.	C will pay D's costs of the action on the standard basis (see (iii) in Example 1)

Tactical considerations

Where the defendant does not accept a Part 36 offer and the claimant beats his own offer at trial, the defendant is likely to pay a heavy price. In contrast, we have seen that a claimant who fails to beat his own offer is usually in no worse position than if his offer had not been made. The result is that, whereas there is no downside for the claimant in making such an offer, a reasonable proposal will place the defendant under considerable pressure.

Since the penalties in r 36.21 are imposed as from the expiry of the deadline for acceptance, the earlier the claimant makes his offer, the greater the pressure on the defendant. It is tactically sensible for a claimant to make an offer as soon as there is enough information to judge its amount and prior to issuing proceedings where practicable.

A defendant faced with a pre-action or Part 36 offer should consider carefully whether it would be appropriate to make a counter offer or Part 36 payment.

12.4.5 Assessing the terms of a Part 36 offer or payment

Since penalties may result from a failure to accept a Part 36 offer or payment, it is important that the recipient is clear about the terms being proposed. He is, therefore, entitled within 7 days of receiving the offer or notice of payment to request clarification. If the information is not provided within 7 days, he may apply to the court for an order that it should be.

The party putting forward the offer or payment should also bear in mind that the court's power to impose penalties or a split costs order is discretionary. The Court of Appeal has emphasised the need for a party considering a payment or offer to be provided with the information needed to assess whether to accept it (see *Ford v GKR Construction and Others* [2000] 1 All ER 802). Where there is a failure to provide material information the court may well consider it unjust to make either a split costs order or impose penalties under r 36.21.

12.4.6 Secrecy

Except in very limited circumstances, neither a Part 36 offer nor a Part 36 payment may be revealed to the trial judge until all questions of liability and quantum have been decided.

12.4.7 Offers other than under Part 36

There is nothing to prevent parties from making offers to settle that do not comply with the procedural requirements of Part 36. Provided the offer is an open one or made 'without prejudice save as to costs' the court is obliged to have regard to it when exercising its discretion as to costs (r 44.3(4)(c)). The Court of Appeal has confirmed that since it is within the general discretion of the court to order costs on an indemnity basis and interest at whatever rate it thinks fit, such an offer could attract the same consequences as one made under Part 36, including the interest and cost penalties set out in r 36.21 (*Petrograde Inc v Texaco Ltd* [2000] CLC 1341). It will all depend on what the court considers just in the circumstances.

Having said this, parties should be cautious about making non-Part 36 offers if they wish them to carry Part 36 consequences, since to do so will certainly increase the uncertainty of the outcome. In particular, a defendant who could make a Part 36 payment, but chooses merely to put forward an offer, will not usually be treated as if a Part 36 payment was made. In *Amber v Stacy* [2001] 2 All ER 88, the defendant made a written offer to settle shortly after the issue of proceedings, followed by a Part 36 payment over a year later. At trial, the claimant succeeded but failed to beat either the original written offer or the Part 36 payment. The Court of Appeal considered whether the defendant should recover his costs only from the deadline for acceptance of the Part 36 payment or whether (and to what extent) the earlier written offer should be taken into account. The Court of Appeal stated that there were 'compelling reasons of principle and policy' why defendants offering a monetary settlement should do so by way of a Part 36 payment: this offered greater clarity and certainty to the claimant. As a result, it was not appropriate for the claimant to pay the whole of the defendant's costs back to the date of the written offer. Nevertheless, the earlier written offer was a relevant factor in the court's exercise of its discretion as to costs. The Court of Appeal ordered the claimant to pay the defendant half his costs from the date of the written offer until the expiry of the deadline for acceptance of the Part 36 payment.

12.5 CLAIMS INVOLVING CHILDREN AND PATIENTS

Where a claim is made by or on behalf of a child or patient, or against a child or patient, no settlement of that claim is valid without the approval of the court. Thus, neither a Part 36 offer nor a Part 36 payment may be accepted without the court's approval.

Approval is required, even if a compromise is reached before the issue of proceedings. In such a case the application for approval should be made under Part 8.

12.6 DISCONTINUANCE (Part 38)

12.6.1 General Provisions

A claimant may decide not to pursue his claim, even though no settlement has been reached. For example, he may conclude that his chances of succeeding at trial or of recovering any money from the defendant are so slim that he would be better to discontinue. A claimant may discontinue a claim at any time and, if there are co-defendants, he may do so against all or any of them. The claimant will need the court's permission to discontinue a claim where:

(a) the court has granted an interim injunction; or
(b) any party has given an undertaking to the court.

If an interim payment has been made, the claimant may discontinue only if:

(a) the defendant who made the payment consents in writing; or
(b) the court gives permission.

Where there are two or more claimants, a claimant may discontinue only if:

(a) all the other claimants consent in writing; or
(b) the court gives permission.

12.6.2 Procedure

The claimant must file and serve a notice of discontinuance on all other parties. If the claimant needs the consent of another party in order to discontinue, a copy of that consent must be attached to the notice.

If the claimant discontinues in a case where consent or the court's permission was not required, any defendant may apply to set aside the notice of discontinuance. The application must be made within 28 days.

12.6.3 Liability for costs

A claimant who discontinues is liable for the defendant's costs unless the court orders otherwise.

If proceedings are only partly discontinued, the claimant is liable only for the costs of the part of the claim he is discontinuing, and those costs must not be assessed until the rest of the case is over unless the court orders otherwise.

Chapter 13

FINAL PREPARATIONS FOR TRIAL, TRIAL AND ASSESSMENT OF COSTS

13.1 FINAL PREPARATIONS FOR TRIAL

13.1.1 Briefing counsel

If the solicitor intends to brief counsel to deal with the trial, then counsel should be instructed to appear as soon as possible once the trial date is known. Very often, of course, counsel will already have been instructed in a case to either advise, draft a statement of case or appear at a case management conference. The brief to counsel should contain copies of all relevant documents which will be required at the trial.

The content of the brief should deal in detail with the facts still in issue and how they are to be proved. Even though the barrister may be familiar with the case, the solicitor should nevertheless take the time to set matters out fully in the brief in case it is passed on to another barrister at a later stage. Occasionally, the barrister originally instructed may be unable to attend the trial in which case the brief will be handed over to another barrister at short notice.

Practice varies as to whether there will be a conference with counsel before the hearing. This will depend on the extent to which there have already been conferences, and the importance and complexity of the case.

When acting for a private or commercial client, it is up to the solicitor to negotiate the brief fee with counsel's clerk following delivery of the brief. In a fast track case, one would try to restrict the brief fee to the maximum amount allowed for the advocacy in a fast track case (see Chapter 13).

In a multi-track case, the fee only covers one day unless agreed otherwise. If the case takes more than one day, counsel will be entitled to charge a 'refresher fee' for each subsequent day.

13.1.2 Attendance of witnesses (Part 34)

Witnesses in general

All witnesses should be kept fully informed of the expected trial date and, once the date has been fixed, should be told of that date without delay. It is sensible at an early stage to check with witnesses whether any particular periods would be inconvenient for them to attend the trial. Details of a witness's availability have to be given to the court on the allocation and listing questionnaires.

Even where witnesses have been kept fully informed and involved, it is unwise to rely on the assumption that they will attend court voluntarily.

Instead, their attendance should be encouraged by serving them with a witness summons. This is a document issued by the court requiring a witness to:

(a) attend court to give evidence; or

Chapter 13 contents
Final preparations for trial
Trial
Costs
Human rights

(b) produce documents to the court.

A witness summons should be served at least 7 days before the date on which the witness is required to attend court. It will then be binding upon the witness, and if the witness fails to attend court, he will be in contempt. If a party wishes to issue a summons less than 7 days before the date of the trial, permission from the court must be obtained.

The witness summons will normally be served by the court unless the party on whose behalf it is issued indicates that he wishes to serve it himself.

At the time of service of a witness summons the witness must be offered or paid:

(a) a sum reasonably sufficient to cover his expenses in travelling to and from the court; and
(b) such sum by way of compensation for loss of time as may be specified by the court.

The danger in not serving a witness with a witness summons is that if he fails to attend the trial, the first question the judge will ask the solicitor or barrister conducting the case is why a witness summons was not served. If a witness summons had been served, there is a greater possibility that the court will be sympathetic enough to grant an adjournment of the trial if that is required because of the crucial nature of the missing witness's evidence.

Expert witnesses

Practice varies as to whether to serve an expert witness with a witness summons. The safest course is to ask the expert whether they wish to be put under this obligation to attend. Some expert witnesses do wish to be put under this obligation because they are busy professional people and the compulsion of the order makes it easier for them to break any other appointments.

Police officers must always be served with a witness summons, because they will not give evidence in a civil matter on behalf of either party unless they are under an obligation to do so.

13.1.3 Preparing trial bundles (Part 39)

Unless the court orders otherwise, the claimant must file the trial bundle not more than 7 days and not less than 3 days before the start of the trial. By para 3.2 of the Practice Direction to Part 39 – Miscellaneous Provisions Relating to Hearings, unless the court orders otherwise, the trial bundle should include a copy of:

'(1) the claim form and all statements of case,
(2) a case summary and/or chronology where appropriate,
(3) requests for further information and responses to the requests,
(4) all witness statements to be relied on as evidence,
(5) any witness summaries,
(6) any notices of intention to rely on hearsay evidence under rule 33.2,
(7) any notices of intention to rely on evidence (such as a plan, photograph etc) under rule 33.6 which is not –

    (a) contained in a witness statement, affidavit or expert's report,
    (b) being given orally at trial,
    (c) hearsay evidence under rule 33.2,

Final Preparations for Trial, Trial and Assessment of Costs 145

> (8) any medical reports and responses to them,
> (9) any expert's reports and responses to them,
> (10) any order giving directions as to the conduct of the trial, and
> (11) any other necessary documents.'

The contents of the trial bundle should be agreed where possible. The parties should also agree where possible:

> '(1) that the documents contained in the bundle are authentic even if not disclosed under Part 31, and
> (2) that documents in the bundle may be treated as evidence of the facts stated in them even if a notice under the Civil Evidence Act 1995 has not been served.'

(para 3.9 of the Practice Direction to Part 39)

Where it is not possible to agree the contents of the bundle, a summary of the points on which the parties are unable to agree should be included.

The party filing the trial bundle should supply identical bundles to all the parties to the proceedings and for the use of the witnesses.

The trial bundle should be accompanied by an estimated length of reading time and an agreed estimate of the likely length of the hearing.

13.2 TRIAL

13.2.1 Venue

For both fast track and multi-track cases, the trial will normally take place at the court where the case is being managed, but it may be at another court if it is appropriate having regard to the needs of the parties and the availability of court resources.

13.2.2 Timetable

In most cases, in both the fast track and multi-track, a trial timetable will have been fixed after filing the listing questionnaires. The timetable may, for example, limit the time for cross-examination and re-examination of each particular witness.

At the trial, the judge may confirm or vary any timetable given previously, or, if none has been given, set his own.

The judge will generally have read the papers in the trial bundle (which, as we saw in the previous chapter, will have been filed with the court prior to the hearing).

A fast track trial should usually be completed within one day. However, if it lasts more than one day, the judge will normally sit on the next court day to complete the trial.

In multi-track cases, the judge will normally sit on consecutive court days until it has been completed.

13.2.3 Order of proceedings

The claimant

If allowed by the judge, the claimant may make an opening speech setting out the background to the case and the facts which remain in issue. If this is allowed by the timetable set by the court, it must be very concise.

THE EVIDENCE

The claimant and his witnesses will then give evidence. In most cases, the witness statements will stand as the evidence-in-chief. If that is the case then, after being sworn, the witness may simply be asked to confirm that his statement is correct. He will be able to amplify what is in his witness statement only if allowed to do so by the judge. If some form of limited examination-in-chief is allowed by the judge, then the usual rule is that a witness cannot be asked leading questions by his own advocate to encourage him to relate the story. It is difficult to define a leading question. Basically, it is one which suggests the answer or assumes a fact which has not yet been proved. For example, a question to the claimant in a breach of contract case, 'did the defendant supply your firm with goods which did not match the sample?' suggests that the goods did not match the sample. It is therefore an objectionable leading question. Instead, the claimant should be asked in general terms, 'describe to the court the condition of the goods when they arrived as compared to the sample provided earlier'.

The next stage is the cross-examination of the witness. There is no bar on leading questions. The purpose of cross-examination is to discredit the person being cross-examined in order to make their evidence appear less believable either on the case overall or in relation to a specific element of it. There are many ways in which this may be done. It may involve highlighting inconsistencies in the evidence given by the witness, or the improbability of the witness's version of events. It may involve alleging that the witness is biased in some way. If the witness has previous convictions, it is even possible for the advocate to cross-examine on these to show the witness's character generally in a bad light.

Sometimes, the witness's evidence will be inconsistent with an earlier statement. This will then give the advocate scope to cross-examine on the previous inconsistent statement to show the court how the witness has given different versions of events at different times and therefore should not be believed.

However, cross-examination does not always involve an aggressive attack on the witness and his credibility. Cross-examination can be conducted in a more subtle fashion and often the best results are achieved by a less confrontational approach. Sometimes, even evidence which is favourable to the other side's case can be extracted from the witness if the right questions are asked.

In addition to the above, however, there is one mandatory rule concerning cross-examination. This is that the cross-examining advocate must put his own party's case to the witness he is cross-examining. Thus, the claimant's advocate must put the claimant's case to the defendant in cross-examination. For example, perhaps the claimant has given evidence that he made known to the defendant a particular purpose for the goods he has bought. The defendant denies this in his witness statement/examination-in-chief.

It must be put to the defendant in cross-examination that the defendant did know of this particular purpose.

It is highly unlikely that the witness being cross-examined in this way will change his story as a result of the allegation being put to him. Nevertheless, it is essential that the cross-examining advocate puts his own client's case to the witness in this way as failure to challenge the opponent's evidence implies acceptance of that evidence.

RE-EXAMINATION

Following cross-examination, the advocate is given the opportunity to ask further questions of their own witness. However re-examination is strictly limited to matters arising out of the cross-examination. It is not possible to introduce new issues at this stage. Accordingly, if some ambiguity has been left as a result of the cross-examination, this might be an opportunity to resolve it and try to restore the witness's credibility on that point. For example, perhaps cross-examination has established that the witness normally wears glasses but that he was not wearing them on the day of the incident in question. Insofar as this detracts from his credibility in implying that perhaps he did not see what he thought he saw, re-examination would be an opportunity to clarify the fact that the witness wears glasses only for reading. As with examination-in-chief, the advocate cannot ask a leading question.

PROBLEM WITNESSES

One problem which can arise with the evidence of a witness is the possibility of the witness unexpectedly being unfavourable to the party who has called him. For example, a witness might change his story during cross-examination. If he does this, there is little that the advocate who called the witness can do to remedy the situation. It is not possible for a party's advocate to cross-examine a witness he has himself called.

However, sometimes matters proceed further than this and the witness proves not merely to be unfavourable to the party who called him, but actually proves to be hostile in giving his evidence. It is difficult to be precise as to when a witness can be said to have passed from merely being unfavourable to being hostile, but it would probably be apparent from the witness's demeanour and lack of co-operation that he has no desire either to see justice done or to give his evidence fairly. One indicator would be the extent to which the witness's evidence is inconsistent with the statement previously given to the party calling him. It is then up to that party to make an application to the court for the witness to be declared hostile and, if he is, the party who called him can then (contrary to the usual rule) cross-examine that witness on the facts of the case and on the previous inconsistent statements. The witness's general character cannot, however, be attacked by the party who called him, nor can the witness be cross-examined about any previous convictions. Having a witness declared hostile should be regarded as a damage limitation exercise. Whilst it may allow the advocate to retain some control over the case, he is clearly not going to win it unless the damage done can be repaired by evidence from another witness. Strictly, by virtue of s 4 of the Civil Evidence Act 1995, it would be open to the court to attach weight to the previous inconsistent statement as evidence. In practice, however, the court is more likely to take the view that this witness is not someone who can be relied upon.

The defendant

The defence will present its evidence in exactly the same way as the claimant.

13.2.4 Children as witnesses

A child who understands the nature of an oath will give sworn evidence. Otherwise, s 96(2) of the Children Act 1989 provides that:

> 'The child's evidence may be heard by the court if, in its opinion –
> (a) he understands that it is his duty to speak the truth; and
> (b) he has sufficient understanding to justify his evidence being heard.'

A child for these purposes is a person under the age of 18. It is for the judge to decide whether the child can give evidence, and, if so, whether it will be given on oath. As a general rule, it will be assumed that children over the age of 14 can give sworn evidence, and the judge will make enquiries of children under that age in order to form an opinion.

The judge will speak to the child to discover whether he appreciates the solemnity of the occasion and the added responsibility to tell the truth which is involved in taking an oath, over and above the ordinary social duty to be truthful. If so, the child can give sworn evidence. If not, but nevertheless the conditions in s 96(2) are satisfied, the child can give unsworn evidence. Children under the age of 11 are normally considered too young to take the oath, whereas children above that age are often able to give sworn evidence.

13.2.5 Closing speeches

After the evidence has been given, usually the defence advocate will make a closing speech followed by the claimant's advocate.

13.2.6 The judgment

The judge will deliver his judgment either immediately, perhaps after a short adjournment if he requires time to collect his thoughts, or (if the case is complex) judgment may be reserved to be delivered at a later date. If the court gives judgment both on the claim and counterclaim, then if there is a balance in favour of one of the parties the court will order the party whose judgment is for the lesser amount to pay the balance.

13.2.7 Interest

Interest up to the date of judgment

Interest will normally be awarded, provided it has been claimed in the particulars of claim. In the absence of any contractual provision to the contrary, or entitlement to interest under the Late Payment of Commercial Debts (Interest) Act 1998, interest on the damages will usually be awarded by the judge in his discretion (under the Supreme Court Act 1981, s 35A or County Court Act 1984, s 69) at the rate of 8 per cent per annum from the date the cause of action arose until the date of judgment. Rather different rules apply to personal injury actions which are beyond the scope of this book.

Interest is a discretionary matter and the judge might choose to award at a different rate or for a different period. For example, if the claimant has been dilatory about pursuing the action then the judge may disallow interest for a period even if he eventually succeeds in his claim.

Interest after judgment

Once judgment has been given different rules apply. In the High Court, interest is payable under s 17 of the Judgments Act 1838 at a rate of 8 per cent (unless there is a contractual right to more). In a county court, interest is payable under the County Courts (Interest on Judgment Debts) Order 1991, providing the judgment was for at least £5,000 (or, if less, that the Late Payment of Commercial Debts (Interest) Act 1998 applies). In neither case is the interest discretionary and it accrues on both the judgment and on costs.

It should be noted that, whilst judgment interest cannot accrue on damages until they have been quantified, interest is payable on costs from the date of judgment even if the amount to be paid has yet to be assessed (*Hunt v RM Douglas (Roofing) Ltd* [1990] 1 AC 398). As a result, it is in the interests of the party paying costs to make a payment on account as soon as possible, even if an interim order requiring such a payment is not made by the court (see **13.3.7**).

13.3 COSTS

13.3.1 The indemnity principle

Although the court has a wide discretion, the general rule is that the loser in litigation will be ordered to pay the winner's costs (r 44.3(2)(a)). Note that the winner (the receiving party) is entitled to an indemnity in respect of the costs he has incurred. In other words, he cannot make a profit out of the paying party by seeking more than his solicitor and client costs. This is known as the indemnity principle (not to be confused with the indemnity basis: see **13.3.3**).

The word 'indemnity' could mislead. In reality, the receiving party will not receive a full indemnity in respect of his costs. The paying party will invariably challenge particular items, arguing that the work was unnecessary or was performed in an unnecessarily expensive way (eg at too high a charge-out rate).

13.3.2 General provisions about costs (Part 44)

At the end of the trial, the court has a discretion as to:

> '(a) whether the costs are payable by one party to another;
> (b) the amount of those costs; and
> (c) when they are to be paid.'

(r 44.3(1) of the CPR 1998)

Whilst the general rule is that the court will order the unsuccessful party to pay the costs of the successful party, this is only a starting point and the court can make a different order for costs if it thinks it appropriate to do so.

All the circumstances will be considered including:

(a) conduct both before and during the proceedings and on particular issues;
(b) success on particular issues;
(c) any payment into court (eg under Part 36) or offers of settlement.

An example of conduct being taken into account in making a decision on costs is the decision of Jacob J in *Mars UK Ltd v Teknowledge Ltd (No 2)* [1999] Masons CLR

322, ChD. In that case, he anticipated that the successful claimant would only be likely to receive 40 per cent of the costs because of the heavy-handed way in which they had rushed into court proceedings against a smaller opponent who had been genuinely attempting to achieve a negotiated settlement.

The order may reflect the decision on particular issues by providing for payment of, for example:

(a) a proportion of a party's costs;
(b) a specified amount of a party's costs;
(c) costs for a particular period;
(d) costs incurred before the proceedings began;
(e) costs of a particular step;
(f) costs of a distinct part of the proceedings;
(g) interest on costs from or until a certain date, including a date before judgment.

Orders whereby the winner receives only part of his costs are becoming increasingly common and a party who raises a number of issues but who succeeds on only some of them can no longer expect to recover the whole of his costs. For example, where both claim and counterclaim succeed, the court may well set off the costs payable on each and direct only payment of the balance.

13.3.3 The basis of assessment (r 44.4)

When the court assesses costs, it will assess those costs either on the standard basis or the indemnity basis. In either case, no costs will be allowed which are unreasonable.

What is the difference between the standard basis and the indemnity basis?

The standard basis
(a) The court will only allow costs which are proportionate to the matters in issue;
(b) any doubt in relation to reasonableness or proportionality is exercised in favour of the paying party.

The indemnity basis
(a) The court will not allow recovery of costs that were unreasonably incurred or unreasonable in amount.
(b) Any doubt in relation to reasonableness is exercised in favour of the receiving party.

The difference between the two bases

Where there is no doubt over the reasonableness of costs, the difference between the two bases is that in assessing on the standard basis the court will only allow those costs that are proportionate to the matters in issue.

In assessing what is proportionate para 11 of PD 44 requires the court to have regard to:

(i) the amount of money involved;
(ii) the importance of the case;
(iii) the complexity of the issues; and the financial position of each party;
(iv) the factors in r 44.5 (see below).

The great majority of costs orders are awarded on the standard basis. An award on the indemnity basis is usually reserved for occasions where there has been culpable behaviour on the part of the paying party (for example pursuing an unjustified claim or defence or where there has been non-compliance with court orders). Where the court does not specify in its order which basis is to apply, the standard basis is used.

13.3.4 Relevant factors in assessing the amount of costs (r 44.5)

As well as the basis (ie standard or indemnity) on which the court is assessing costs, the court will also take into account the following factors in deciding the amount of costs the receiving party is entitled to:

(a) the conduct of all the parties, including conduct before as well as during the proceedings and the efforts made, if any, before and during the proceedings in order to try to resolve the dispute;
(b) the amount or value of any money or property involved;
(c) the importance of the matter to all the parties;
(d) the particular complexity of the matter or the difficulty or novelty of the questions raised;
(e) the skill, effort, specialised knowledge and responsibility involved;
(f) the time spent on the case;
(g) the place where and the circumstances in which work or any part of it was done.

13.3.5 Procedure for assessing costs

Where the court orders one party to pay costs to another, the court will either make a summary assessment of costs there and then, or order detailed assessment of the costs by the costs officer. (The costs officer is the district judge or, in London, the costs judge.)

13.3.6 Fast-track costs (Part 46)

Trial costs

In fast-track cases, there is a specified figure for the advocate for preparing for and appearing at the trial.

Value of the claim	Amount of fast-track trial costs which the court may award
Up to £3,000	£350
More than £3,000 but not more than £10,000	£500
More than £10,000	£750

The court may not award more or less than the amount shown except in limited circumstances. For example, an additional £250 can be awarded where it is necessary for a legal representative to attend to assist the advocate. Therefore, if a barrister is instructed to conduct the fast-track trial and a representative from the solicitor's office attends court with the barrister, £250 can be awarded for that attendance provided the court thinks that it was necessary.

Valuing the claim

If the claimant succeeds, then the value of the claim is based on the amount awarded, excluding any interest or reduction for contributory negligence.

If the defendant was successful, then the value of the claim is based on the amount claimed by the claimant.

Improper or unreasonable behaviour by one of the parties may lead to a departure from the specified figure.

If there is more than one claimant or defendant but the successful parties only used one advocate, there will be only one award. If the successful parties used separate advocates, there will be a separate award for each party.

Summary assessment of other fast track costs

The fast-track trial costs are in addition to the rest of the costs in bringing the claim. The usual practice on fast-track cases is for these to be summarily assessed at the end of the case. In fast-track cases, therefore, the party should always file and serve a statement of costs (see Chapter 9) at least 24 hours prior to the hearing. Because the costs of the entire case are being summarily assessed by the court there and then, and because counsel will not be familiar with the way in which solicitors' costs are incurred in preparing the case for trial, there is a strong argument for using a solicitor advocate rather than counsel at the trial of a fast-track action. Where the receiving party has funded the litigation by way of a conditional fee agreement the court will as part of its summary assessment assess whether the paying party should pay some or all of any success fee due to the winner's solicitor and any after-the-event insurance premium that was paid (see **13.3.8** below).

13.3.7 Multi-track cases

In multi-track cases there are no specified trial costs. Although the judge does have the power to make a summary assessment of costs, in multi-track cases the court will usually order detailed assessment.

Detailed assessment proceedings are commenced by the receiving party serving on the paying party:

(a) notice of commencement in Form N252 (see Appendix A); and
(b) a copy of the bill of costs.

This action must be taken within 3 months of the date of the judgment or order.

The bill of costs is a rather complex document, which should be prepared in the form described by para 4 of PD 43. A copy of an example of a bill of costs appears in Appendix B. Preparing a bill of costs is a specialist task, usually undertaken by either an in-house costs draftsman or a firm of independent costs draftsmen. A claim can be included for the reasonable costs of preparing and checking the bill.

The first part of the bill sets out background information including a brief description of the history of the action and a statement of the grade of fee earner(s) involved (together with the hourly charge-out rate claimed for each). If the litigation was funded by way of a conditional fee agreement this will be stated, together with the success fee that was agreed. Similarly, if the receiving party has been publicly funded, the relevant details must be set out in the background information.

The main body of the bill comprises a breakdown of the work performed, divided into different categories of work as set out in para 4.6 of the Practice Direction:

(1) attendances on the court and counsel;
(2) attendances on and communications with the receiving party;
(3) attendances on and communications with witnesses including any expert witnesses;
(4) attendances to inspect any property or place for the purposes of the proceedings;
(5) attendances on and with other persons;
(6) communications with the court and with counsel;
(7) work done on documents: preparing and considering documentation;
(8) work done in connection with negotiations with a view to settlement (if not already covered under another head);
(9) attendances on and communications with agents and work done by them;
(10) other work done which was of or incidental to the proceedings and which is not already covered above.

The work done within each of these heads is set out chronologically in numbered items. As can be seen from the model bill in Appendix B, the information is presented in columns, with the amount claimed for profit costs, disbursements and VAT being shown separately.

Communications in the context of paragraph 4.6 means letters out and telephone calls. Most will be classed as routine and charged at a standard rate of 6 minutes (thus a routine letter drafted by an assistant charging a rate of £140 per hour would be charged at £14). Where letters out or telephone calls are sufficiently complex/lengthy not to be classed as routine, they may be charged according to the time actually spent on them. Letters in are not charged for separately.

Local travelling expenses (generally within a 10 mile radius of the court) cannot be claimed, but the solicitor is entitled to claim at up to the hourly rate for time spent travelling and waiting (depending on the amount he charged his client).

Office expenses such as the cost of postage, telephone bills and couriers cannot be charged except in unusual circumstances.

Late commencement of the assessment process

Permission is not required to commence detailed assessment proceedings out of time, but if the receiving party does not commence the process within 3 months, the court may disallow all or part of the costs or disallow all or part of any interest accruing on the costs. Since interest will be accumulating on the costs even though they have not yet been quantified, the usual sanction, however, will be to disallow all or part of the interest that would otherwise be payable to the receiving party (r 47.8).

It is open to the paying party to apply for an order that the receiving party lose their right to costs unless detailed assessment proceedings are commenced by a certain date.

Challenging the bill

The paying party has 21 days from receipt of the notice of commencement to serve points of dispute on the receiving party (r 47.9). If he does not do so, the receiving party can apply for a default costs certificate which will include an order to pay the costs. The default costs certificate will be set aside only if good reason is shown by the paying party. If the paying party serves the points of dispute late (but before the default certificate is issued), the paying party may not be heard further unless the court gives permission.

On receipt of the points of dispute, the receiving party may serve a reply within 21 days (r 47.13). The receiving party must file a request for an assessment hearing within 3 months of the expiry of the period for commencing detailed assessment proceedings.

There will then be a detailed assessment hearing, at which the court will decide what costs are to be paid. The receiving party must, within 14 days of the hearing, file a completed bill showing the amount of costs finally due.

The receiving party will normally be entitled to the costs of the detailed assessment proceedings but the court may take into account:

(a) the conduct of the parties;
(b) the amount of any reduction from the original amount claimed;
(c) the reasonableness of claiming or challenging any particular item.

The court must also take into account any written offer expressed to be 'without prejudice save as to the costs of the detailed assessment proceedings'.

No time is specified for service of such an offer, but any offer made more than 14 days after:

(a) service of the notice of commencement (paying party);
(b) service of the points of dispute (receiving party),

will be given less weight unless good reason is shown.

Appeals

Where the assessment was by a judge, the appeals process is governed by Part 52. An appeal from a detailed or summary assessment by a district judge is made to a circuit judge. An appeal from an assessment by a circuit judge, is made to a High Court judge. Permission to appeal is required either from the original court or the appeal court. If permission is not sought at the original assessment, it must be sought from the appeal court within 14 days. The appeal takes the form of a review of the original decision, rather than a re-hearing.

Part 52 does not apply where the detailed assessment was performed by an officer of the court. In this case, r 47.20 applies (as supplemented by paras 47 and 48 of PD 47). Permission to appeal is not required and the appeal takes the form of a re-hearing either by a costs judge or a district judge of the High Court.

Agreeing costs

Rather than go through the detailed assessment procedure, it is always open to the parties to agree the figure for costs payable by one side to another. Very often, the parties will attempt to agree a figure for costs, and only proceed to a detailed assessment if they are unable to reach agreement.

Interim orders

The detailed assessment of costs procedure initially means that there will be some delay in the successful party receiving their costs from the unsuccessful party. Rule 44.3(8) of the CPR 1998 allows the court at trial to order an interim payment of part of these costs, and in *Mars UK Ltd v Teknowledge Ltd (No 2)* [1999] Masons CLR 322, ChD, Jacob J indicated that the court should make an order for the interim payment of costs in most cases.

Conditional fee agreements

A winning party who has funded the litigation by a conditional fee agreement (CFA) is likely to have agreed to pay their solicitor a success fee and may also have paid a premium for after-the-event insurance. Where a costs order is made in that party's favour, the costs payable include the success fee and premium. These items are referred to as the additional liability to distinguish them from the base costs.

Rule 44.3B sets out a number of limits on the recovery of the additional liability, including that the following may not be recovered:

(i) Any proportion of the success fee that compensates the solicitor for costs resulting from the postponement of the payment of his fees and expenses. For example, the solicitor will sometimes have funded the disbursements by way of a loan. Any part of the success fee intended to compensate the solicitor for the interest payable on the loan is not recoverable from the paying party.
(ii) The success fee applicable to any period during which the required notice of funding had not been filed (see **2.5.2**).
(iii) Any success fee if the receiving party has failed to disclose the required risk assessment information (see below).

Where (ii) or (iii) apply the receiving party may apply for relief from sanctions.

In addition, the paying party is, of course, only liable for the success fee and premium to the extent that these are reasonable and (where the standard basis applies) proportionate. The Practice Direction makes clear, however, that the success fee should not be reduced simply because when it is added to the base costs the total appears disproportionate. In considering the success fee the court will consider the circumstances as they reasonably appeared to the solicitor when the CFA was entered into. Relevant factors include the extent of the risk that the fees and expenses would not be payable, whether the solicitor was liable under the CFA for any disbursements and what other methods of financing the case were available.

A party wishing to recover an additional liability from his opponent is obliged by r 44.15 to file with the court and serve on every other party a notice of funding in Form N251 within 7 days of entering the CFA or when he issues the claim form (if later). There is, however, no requirement to disclose the amount of the success fee or how that figure was arrived at until the assessment of costs stage.

Where the court has ordered a detailed assessment, the receiving party must on commencing those proceedings file and serve on the paying party a statement of the reasons for the success fee (in accordance with reg 3 of the Conditional Fee Agreement Regulations 2000), together with a copy of the after-the-event insurance certificate giving details of the extent of the cover provided and the premium paid (see para 32 of PD 47).

Where the court decides to perform a summary assessment of the additional liability, the party must make available:

(i) the Form N251 ;
(ii) all estimates and statements of costs that have been filed during the course of the action; and

(iii) a copy of the risk assessment prepared when the CFA was entered into (see para 14 of PD 44).

Under reg 3(2)(b) of the Conditional Fee Agreements Regulations 2000, any amount of the success fee which is disallowed on assessment ceases to be payable by the receiving party unless the court orders otherwise. If the receiving party's solicitor applies to the court for such an order, the matter may well have to be adjourned to a separate hearing.

13.4 HUMAN RIGHTS

The court's ability to restrict the evidence heard at trial and to control the trial timetable raise the possibility of a challenge under Article 6(1). As discussed at **11.15.2**, provided the court is careful in exercising its powers to apply the overriding objective, it is likely to be difficult for litigants to challenge such case management decisions successfully.

The right to a fair trial includes an obligation on the part of the court to give reasons for its decisions (see, eg, *Van de Hurk v Netherlands* (1994) 18 EHRR 481). A failure at the end of a trial to give a sufficiently reasoned judgment would, therefore, be a breach of Article 6(1).

The approach taken by the European Court of Human Rights has already received support from the Court of Appeal in *Hyams v Pender* [2000] 1 WLR 32. The defendant had sought permission to appeal a county court possession order. The application had been decided by the court on paper (ie without a hearing) and had been refused 'for non-compliance with Practice Direction (Part 52)'. The defendant appealed the refusal to the Court of Appeal, which, whilst dismissing the appeal, stated that the right to reasons meant that the judge should have identified how the Practice Direction had not been complied with.

Chapter 14

ENFORCEMENT OF MONEY JUDGMENTS

14.1 INTRODUCTION

Once a party has obtained a judgment against his opponent, the opponent will usually pay the amount he has been ordered to pay without any further action being necessary. If, however, the losing party fails to pay the amount he has been ordered to pay, then the winning party will have to take steps to enforce the judgment debt. The judgment will not be enforced by the court automatically, and unless the winning party takes enforcement action, he will not receive the money that he was awarded. The winning party will have to consider with his solicitor the best method of enforcing payment.

Where the opponent is not insured, the question of enforcement is one which should be considered before proceedings are ever commenced, because it is obviously not worth obtaining a judgment against a party who does not have the means to pay. The solicitor should consider the question of enforcement with their client at the outset, and proceedings should not be commenced at all unless he or she is satisfied that the defendant's whereabouts are known, that prima facie he has the means to pay the amount in issue, and has assets which can be taken from him to enforce payment if necessary.

The CPR themselves do not yet deal with enforcement and so one has to look at the 'old' High Court and county court rules, contained respectively in Sch 1 and 2 to the CPR 1998.

Chapter 14 contents
Introduction
Interest on judgment debts
Tracing the other party
Investigating the judgment debtor's means
Methods of enforcement

14.2 INTEREST ON JUDGMENT DEBTS

14.2.1 High Court judgments

Interest accrues on all High Court judgments from the date judgment is pronounced. The current rate of interest is 8 per cent per annum, although this may be altered from time to time by statutory instrument. The rate applicable to any particular judgment is the rate in force when the judgment was made. Where judgment is entered for damages to be assessed, interest begins to run from the date when damages are finally assessed or agreed, ie the date of the final judgment. Interest on an order for the payment of costs runs from the date of the judgment, not from the date of the final costs certificate. Therefore, interest is accruing on the costs before the paying party knows how much he has to pay in costs. He can alleviate the situation by making a payment on account of costs.

14.2.2 County court judgments

Interest accrues on county court judgments of £5,000 or more, although the Lord Chancellor's Department is considering whether to allow interest on judgment debts below £5,000. The current rate of interest is 8 per cent per annum, subject to alteration by statutory instrument, and the rate applicable is the rate in force when the judgment was made.

Where under the terms of the judgment payment is deferred, or to be in instalments, interest will not accrue until that date, or until an instalment falls due.

Where enforcement proceedings are taken the judgment debt ceases to carry interest unless the enforcement proceedings fail to produce any payment, in which case interest will continue to accrue on the judgment debt as if the enforcement proceedings had never been issued. 'Enforcement proceedings' include an application for an oral examination (see **14.4.2**). If an attachment of earnings order is in force, interest does not accrue.

Care needs to be taken as regards interest in the county court. If enforcement proceedings are taken and anything at all is recovered, then the balance of the debt will become interest free.

When applying to enforce interest in the county court, a party must supply a certificate setting out the amount of interest claimed, the sum on which it is claimed, the dates from and to which interest has accrued, and the rate of interest applied.

14.3 TRACING THE OTHER PARTY

There are a number of methods of enforcement available, but before commencing enforcement proceedings, the other party's whereabouts need to be established. If the other party's whereabouts are not known, consideration should be given to employing an enquiry agent to trace him. If this is to be done, the enquiry agent should be given as much information as possible to assist his enquiries (eg the other party's last known address, his last known employer, details of any known relatives). A limit should be placed on the costs which may be incurred by the enquiry agent, so that a disproportionate amount of money is not wasted in attempts to trace the defendant, which might be unsuccessful in the end. In practice, these enquiries are likely to have been made at the outset of the case, since there is little point in suing a defendant you cannot trace.

14.4 INVESTIGATING THE JUDGMENT DEBTOR'S MEANS

The next thing to consider is what assets the judgment debtor has, since the method of enforcement chosen will depend upon what type of assets are available to pay the judgment debt. The winning party may already have enough information about his opponent for a decision to be made, otherwise further enquiries will have to be made.

There are two ways to investigate the judgment debtor's assets: the winning party can either instruct an enquiry agent to make investigations; or he can apply to the court for an oral examination of the judgment debtor.

14.4.1 Instructing an enquiry agent

The enquiry agent should be given as much information as possible to assist their enquiries, and a limit should be placed on the amount of costs to be incurred, to avoid spending a disproportionate amount on these preliminary enquiries. Even so, this method of carrying out the investigations is likely to be considerably more expensive than applying to the court for an oral examination of the judgment debtor. However, the enquiry agent may be able to discover assets which are not disclosed on an oral examination, and they may produce results more quickly, depending on the speed with which the oral examination can be dealt with by the court.

14.4.2 Oral examination (RSC Ord 48, r 1; CCR Ord 25, r 3)

An order for an oral examination is a court order requiring the judgment debtor to attend before an officer of the court and be examined on oath as to his means. The judgment creditor obtains the order by making an application without notice to either the High Court or a county court. If the judgment debtor is a company, the order can be made against an officer of the company. The order requires the judgment debtor to produce all relevant books or documents.

(1) Application to the High Court

(a) The application without notice is made by filing evidence showing that the applicant is entitled to enforce the judgment, identifying the judgment, and stating the amount remaining unpaid under it at the time of the application.
(b) The evidence is placed before the master or district judge, and if he or she is satisfied that an order for an oral examination should be made, they will make the order.
(c) The order must be served personally upon the judgment debtor, and he should be offered 'conduct money' at the time of service. 'Conduct money' means the debtor's reasonable travelling costs to and from the court. There is no requirement to tender this in the first instance, but if it is offered, it will mean that the order can be enforced by committal proceedings if the debtor fails to comply with it.
(d) The examination will take place before a senior clerk of the court office. It will be held at the most convenient court, which will be the High Court office or county court for the district in which the debtor resides.
(e) The judgment creditor's representative has to attend the hearing, and should be prepared to examine the debtor as to his means. The examination is intended to be not merely an examination, but a cross-examination of the most severe kind. It is useful, if possible, to obtain some evidence of the debtor's means beforehand, to enable probing questions to be asked. If, for example, the debtor denies that he owns a motor car, it is useful to be able to ask, 'In that case, who owns the BMW registration number ABC 123 which is parked in your driveway most evenings?'. The court officer will take a note of the evidence given.
(f) At the end of the examination the debtor is asked to sign a form containing a note of the evidence which he has given. The court may allow the costs of the examination, if any valuable information has been obtained, and so the judgment creditor's representative should ask for an order for costs.
(g) If the judgment debtor fails to attend the oral examination, an application can be made for his committal to prison. In practice, a suspended committal order will

be made in the first instance, and this will usually be sufficient to persuade the debtor to attend the next hearing.

(2) Application to a county court
(a) The application is made by completing the prescribed application form and filing this at court.
(b) The district judge will then make the order if he or she considers it appropriate.
(c) The order must then be served on the judgment debtor, and service may be either personal or by post.
(d) The judgment debtor then has to attend court on the appointed day and the examination will take place before an officer of the court. It will take place in the county court for the district where the debtor resides or carries on business, and the proceedings may have to be transferred for this purpose. The procedure at the examination will be the same as for a High Court examination.
(e) If the debtor fails to attend, the hearing will be adjourned, and notice of the adjourned hearing must be served personally on the debtor. Conduct money should be tendered if the debtor requests it. If the debtor fails to attend the adjourned hearing, he may be committed to prison. A suspended committal order will be made in the first instance, which usually has the effect of persuading the debtor to attend at the next hearing.

14.5 METHODS OF ENFORCEMENT

There are four common methods of enforcement to choose from, which are:
(a) execution (ie, seizure and sale of the debtor's goods);
(b) charging order (ie, a charge on the debtor's land or securities);
(c) garnishee order (ie, an order requiring a third party who owes money to the debtor to pay it directly to the creditor);
(d) attachment of earnings order (ie, an order requiring the debtor's employer to make deductions from his earnings and pay it to the creditor).

The solicitor must decide in the light of the information he has obtained about the judgment debtor, which method of enforcement is most suitable.

Each method of enforcement mentioned is now considered in more detail.

14.5.1 Execution (RSC Ord 46; CCR Ord 26, r 1)

This process enables the sheriff's officer (High Court) or court bailiff (county court) to seize and sell the debtor's goods to pay the judgment debt and costs and the costs of enforcement. The items seized are sold by public auction. After deducting the expenses of sale, the judgment debt and costs are paid, and any surplus proceeds are returned to the debtor.

(1) Choice of court

(A) HIGH COURT

A party who has obtained a judgment in the High Court may issue a writ of fieri facias in that court, regardless of the amount to be enforced.

Enforcement of Money Judgments 161

(B) COUNTY COURT

Where a party has obtained judgment in a county court, and the amount to be enforced by execution is £5,000 or more, it must be enforced in the High Court unless the proceedings originated under the Consumer Credit Act 1974.

Where the sum to be enforced is less than £600, it must be enforced in a county court.

In the case of county court judgments of £600 or more but less than £5,000, the judgment creditor can choose whether to issue execution in the High Court or the county court. If he chooses to use the High Court, the county court judgment must first be transferred to the High Court. The advantage of this is that interest then accrues on the judgment debt.

A party with a county court judgment for £5,000 or more will be able to issue a part warrant in that court, for example where an instalment order or the final balance is less than £5,000.

(2) Procedure in the High Court

(a) The judgment creditor completes two copies of a writ of fieri facias and a praecipe for a writ of fieri facias.
(b) He delivers these documents to the court office, together with the judgment and the costs officer's certificate where the enforcement relates to costs.
(c) The court seals the writ and returns one copy of it to the judgment creditor.
(d) The judgment creditor forwards the sealed copy writ to the under-sheriff for the county where the debtor resides or carries on business.
(e) The under-sheriff sends the writ to his officer for execution.

(3) Procedure in the county court

(a) The judgment creditor completes the form of request for a warrant of execution.
(b) The judgment creditor files this at court, together with the fee.
(c) The warrant is executed by the bailiff of the county court for the district where the debtor resides or carries on business.

(4) Items exempt from seizure

Certain items cannot be seized. These are:

(a) goods on hire or hire-purchase;
(b) tools, books, vehicles and other items of equipment which are necessary to the debtor for use personally in his job or business;
(c) clothing, bedding, furniture, household equipment and provisions which are necessary for satisfying the basic domestic needs of the debtor and his family.

'Necessary items' are items which are so essential that without them a debtor could not continue his existing job or business.

MOTOR VEHICLES

It should be the exception rather than the rule that a debtor is allowed to retain a motor vehicle as a necessary item. It is for the debtor to satisfy the sheriff/bailiff that the vehicle is necessary to allow him to continue his job or business. The fact that a debtor claims to need a vehicle to get to and from his place of work should not by itself be considered grounds to exempt the vehicle. The sheriff/bailiff must be satisfied that no reasonable alternative is available.

HOUSEHOLD ITEMS

Items such as stereo equipment, televisions, videos, or microwave ovens where there is also a conventional cooker, are not considered to be necessary for satisfying the basic domestic needs of the debtor and his family.

It is always helpful to inform the sheriff/bailiff of specific items which could be seized, for example tell him the make, type and registration number of the debtor's car.

(5) 'Walking possession'

In practice, the debtor's goods are not usually removed immediately. The debtor and the sheriff/bailiff will enter into an agreement for 'walking possession'. This means that the sheriff/bailiff agrees not to remove the goods at once and, in return, the debtor agrees not to dispose of them nor permit them to be moved. This gives the debtor a further opportunity to pay the sum due, and he may apply for suspension of the writ or warrant. If this is granted, it means that the writ of fieri facias/warrant of execution is suspended on condition that the debtor pays the sum due by specified instalments.

The sheriff/bailiff must not effect a forcible entry to any premises and must not take goods from the debtor's person.

14.5.2 Charging order on land (RSC Ord 50; CCR Ord 31)

A judgment creditor may apply to the court for an order charging the judgment debtor's land with the amount due under a judgment. A charging order can also be made in respect of land which the debtor owns jointly with another person, in which case the order is a charge upon the debtor's beneficial interest, rather than upon the land itself.

(1) Restrictions on making a charging order

Where the court has made an order for payment of the sum due by instalments, a charging order will not be made as long as the debtor is up to date with the instalment payments.

(2) Registration of the charging order

Once a charging order has been made, it should be registered if possible.

If the judgment debtor is the sole owner of the land, the charging order can be registered, at the Land Charges Department as an order affecting land if the title is unregistered, or at HM Land Registry as a notice if the land is registered.

Where the land is jointly owned, the debtor technically has an interest only in the proceeds of sale under the trust for sale, rather than an interest in the land itself. Therefore, in the case of unregistered land, the charging order is not registrable because it is not an order relating to land. In the case of registered land, the charging order can be protected by entry of a caution.

If the creditor does not know whether the land is registered, he should make an Index Map Search before applying for a charging order. If the creditor does not know whether the land is jointly owned, he should make a search of the title in the case of registered land, again before applying for a charging order.

(3) Notice

Whether or not the charging order is registered, written notice of it should be given to any prior chargee(s) to prevent any tacking of later advances. A search may be necessary at HM Land Registry (registered land) or the Land Charges Department (unregistered land) to discover the existence of prior incumbrances.

Once this has been done, the creditor has security for the debt, but he still has not obtained the sum due.

(4) Order for sale

In order to obtain the money, the creditor can apply to the court for an order for sale of the land charged. The judgment will then be satisfied out of the proceeds of sale.

(5) Choice of court

(A) HIGH COURT

The application for a charging order may only be made to the High Court if the judgment to be enforced is a High Court judgment for a sum exceeding £5,000.

(B) COUNTY COURT

If the judgment to be enforced is a county court judgment or a High Court judgment for £5,000 or less, the application for a charging order must be made to a county court. If it is a High Court judgment for more than £5,000, the application may be made to the county court, or the creditor may choose the High Court (see (A) above). The appropriate county court will normally be the court for the district in which the debtor resides or carries on business.

(6) Procedure in the High Court

(a) The judgment creditor files a witness statement or affidavit in support of the application. This must state the name and address of the judgment debtor and, if known, of every other creditor of his whom the applicant can identify. It must certify the amount of money remaining due under the judgment, identify the subject matter of the intended charge, and verify that the interest to be charged is owned beneficially by the judgment debtor.

(b) The judgment creditor must also file a draft charging order nisi (an order to show cause).

(c) The master or district judge considers the application in the absence of the parties and, if satisfied, makes the charging order nisi.

(d) The charging order nisi should be registered either at the Land Charges Department or at HM Land Registry, if registration is possible.

(e) The charging order nisi, indorsed with a hearing date, together with a copy of the supporting affidavit or witness statement, must be served on the judgment debtor at least 7 days before the return day. Ordinary service is required.

(f) At the hearing, which will take place before the master or district judge, a charging order absolute will be made unless the judgment debtor shows cause why this should not be done.

(g) The creditor now has a charge on the debtor's land which can be enforced by an order for sale of the property.

(h) In order to enforce the charging order by sale of the property charged, fresh proceedings would have to be commenced in the Chancery Division.

(7) Procedure in the county court

The county court procedure is the same as the procedure in the High Court. When a charging order has been obtained in a county court, it can be enforced by applying for an order for sale in a county court.

14.5.3 Charging order on securities

A judgment creditor can also obtain a charging order on a judgment debtor's beneficial interest in certain specified securities.

The procedure is similar to the procedure for obtaining a charging order on land.

14.5.4 Garnishee proceedings (RSC Ord 49; CCR Ord 30)

Where a person (who is called the garnishee) owes money to the judgment debtor, the court can make an order requiring the garnishee to pay the judgment creditor the whole of that debt or such part of it as is sufficient to satisfy the judgment debt and costs. This is known as a garnishee order. A bank account or building society account is often the target of such an order. Judgment debtors who are self-employed often have trade debts due to them. It is possible to find out on oral examination what these debts are and then to take garnishee proceedings accordingly.

The debt must belong to the judgment debtor solely and beneficially. This means, for example, that the judgment creditor cannot garnish the husband and wife's joint bank account if the husband alone is the judgment debtor. Also, the garnishee must be within the jurisdiction.

(1) Choice of court

(A) HIGH COURT

Where a person has obtained a judgment for £50 or more, he may apply to the High Court for a garnishee order to enforce payment.

(B) COUNTY COURT

Where a person has obtained a county court judgment for at least £50, the county court may make a garnishee order.

(2) Procedure in the High Court

(a) The judgment creditor files an affidavit or witness statement, setting out the name and last known address of the judgment debtor, details of the date and amount of the judgment, the amount which remains unpaid, and details of the garnishee.
(b) The judgment creditor also files a draft garnishee order nisi (also called an order to show cause).
(c) The master or district judge considers the evidence and, if he or she is satisfied, the garnishee order nisi is issued. This is indorsed with a hearing date when the garnishee is required to attend and show cause why he should not pay his debt directly to the judgment creditor.
(d) The judgment creditor must serve the garnishee order nisi personally upon the garnishee at least 15 days before the return day. He must also serve it on the

judgment debtor by ordinary service at least 7 days thereafter and at least 7 days before the return day.
(e) The order binds the garnishee as soon as it is served upon him, and he must retain the money in question in his possession until the court has made a final order at the hearing.
(f) At the hearing, the master or district judge has a discretion as to whether or not to make the order absolute. Provided the garnishee does not dispute his liability, a garnishee order absolute will usually be made.
(g) The garnishee must then pay the debt which he owes to the judgment debtor to the judgment creditor.

Any payment made by the garnishee in compliance with an order absolute will discharge the garnishee's liability to the judgment debtor to the extent of the amount paid.

If the garnishee fails to pay his debt to the judgment creditor, the judgment creditor can enforce the order against the garnishee in the same manner as for any other money judgment.

(3) Procedure in the county court

The application is made to the county court which gave the judgment, but a garnishee who is disputing liability may apply for transfer to his local court.

The procedure is the same as for the High Court, except that the garnishee order nisi may be served either personally or by post upon the garnishee.

(4) Garnishee proceedings against a deposit-taking institution

A bank or building society account, provided that it is in credit, is an ideal target for garnishee proceedings. Once the garnishee order nisi is served, the account is frozen and, upon the making of the garnishee order absolute, the money in the account must be paid over to the judgment creditor.

There are some special points to bear in mind when garnishee proceedings are taken against a deposit-taking institution.

(a) The evidence in support must state whether the witness knows the name and address of the branch where the account is held and the account number. This information should be obtained from the judgment debtor at the oral examination.
(b) The order must be served on the registered or head office of the institution, and it is also desirable to serve a copy on the branch concerned.
(c) In making an order, any conditions applicable to the account in question which purport to restrict withdrawals will be disregarded, for example conditions requiring an account holder to give notice, or to produce a deposit book.
(d) An order against a building society cannot require a payment which would reduce the balance in the account to a sum less than £1.
(e) Before paying the judgment creditor, the deposit-taking institution is entitled to deduct a prescribed sum (currently £50) in respect of administrative expenses.

Deposit-taking institutions do not usually attend the hearing to 'show cause'. Instead, they usually write to the court confirming that they will comply with any order made.

If the institution in question does not hold any money to the credit of the judgment debtor, in the county court it may give notice to that effect to the court, and the garnishee proceedings against it are then automatically stayed unless the judgment creditor disputes the notice.

(5) Costs

The costs of a successful application are usually fixed and may be retained by the judgment creditor out of the money recovered from the garnishee in priority to the judgment debt.

The costs of an unsuccessful application are in the discretion of the court and may be ordered against the judgment debtor or judgment creditor as the court thinks fit.

14.5.5 Attachment of earnings (CCR Ord 27)

An attachment of earnings order is an order which compels the judgment debtor's employer to make regular deductions from the debtor's earnings and pay them into court. The High Court has no power to make an attachment of earnings order. If the judgment has been obtained in the High Court, the proceedings will have to be transferred to the county court before this method of enforcement can be used. The amount remaining due under the judgment must be at least £50 for an attachment of earnings application to be made. Also, the debtor must be employed; an order cannot be made if the debtor is unemployed or self-employed.

Procedure

(a) The judgment creditor completes the prescribed application form and files it at court.
(b) The court informs the debtor of the application, and requires him either to pay the sum due, or file a statement of means in the prescribed form. The court will make a diary entry for return of the form.
(c) If the debtor returns the form, the court staff will make an attachment of earnings order. The court staff will fix the repayment rate by applying certain guidelines which they are given to the debtor's statement of means. If necessary, the application will be referred to the district judge. The order will specify the 'normal deduction rate' and the 'protected earnings rate'. The latter is the amount which the debtor is allowed to retain out of his earnings in any event. If his earnings for a particular week are equal to or less than the 'protected earnings rate', then the creditor will receive nothing that week.
(d) The order will be sent to the parties, and to the debtor's employer, with instructions to deduct the amount ordered from the debtor's pay and forward it to the court. The employer is entitled to deduct an additional sum (currently £1) in respect of his administrative costs for each deduction which he makes in accordance with the order.
(e) If either party objects to the order which has been made, he can apply for the matter to be reconsidered by the district judge. If such an application is made, there will be a hearing before the district judge. In the meantime, the employer will be required to make deductions as ordered unless and until the order is varied.
(f) If the debtor informs the court that he is unemployed or self-employed, the application will be dismissed.
(g) If the debtor does not respond to the initial notice sent to him by the court, an order to produce a statement of means will be served on him personally by the court bailiff. This order is automatically issued by the court. If the creditor has

provided the name and address of the debtor's employer, the employer will also be contacted at this stage for a statement of earnings.

(h) If the debtor still does not respond when the order is served on him by the court bailiff, then the court will automatically issue a notice to show cause. This will be served on the debtor by the court bailiff, and it will give notice of a hearing before the district judge which the debtor is required to attend. Failure to attend will lead to his committal to prison.

14.5.6 Insolvency

(1) Bankruptcy

Where the judgment debt is for £750 or more, the judgment creditor may decide to petition for bankruptcy of the judgment debtor. However, he will not be able to do this if he has already registered a charging order because he is then in the position of a secured creditor, and a secured creditor cannot petition for bankruptcy unless he gives up his security.

Bankruptcy procedure is not dealt with in detail here (for more detail, please refer to the LPC Resource Book *Business Law and Practice* (Jordans)). Briefly, the first step is for the judgment creditor to serve on the judgment debtor a statutory demand in the prescribed form, unless execution has been levied and remains unsatisfied, in whole or in part, in which case there is no need for a statutory demand. Three weeks after service of the statutory demand, the petitioner may file the bankruptcy petition. In addition, an affidavit is required to verify the truth of the petition. The court will issue the petition indorsed with the date and place of hearing. The petition must be served on the debtor at least 14 days before the hearing. At the hearing, the judgment creditor must prove that the debt is still outstanding, and the court will usually then make a bankruptcy order, although the petition may be dismissed, stayed or adjourned. If a bankruptcy order is made, all the debtor's property vests in the trustee in bankruptcy.

(2) Winding up

If the judgment debtor is a company, the judgment creditor may consider winding up the company. The procedure for this is very similar to the bankruptcy procedure for individuals.

14.5.7 Enforcement outside the jurisdiction

The methods of enforcing English judgments abroad, or enforcing a foreign judgment in England, depend on the arrangements which have been made with the foreign country in question either by Treaty or Convention. These arrangements are as follows.

(1) The EU

Article 26 of the Brussels Convention on Jurisdiction and the Enforcement of Judgments 1968, as incorporated into English law by the Civil Jurisdiction and Judgments Act 1982, requires all Member States to recognise and enforce the judgments of other Member States.

To enforce a judgment obtained in the High Court in another EU country, the first step is to obtain a certified copy of the judgment. The application for the certified copy is made without notice, supported by evidence contained in a witness statement or affidavit. RSC Ord 71, r 36 (set out in Sch 1 to the CPR 1998) sets out the matters which must be dealt with in the witness statement or affidavit.

When the court issues the certified copy, annexed to it will be a copy of the claim form. The creditor's solicitors, assuming they do not have a branch in the State in question, will send the certificate to agents in the State so that they can follow the appropriate local procedure. The creditor's solicitors will probably need to supply a translation of the judgment.

To register a foreign judgment in England, the creditor applies without notice to the Royal Courts of Justice in London, the application being supported by evidence contained in a witness statement or affidavit. The judgment, or a certified copy of the judgment, must be exhibited to the witness statement or affidavit.

RSC Ord 71, r 28 sets out the matters which must be dealt with in the witness statement or affidavit.

If leave to register is granted, notice of registration has to be served on the debtor. The notice gives details of the judgment and the order for registration, the creditor's address for service, and the debtor's right of appeal. If the debtor does wish to appeal against the order for registration, he has one month to do so.

If there is no appeal, or the appeal fails, the creditor then registers the judgment with the High Court in London and proceeds to enforce it in the usual way.

(2) Countries outside the EU

Similar provisions to those outlined above apply to countries covered by the Administration of Justice Act 1920 and the Foreign Judgments (Reciprocal Enforcement) Act 1933. The countries covered by these Acts are mainly Commonwealth States.

For countries not covered by these Acts, such as the USA, enforcement of judgments of the courts of these countries is covered by common law. Usually, the creditor will treat the foreign judgment as a contract containing an implied promise to pay the judgment debt. He will issue proceedings in England alleging breaches of that contract, and if the debtor attempts to defend those proceedings, will apply for summary judgment under Part 24 of the CPR 1998.

Enforcement abroad is a matter for the law and courts of the country where the creditor is seeking to enforce an English judgment.

Chapter 15

ALTERNATIVE DISPUTE RESOLUTION

This chapter develops further the concept that it may be possible to use less confrontational modes of dispute resolution to reach a quick, cheap and commercially realistic solution. It explains: (i) how alternative dispute resolution differs from arbitration and litigation; (ii) the advantages and disadvantages of alternative dispute resolution; (iii) the various types of methods available to resolve disputes; and (iv) the organisations which may be able to help if the parties do choose to use some method of dispute resolution instead of arbitration or litigation.

Chapter 15 contents
The nature of ADR
Advantages of ADR
Disadvantages of ADR
Types of ADR
Organisations providing ADR
Using ADR
Choosing ADR
Summary

15.1 THE NATURE OF ADR

Alternative dispute resolution (ADR) is a means of resolving disputes by using an independent third party who may help the parties to reach their own solution, but who cannot impose a solution. It is voluntary and without prejudice. The parties choose the process and either of them can withdraw at any time before a solution is agreed. If either of them does not like the proposed solution, they do not have to accept it.

15.1.1 How ADR differs from other forms of dispute resolution

Litigation is not voluntary (save in the sense that the claimant chooses to issue a claim in the first place). Once the case is started, usually neither party can withdraw without paying the opponent's costs. If the parties are unable to negotiate a settlement, the court will impose its own solution. The winner will enforce that solution.

Arbitration is voluntary in the sense that the parties voluntarily entered into an arbitration agreement. When a dispute arises, however, one party can force the other to arbitrate against his will, because of the original contractual agreement to do so. The arbitrator will impose a solution which the winner can enforce.

Negotiation is both voluntary and non-binding, but it is not the same as ADR. In a negotiation there is no independent third party. The negotiators are identified with their respective 'sides' and may only see the case from their side's point of view. In ADR, there is a third party who is totally independent and who can see both sides' points of view.

15.1.2 The independent third party

The independence of the third party is an essential feature of ADR, as is the fact that he or she cannot impose a solution. As the parties know that he is independent and cannot do anything to harm them, they are more likely to trust and be open with him. They are less likely to be aggressive towards each other in his presence. They will not want to be seen by him as an obstacle towards a settlement and are likely to be more accommodating in his presence. He may therefore be able to defuse the dispute and make settlement more likely.

The third party can help the parties to settle their dispute in another way. A commercially minded neutral may come up with ideas which the parties may not have thought of and which solve the problem without either side losing face.

15.2 ADVANTAGES OF ADR

The CPR 1998 specifically recognise the advantages of ADR. Rule 1.4(2)(e), in giving guidance on how to further the overriding objective of dealing with cases justly, talks about:

> 'encouraging the parties to use an alternative dispute resolution procedure if the court considers that appropriate and facilitating the use of such procedure.'

In a *Practice Statement (Alternative Dispute Resolution) (No 2)* [1996] 1 WLR 1024, Waller J said:

> 'the settlement of actions by means of ADR (i) significantly helps to save litigants the ever mounting cost of bringing their actions to trial; (ii) saves them the delay of litigation in reaching finality in their disputes; (iii) enables them to achieve settlement of their disputes while preserving their existing commercial relationships and market reputation; (iv) provides them with a wider range of settlement solutions than those offered by litigation; and (v) is likely to make a substantial contribution to the more efficient use of judicial resources ... .'

Some of these points are amplified below.

15.2.1 Cheapness and speed

Apart from the fact that an independent third party can find it easier to lead the parties to a settlement, ADR has many other attractions. It can be significantly cheaper than both arbitration and litigation. This is because it is quicker. A skilled neutral can, in most cases which are suitable for ADR, help the parties to resolve their dispute in a relatively short period of time.

The parties do, of course, have to pay the third party for his services. They will usually instruct lawyers to help them on the day and they will have to pay those lawyers. If ADR works, however, there will be a significant reduction in the amount of time the lawyers spend in preparing and presenting the case. This will save costs. Even more importantly, the client saves on the indirect costs involved in their employees and executives having to spend time reading court documents, consulting lawyers and attending court.

However, clients should not be given the impression that ADR comes at bargain basement prices. Any lawyer representing the client will want to be fully prepared, and that will take time (including the client's time in dealing with the lawyer's enquiries) and will cost money.

15.2.2 Flexibility

Speed and cheapness are the principal attractions of ADR but it is also very flexible. The parties can choose one of several forms of ADR. They can choose the procedure to be followed in conjunction with their chosen neutral. They do not have to comply with any statutes or rules of court. There is not even any case-law limiting what the parties or the neutral can do.

15.2.3 Preserving a business relationship

ADR shares with arbitration the virtue of privacy. It is also ideal for cases where the parties to the dispute are going to have to continue to deal with each other. The fact that they have chosen a non-confrontational method of solving their problem makes it much easier for them to continue their relationship, since the solution is theirs and has not been imposed upon them.

15.2.4 Commercial reality

A third party unconnected with the dispute may be able to assist the parties to arrive at realistic and workable settlement terms.

15.3 DISADVANTAGES OF ADR

15.3.1 It does not bind the parties to the procedure

As a general principle, no one can be forced to resolve a dispute by any form of ADR against their wishes. If one party suggests ADR, the other parties do not have to agree, and, even if the parties have started to resolve a dispute by ADR, most ADR agreements allow any party to withdraw at any stage before a solution has been agreed. It will then be necessary to resort to litigation or, if there is an arbitration agreement, to arbitration.

The House of Lords has, however, in *Channel Tunnel Group Ltd and France Manche SA v Balfour Beatty Construction Ltd* [1993] 2 WLR 262 indicated that the court does have an inherent jurisdiction to stay litigation which has been commenced in breach of an agreed method of resolving disputes. This is the case even if that method is not technically an arbitration agreement under the Arbitration Act 1996. This may mean that a party who litigates in breach of an ADR agreement will have to abandon the litigation until the ADR process has been exhausted. The principles governing this have yet to be worked out by the courts. Forcing parties to use ADR may also be of limited practical benefit, since they will be less likely to reach a settlement.

15.3.2 The awards are not so easily enforceable

There is no equivalent of s 66 of the Arbitration Act 1996 (see **2.8.1**) enabling ADR awards to be enforced as if they were court judgments. However, if the parties do agree to terms suggested as a result of ADR, they have entered into a contract. If one of the parties does not carry out that contract, he can be sued for breach of contract and the claimant would usually expect to obtain summary judgment under Part 24 of the CPR 1998 without any difficulty.

It is standard practice in many forms of ADR to provide that no agreement will be binding upon the parties unless it is placed in writing and signed by the parties.

A party who has commenced court proceedings, but then resolved the dispute by ADR, can record the agreement reached in a consent order, which can be enforced by the usual methods.

15.3.3 The facts may not be fully disclosed

The speed of ADR has an associated disadvantage. Because there is no equivalent of disclosure, there is a risk that the parties may resolve the dispute without knowing all the facts. This may lead to the wrong decision. Many businessmen, however, take the view that a quick decision, even if it is not completely accurate, is better than wasting time and money on a protracted dispute in order to get a more correct decision. They often feel that litigation is a lottery anyway.

15.3.4 ADR is not appropriate for all cases

ADR is not appropriate in the following cases:

(1) where the client needs an injunction (after which ADR may then be appropriate);
(2) where there is no dispute. If the case is a simple debt collection matter, the creditor should issue a claim form followed by a Part 24 application, or consider insolvency proceedings;
(3) The client needs a ruling on a point of law.

15.4 TYPES OF ADR

15.4.1 Mediation and conciliation

Mediation and conciliation are usually interchangeable terms. For ease of reference the term mediation will be used to cover both processes in this chapter.

In a typical mediation, the third party who has been selected as mediator will have written statements from both parties. Following that, the mediator will discuss the case with them. They will tell him what they think about each party's case on a without prejudice basis. The mediator will not pass on to the other party information which is confidential, unless he is given permission to do so.

These discussions help the mediator to identify the real areas of disagreement and the points which are most important to the respective parties. He can then move the parties towards constructive solutions to the problem.

The method of mediation described above assumes that the mediator and the parties will meet in the same building. This enables things to be dealt with quickly because, if necessary, the parties can meet face to face to iron out their differences. There are, however, other forms of mediation. The parties do not have to meet. The matter can be dealt with by correspondence and telephone conversations.

It is vital that the parties are represented at the mediation by people who have authority to instruct their lawyers to reach agreement.

15.4.2 'Med-arb'

Under this form of ADR, the parties agree to submit their dispute to mediation and that, if this does not work, they will refer the matter to arbitration. They may, if they wish, use the person who has been acting as their mediator as their arbitrator. This will save costs because the arbitrator will already know the facts of the case. There is a risk, however, that, during the mediation, he will have become privy to confidential information belonging to one of the parties. This would compromise his position as arbitrator, so any agreement for 'med-arb' should give either party the right to object to the mediator becoming the arbitrator.

15.4.3 'Mini-trial' or 'structured settlement procedure'

Under this procedure, the parties appoint a neutral who will sit as chairman of a tribunal composed of himself and a senior representative of each of the parties. These representatives may not be immediately connected with the dispute and should have authority to reach such compromise as they see fit. They will then hear and/or read the cases of the two parties (sometimes with an expert) after which they will negotiate with each other with the help of the independent arbiter.

15.4.4 Expert appraisal

The parties can refer all or part of their dispute to an expert in the disputed field for his opinion. His opinion is not binding on the parties, but could influence their approach to subsequent negotiations. It will be for the parties to choose the appropriate procedure which could even involve a short trial before the expert makes his recommendation.

15.4.5 Judicial appraisal

The Centre for Dispute Resolution (CEDR) has a scheme whereby former judges and senior counsel are available to give a quick preliminary view on the legal position, having heard representations from both parties. It is a matter for agreement between the parties as to whether this opinion is to be binding on them or not.

15.4.6 Expert determination

Expert determination is a halfway house between arbitration and ADR. As in arbitration, the parties select an expert to decide the case for them. They agree to accept his decision and, if one fails to do so, the other can sue for breach of contract. The expert's decision cannot, however, be enforced as a court order and he does not have the powers of an arbitrator under the Arbitration Act 1996. Also, unlike an arbitrator, he can be sued in negligence by a party who thinks his decision was wrong.

15.4.7 Final offer arbitration

The parties can instruct their chosen neutral that they will both make an offer of the terms on which they will settle and that he must choose one of those two offers and no other solution. Neither party can afford to make an unrealistic offer because that will mean that the neutral will choose the opponent's offer, so, at least in theory, the offers are likely to be realistic.

15.5 ORGANISATIONS PROVIDING ADR

Anyone can provide help in resolving disputes, but the job is not as easy as it sounds. It should be done by someone who has been trained. The two main organisations who have pioneered ADR in commercial matters, in this country, are the Centre for Dispute Resolution (CEDR) and ADR Group.

CEDR is an independent, non-profit making organisation promoting ADR, which runs training courses and maintains a panel of neutrals.

ADR Group is a private company which undertakes mediation and training and has established a network of mediators in firms of solicitors throughout the country.

Two other organisations which are very active in the field of ADR, although their principal raison d'être arose from other functions, are the Chartered Institute of Arbitrators and the Academy of Experts.

Finally, there is Mediation UK, whose general services include all forms of mediation.

Many professional bodies, like the Royal Institution of Chartered Surveyors (RICS), provide ADR services for disputes involving their members.

The judges of the commercial list in the High Court may be prepared to offer their services to help litigants to resolve their disputes without going to trial.

15.6 USING ADR

Parties to a dispute can always reach an ad hoc agreement, when the dispute arises, to use any form of ADR they see fit to solve their problems. It is more pro-active, however, to agree in the original contract that, if any dispute does arise between the parties, they will resolve it by some specified form of ADR.

Such contracts may not be effective (see **15.3.1**), because a party cannot be forced to reach a consensual solution, but they do give the parties an opportunity to resolve their disputes peaceably. There is a very strong case for recommending that existing contracts which include an arbitration agreement should be amended, so that the agreement provides for mediation before the parties go to formal arbitration (which they would only do if mediation failed).

15.6.1 Disclosure obligations

An agreement to use ADR should include clauses dealing with some of the potential pitfalls associated with ADR. The parties should decide whether to have a clause requiring full disclosure. The drawback of such a clause is that, the more information the parties have to provide for each other, the longer the proceedings may take and the more expensive they will be. Its advantage is that it would be possible to set aside a settlement reached, as a result of ADR, on discovering that one of the parties had concealed vital information. To prevent vexatious applications to set aside any settlement, it might be wise to stipulate in the disclosure clause that a settlement can only be challenged for fundamental non-disclosure of matters which would significantly have affected the result of the ADR process.

15.6.2 Confidentiality

A confidentiality clause in the agreement will encourage full disclosure. The mediator is always under a duty of confidentiality, but the parties will be more likely to disclose information to each other if they know that the other party has agreed not to divulge the information to anyone else. However, if the parties are commercial rivals, who need to keep their methods secret from each other, disclosure and confidentiality clauses are pointless.

15.6.3 Other matters

An ADR agreement should explain how the mediator or other arbiter will be appointed and specify the procedure he should follow. It should also specify that the representatives who attend any ADR process must have full authority to settle the dispute there and then.

15.7 CHOOSING ADR

A solicitor should discuss with the client the possible uses of ADR whenever a dispute arises in a commercial matter. If the client is willing (or has already agreed) to use ADR, it should be used unless it is obviously inappropriate, for example, because an injunction is required or the other party cannot be trusted to comply with an award or to co-operate in the process. There is no point, however, in proceeding with ADR if it looks like failing. In such cases, at the first sign of non-co-operation or lack of trust (eg where the opponent will not help in the selection of the neutral), litigation or arbitration should be used. This does not mean abandoning ADR. It may be appropriate to continue with ADR in conjunction with litigation, using the latter as a spur to co-operation with the former.

Not surprisingly, given r 1.4(2)(e) (see **15.2**), parties who do choose to litigate may well receive judicial encouragement (and sometimes a degree of pressure) at the case management conference and other hearings to attempt ADR.

15.8 SUMMARY

Alternative dispute resolution involves an independent third party who helps the parties to a dispute to resolve that dispute. The parties are usually free to dispense with his services whenever they see fit. It can provide a quick and cheap means of resolving a dispute in a commercially sensible manner, although the result may not be entirely in accordance with the parties' legal rights and cannot be enforced in the same way as a court judgment or an arbitrator's award.

Solicitors advising clients should be aware of the wide range of ADR techniques and of the organisations who offer help with these techniques. It may be helpful to include ADR agreements in commercial contracts, but careful thought needs to be given to the details of such agreements on matters like disclosure and confidentiality.

Appendix A

COURT FORMS

1. Forms N1 and N1A – Claim form and notes for claimant
2. Form N251 – Notice of funding
3. Form N1C – Notes for defendant on replying to the claim form
4. Form N9, including Forms N9A–N9D – Response pack
5. Form N211, including Forms N211A and N211C – Part 20 claim form
6. Form N150 – Allocation questionnaire
7. Form N242A – Notice of payment into court
8. Form N243A – Notice of acceptance and request for payment
9. Form N170 – Listing questionnaire
10. Form N244 – Application notice
11. Form N260 – Statement of costs
12. Form N265 – List of documents
13. Form N252 – Notice of commencement of assessment of bill of costs

1 FORMS N1 AND N1A – CLAIM FORM AND NOTES FOR CLAIMANT

Claim Form

In the

Claim No.

Claimant

SEAL

Defendant(s)

Brief details of claim

Value

Defendant's name and address

	£
Amount claimed	
Court fee	
Solicitor's costs	
Total amount	
Issue date	

The court office at

is open between 10 am and 4 pm Monday to Friday. When corresponding with the court, please address forms or letters to the Court Manager and quote the claim number.

N1 Claim form (CPR Part 7) (10.00) *Printed on behalf of The Court Service*

	Claim No.	

Does, or will, your claim include any issues under the Human Rights Act 1998? ☐ Yes ☐ No

Particulars of Claim (attached)(to follow)

Statement of Truth
*(I believe)(The Claimant believes) that the facts stated in these particulars of claim are true.
* I am duly authorised by the claimant to sign this statement

Full name _____

Name of claimant's solicitor's firm _____

signed _____ position or office held _____
*(Claimant)(Litigation friend)(Claimant's solicitor) (if signing on behalf of firm or company)
*delete as appropriate

Claimant's or claimant's solicitor's address to which documents or payments should be sent if different from overleaf including (if appropriate) details of DX, fax or e-mail.

Notes for claimant on completing a claim form

Further information may be obtained from the court in a series of free leaflets.

- Please read all of these guidance notes before you begin completing the claim form. The notes follow the order in which information is required on the form.
- Court staff can help you fill in the claim form and give information about procedure once it has been issued. But they cannot give legal advice. If you need legal advice, for example, about the likely success of your claim or the evidence you need to prove it, you should contact a solicitor or a Citizens Advice Bureau.
- If you are filling in the claim form by hand, please use black ink and write in block capitals.
- Copy the completed claim form and the defendant's notes for guidance so that you have one copy for yourself, one copy for the court and one copy for each defendant. Send or take the forms to the court office with the appropriate fee. The court will tell you how much this is.

Notes on completing the claim form

Heading

You must fill in the heading of the form to indicate whether you want the claim to be issued in a county court or in the High Court (The High Court means either a District Registry (attached to a county court) or the Royal Courts of Justice in London). There are restrictions on claims which may be issued in the High Court (see 'Value' overleaf).

Use whichever of the following is appropriate:

'In the ....County Court'
(inserting the name of the court)

or

'In the High Court of Justice.........................Division'
(inserting e.g. 'Queen's Bench' or 'Chancery' as appropriate)
'..........................District Registry'
(inserting the name of the District Registry)

or

'In the High Court of Justice.........................Division,
(inserting eg. 'Queen's Bench' or 'Chancery' as appropriate)
Royal Courts of Justice'

Claimant and defendant details

As the person issuing the claim, you are called the 'claimant'; the person you are suing is called the 'defendant'. Claimants who are under 18 years old (unless otherwise permitted by the court) and patients within the meaning of the Mental Health Act 1983, must have a litigation friend to issue and conduct court proceedings on their behalf. Court staff will tell you more about what you need to do if this applies to you.

You must provide the following information about yourself **and** the defendant according to the capacity in which you are suing and in which the defendant is being sued. When suing or being sued as:-

an individual:

All known forenames and surname, whether Mr, Mrs, Miss, Ms or Other (e.g. Dr) and residential address (**including** postcode and telephone number) in England and Wales. Where the defendant is a proprietor of a business, a partner in a firm or an individual sued in the name of a club or other unincorporated association, the address for service should be the usual or last known place of residence **or** principal place of business of the company, firm or club or other unincorporated association.

Where the individual is:

under 18 write '(a child by Mr Joe Bloggs his litigation friend)' after the child's name. If the child is conducting proceedings on their own behalf write '(a child)' after the child's name.

a patient within the meaning of the Mental Health Act 1983 write '(by Mr Joe Bloggs his litigation friend)' after the patient's name.

trading under another name

you must add the words 'trading as' and the trading name e.g. 'Mr John Smith trading as Smith's Groceries'

suing or being sued in a representative capacity

you must say what that capacity is e.g. 'Mr Joe Bloggs as the representative of Mrs Sharon Bloggs (deceased)'.

suing or being sued in the name of a club or other unincorporated association

add the words 'suing/sued on behalf of' followed by the name of the club or other unincorporated association.

a firm

enter the name of the firm followed by the words 'a firm', e.g. 'Bandbox - a firm' and an address for service which is either a partner's residential address or the principal or last known place of business.

a corporation (other than a company)

enter the full name of the corporation and the address which is either its principal office **or** any other place where the corporation carries on activities and which has a real connection with the claim.

a company registered in England and Wales

enter the name of the company and an address which is either the company's registered office **or** any place of business that has a real, or the most, connection with the claim e.g. the shop where the goods were bought.

an overseas company (defined by s744 of the Companies Act 1985)

enter the name of the company and either the address registered under s691 of the Act **or** the address of the place of business having a real, or the most, connection with the claim.

Brief details of claim

Note: The facts and full details about your claim and whether or not you are claiming interest, should be set out in the 'particulars of claim' *(see note under 'Particulars of Claim')*.

You must set out under **this** heading:
- a concise statement of the nature of your claim
- the remedy you are seeking e.g. payment of money; an order for return of goods or their value; an order to prevent a person doing an act; damages for personal injuries.

Value

If you are claiming a **fixed amount of money** (a 'specified amount') write the amount in the box at the bottom right-hand corner of the claim form against 'amount claimed'.

If you are not claiming a fixed amount of money (an 'unspecified amount') under 'Value' write "I expect to recover" followed by whichever of the following applies to your claim:

- "not more than £5,000" **or**
- "more than £5,000 but not more than £15,000" **or**
- "more than £15,000"

If you are **not able** to put a value on your claim, write "I cannot say how much I expect to recover".

Personal injuries

If your claim is for 'not more than £5,000' and includes a claim for personal injuries, you must also write "My claim includes a claim for personal injuries and the amount I expect to recover as damages for pain, suffering and loss of amenity is" followed by either:

- "not more than £1,000" **or**
- "more than £1,000"

Housing disrepair

If your claim is for 'not more than £5,000' and includes a claim for housing disrepair relating to residential premises, you must also write "My claim includes a claim against my landlord for housing disrepair relating to residential premises. The cost of the repairs or other work is estimated to be" followed by either:

- "not more than £1,000" **or**
- "more than £1,000"

If within this claim, you are making a claim for other damages, you must also write:

"I expect to recover as damages" followed by either:

- "not more than £1,000" **or**
- "more than £1,000"

Issuing in the High Court

You may only issue in the High Court if one of the following statements applies to your claim:-

"By law, my claim must be issued in the High Court. The Act which provides this is ....(specify Act)"

or

"I expect to recover more than £15,000"

or

"My claim includes a claim for personal injuries and the value of the claim is £50,000 or more"

or

"My claim needs to be in a specialist High Court list, namely................................(state which list)".

If one of the statements does apply and you wish to, or must by law, issue your claim in the High Court, write the words "I wish my claim to issue in the High Court because" followed by the relevant statement e.g. "I wish my claim to issue in the High Court because my claim includes a claim for personal injuries and the value of my claim is £50,000 or more."

Defendant's name and address

Enter in this box the full names and address of the defendant receiving the claim form (i.e. one claim form for each defendant). If the defendant is to be served outside England and Wales, you may need to obtain the court's permission.

Particulars of claim

You may include your particulars of claim on the claim form in the space provided or in a separate document which you should head 'Particulars of Claim'. It should include the names of the parties, the court, the claim number and your address for service and also contain a statement of truth. You should keep a copy for yourself, provide one for the court and one for each defendant. Separate particulars of claim can either be served

- with the claim form **or**
- within 14 days after the date on which the claim form was served.

If your particulars of claim are served separately from the claim form, they must be served with the forms on which the defendant may reply to your claim.

Your particulars of claim must include

- a concise statement of the facts on which you rely
- a statement (if applicable) to the effect that you are seeking aggravated damages or exemplary damages
- details of any interest which you are claiming
- any other matters required for your type of claim as set out in the relevant practice direction

Address for documents

Insert in this box the address at which you wish to receive documents and/or payments, if different from the address you have already given under the heading 'Claimant'. The address must be in England or Wales. If you are willing to accept service by DX, fax or e-mail, add details.

Statement of truth

This must be signed by you, by your solicitor or your litigation friend, as appropriate.

Where the claimant is a registered company or a corporation the claim must be signed by either the director, treasurer, secretary, chief executive, manager or other officer of the company or (in the case of a corporation) the mayor, chairman, president or town clerk.

Appendix A

2 FORM N251 – NOTICE OF FUNDING

Notice of Funding of Case or Claim

Notice of funding by means of a conditional fee agreement, insurance policy or undertaking given by a prescribed body should be given to the court and all other parties to the case:
- on commencement of proceedings
- on filing an acknowledgment of service, defence or other first document; and
- at any later time that such an arrangement is entered into, changed or terminated

In the	
Claim No.	
Claimant (include Ref.)	
Defendant (include Ref.)	

Take notice that in respect of [all claims herein][the following claims   ] the case of   *(specify name of party)*

[is now][was] being funded by:
(Please tick those boxes which apply)

- ☐ a conditional fee agreement dated   which provides for a success fee;
- ☐ an insurance policy issued on *(date)*   by *(name of insurers)*   ;
- ☐ an undertaking given on *(date)*   by *(name of prescribed body)*   in the following terms

The funding of the case has now changed:

- ☐ the above funding has now ceased
- ☐ the conditional fee agreement has been terminated
- ☐ a conditional agreement dated   which provides for a success fee has been entered into
- ☐ the insurance policy dated   has been cancelled
- ☐ an insurance policy has been issued by *(name of insurer)* on *(date)*
- ☐ the undertaking given on *(date)*   has been terminated
- ☐ an undertaking has been given on *(date)*   by *(name of prescribed body)* in the following terms

Signed   **Date**
Solicitor for the (claimant) (defendant) (Part 20 defendant)
(respondent)(appellant)

The court office at
is open between 10 am and 4 pm Monday to Friday. When corresponding with the court, please address forms or letters to the Court Manager and quote the claim number.

N251 Notice of funding of case or claim (7.00)   *The Court Service Publications Unit*

3 FORM N1C – NOTES FOR DEFENDANT ON REPLYING TO THE CLAIM FORM

Notes for defendant on replying to the claim form

Please read these notes carefully - they will help you decide what to do about this claim.
Further information may be obtained from the court in a series of free leaflets

- If this claim form was received with the particulars of claim completed or attached, you must reply within 14 days of the date it was served on you. If the words 'particulars of claim to follow' are written in the particulars of claim box, you should not reply until after you are served with the particulars of claim (which should be no more than 14 days after you received the claim form). If the claim was sent by post, the date of service is taken as the second day after posting (see post mark). If the claim form was delivered or left at your address, the date of service will be the day after it was delivered.
- You may either
    - pay the total amount i.e. the amount claimed, the court fee, and solicitor's costs (if any)
    - admit that you owe all or part of the claim and ask for time to pay or
    - dispute the claim
- If you do not reply, judgment may be entered against you.
- The notes below tell you what to do.
- The response pack will tell you which forms to use for your reply. (The pack will accompany the particulars of claim if they are served after the claim form).
- Court staff can help you complete the forms of reply and tell you about court procedures. But they cannot give legal advice. If you need legal advice, for example about the likely success of disputing the claim, you should contact a solicitor or a Citizens Advice Bureau immediately.

Registration of Judgments: If the claim results in a judgment being made against you in a **county court**, your name and address may be entered in the Register of County Court Judgments. This may make it difficult for you to obtain credit.
Costs and Interest: Additional costs and interest may be added to the amount claimed on the front of the claim form if judgment is entered against you. In a county court, if judgment is for £5,000 or more, or is in respect of a debt which attracts contractual or statutory interest for late payment, the claimant may be entitled to further interest.

Your response and what happens next

How to pay

Do not bring any payments to the court - they will not be accepted.

When making payments to the claimant, quote the claimant's reference (if any) and the claim number.

Make sure that you keep records and can account for any payments made. Proof may be required if there is any disagreement. It is not safe to send cash unless you use registered post.

Admitting the Claim
Claim for specified amount

If you admit all the claim, take or send the money, including the court fee, any interest and costs, to the claimant at the address given for payment on the claim form, within 14 days.

If you admit all the claim and you are asking for time to pay, complete Form N9A and send it to the claimant at the address given for payment on the claim form, within 14 days. The claimant will decide whether to accept your proposal for payment. If it is accepted, the claimant may request the court to enter judgment against you and you will be sent an order to pay. If your offer is not accepted, the court will decide how you should pay.

If you admit only part of the claim, complete Form N9A and Form N9B (see 'Disputing the Claim' overleaf) and send them to the court within 14 days. The claimant will decide whether to accept your part admission.

If it is accepted, the claimant may request the court to enter judgment against you and the court will send you an order to pay. If your part admission is not accepted, the case will proceed as a defended claim.

Claim for unspecified amount

If you admit liability for the whole claim but do not make an offer to satisfy the claim, complete Form N9C and send it to the court within 14 days. A copy will be sent to the claimant who may request the court to enter judgment against you for an amount to be decided by the court, and costs. The court will enter judgment and refer the court file to a judge for directions for management of the case. You and the claimant will be sent a copy of the court's order.

If you admit liability for the claim and offer an amount of money to satisfy the claim, complete Form N9C and send it to the court within 14 days. The claimant will be sent a copy and asked if the offer is acceptable. The claimant must reply to the court within 14 days and send you a copy. If a reply is not received, the claim will be stayed. If the amount you have offered is **accepted -**

- the claimant may request the court to enter judgment against you for that amount.
- if you have requested time to pay which is not accepted by the claimant, the rate of payment will be decided by the court.

If your offer in satisfaction is **not accepted** -
- the claimant may request the court to enter judgment against you for an amount to be decided by the court, and costs; and
- the court will enter judgment and refer the court file to a judge for directions for management of the case. You and the claimant will be sent a copy of the court's order.

Disputing the claim

If you are being sued as an individual for a specified amount of money and you dispute the claim, the claim may be transferred to a local court i.e. the one nearest to or where you live or carry on business if different from the court where the claim was issued.

If you need longer than 14 days to prepare your defence or to contest the court's jurisdiction to try the claim, complete the Acknowledgment of Service form and send it to the court within 14 days. This will allow you 28 days from the date of service of the particulars of claim to file your defence or make an application to contest the court's jurisdiction. The court will tell the claimant that your Acknowledgment of Service has been received.

If the case proceeds as a defended claim, you and the claimant will be sent an Allocation Questionnaire. You will be told the date by which it must be returned to the court. The information you give on the form will help a judge decide whether your case should be dealt with in the small claims track, fast track or multi-track. After a judge has considered the completed questionnaires, you will be sent a notice of allocation setting out the judge's decision. The notice will tell you the track to which the claim has been allocated and what you have to do to prepare for the hearing or trial. **Leaflets telling you more about the tracks are available from the court office.**

Claim for specified amount

If you wish to dispute the full amount claimed or wish to claim against the claimant (a counterclaim), complete Form N9B and send it to the court within 14 days.

If you admit part of the claim, complete the Defence Form N9B and the Admission Form N9A and send them both to the court within 14 days. The claimant will decide whether to accept your part admission in satisfaction of the claim (see under 'Admitting the Claim - specified amount'). If the claimant does not accept the amount you have admitted, the case will proceed as a defended claim.

If you dispute the claim because you have already paid it, complete Form N9B and send it to the court within 14 days. The claimant will have to decide whether to proceed with the claim or withdraw it and notify the court and you within 28 days. If the claimant wishes to proceed, the case will proceed as a defended claim.

Claim for unspecified amount/return of goods/non-money claims

If you dispute the claim or wish to claim against the claimant (counterclaim), complete Form N9D and send it to the court within 14 days.

Personal injuries claims:

If the claim is for personal injuries and the claimant has attached a medical report to the particulars of claim, in your defence you should state whether you:
- agree with the report **or**
- dispute all or part of the report **and** give your reasons for doing so **or**
- neither agree nor dispute the report **or** have no knowledge of the report

Where you have obtained your own medical report, you should attach it to your defence.

If the claim is for personal injuries and the claimant has attached a schedule of past and future expenses and losses, in your defence you must state which of the items you:
- agree **or**
- dispute **and** supply alternative figures where appropriate **or**
- neither agree nor dispute or have no knowledge of

Address where notices can be sent

This must be either your solicitor's address, your own residential or business address in England and Wales or (if you live elsewhere) some other address within England and Wales.

Statement of truth

This must be signed by you, by your solicitor or your litigation friend, as appropriate.

Where the defendant is **a registered company or a corporation** the response must be signed by either the director, treasurer, secretary, chief executive, manager or other officer of the company **or** (in the case of a corporation) the mayor, chairman, president or town clerk.

4 FORM N9, INCLUDING FORMS N9A–N9D – RESPONSE PACK

Response Pack

You should read the 'notes for defendant' attached to the claim form which will tell you when and where to send the forms

Included in this pack are:
- either **Admission Form N9A** (if the claim is for a specified amount) or **Admission Form N9C** (if the claim is for an unspecified amount or is not a claim for money)
- either **Defence and Counterclaim Form N9B** (if the claim is for a specified amount) or **Defence and Counterclaim Form N9D** (if the claim is for an unspecified amount or is not a claim for money)
- **Acknowledgment of service** (see below)

Complete

If you admit the claim or the amount claimed and/or you want time to pay	▶	the admission form
If you admit part of the claim	▶	the admission form and the defence form
If you dispute the whole claim or wish to make a claim (a counterclaim) against the claimant	▶	the defence form
If you need 28 days (rather than 14) from the date of service to prepare your defence, or wish to contest the court's jurisdiction	▶	the acknowledgment of service
If you do nothing, judgment may be entered against you		

Acknowledgment of Service

Defendant's full name if different from the name given on the claim form

In the

Claim No.

Claimant (including ref.)

Defendant

Address to which documents about this claim should be sent (including reference if appropriate)

if applicable

fax no.

DX no.

Tel. no.   Postcode

e-mail

Tick the appropriate box

1. I intend to defend all of this claim ☐
2. I intend to defend part of this claim ☐
3. I intend to contest jurisdiction ☐

If you file an acknowledgment of service but do not file a defence within 28 days of the date of service of the claim form, or particulars of claim if served separately, judgment may be entered against you.

If you do not file an application within 28 days of the date of service of the claim form, or particulars of claim if served separately, it will be assumed that you accept the court's jurisdiction and judgment may be entered against you.

Signed _____
(Defendant)(Defendant's solicitor)
(Litigation friend)

Position or office held _____
(if signing on behalf of firm or company)

Date _____

The court office at

is open between 10 am and 4 pm Monday to Friday. When corresponding with the court, please address forms or letters to the Court Manager and quote the claim number.

N9 -w3- Response Pack (4.99)   *Produced on behalf of The Court Service*

Appendix A 187

Admission (specified amount)

- You have a limited number of days to complete and return this form
- Before completing this form, please read the notes for guidance attached to the claim form

In the	
Claim No.	
Claimant (including ref.)	
Defendant	

When to fill in this form
- Only fill in this form if you are admitting all or some of the claim **and** you are asking for time to pay

How to fill in this form
- Tick the correct boxes and give as much information as you can. **Then sign and date the form.** If necessary provide details on a separate sheet, add the claim number and attach it to this form.
- Make your offer of payment in box 11 on the back of this form. **If you make no offer the claimant will decide how much and when you should pay.**
- If you are not an individual, you should ensure that you provide sufficient details about the assets and liabilities of your firm, company or corporation to support any offer of payment made in box 11.
- You can get help to complete this form at **any** county court office or Citizens Advice Bureau.

Where to send this form
- **If you admit the claim in full**
  Send the completed form to the address shown on the claim form as one to which documents should be sent.
- **If you admit only part of the claim**
  Send the form **to the court** at the address given on the claim form, together with the defence form (N9B).

How much of the claim do you admit?
- [ ] I admit the full amount claimed as shown on the claim form **or**
- [ ] I admit the amount of £ _____

1 Personal details

Surname	
Forename	

- [ ] Mr [ ] Mrs [ ] Miss [ ] Ms
- [ ] Married [ ] Single [ ] Other *(specify)* _____

Age _____

Address _____

Postcode _____

Tel. no. _____

2 Dependants *(people you look after financially)*

Number of children in each age group

under 11 ____ 11-15 ____ 16-17 ____ 18 & over ____

Other dependants *(give details)* _____

3 Employment

- [ ] I am employed as a _____
  My employer is _____
  Jobs other than main job *(give details)* _____

- [ ] I am self employed as a _____
  Annual turnover is.................. £ _____

  - [ ] I am not in arrears with my national insurance contributions, income tax and VAT
  - [ ] I am in arrears and I owe............ £ _____

  Give details of:
  (a) contracts and other work in hand _____
  (b) any sums due for work done _____

- [ ] I have been unemployed for ____ years ____ months
- [ ] I am a pensioner

4 Bank account and savings

- [ ] I have a bank account
  - [ ] The account is in credit by........ £ _____
  - [ ] The account is overdrawn by.... £ _____
- [ ] I have a savings or building society account
  The amount in the account is.......... £ _____

5 Residence

I live in [ ] my own house [ ] lodgings
          [ ] my jointly owned house [ ] council accommodation
          [ ] rented accommodation

N9A -w3- Form of admission (specified amount) (4.99) Produced on behalf of The Court Service

6 Income

My usual take home pay *(including overtime, commission, bonuses etc)*	£	per
Income support	£	per
Child benefit(s)	£	per
Other state benefit(s)	£	per
My pension(s)	£	per
Others living in my home give me	£	per
Other income *(give details below)*		
	£	per
	£	per
	£	per
Total income	**£**	**per**

8 Priority debts *(This section is for arrears only. Do not include regular expenses listed in box 7.)*

Rent arrears	£	per
Mortgage arrears	£	per
Council tax/Community Charge arrears	£	per
Water charges arrears	£	per
Fuel debts: Gas	£	per
Electricity	£	per
Other	£	per
Maintenance arrears	£	per
Others *(give details below)*		
	£	per
	£	per
Total priority debts	**£**	**per**

7 Expenses

(Do not include any payments made by other members of the household out of their own income)

I have regular expenses as follows:

Mortgage *(including second mortgage)*	£	per
Rent	£	per
Council tax	£	per
Gas	£	per
Electricity	£	per
Water charges	£	per
TV rental and licence	£	per
HP repayments	£	per
Mail order	£	per
Housekeeping, food, school meals	£	per
Travelling expenses	£	per
Children's clothing	£	per
Maintenance payments	£	per
Others *(not court orders or credit debts listed in boxes 9 and 10)*		
	£	per
	£	per
	£	per
Total expenses	**£**	**per**

9 Court orders

Court	Claim No.	£	per
Total court order instalments		**£**	**per**

Of the payments above, I am behind with payments to *(please list)*

10 Credit debts

Loans and credit card debts *(please list)*

	£	per
	£	per
	£	per

Of the payments above, I am behind with payments to *(please list)*

11 Offer of payment

☐ I can pay the amount admitted on [ ]
or
☐ I can pay by monthly instalments of £ [ ]

If you cannot pay immediately, please give brief reasons below

12 Declaration

I declare that the details I have given above are true to the best of my knowledge

Signed [ ]

Date [ ]

Position or office held *(if signing on behalf of firm or company)* [ ]

Defence and Counterclaim (specified amount)

In the

Claim No.

Claimant (including ref.)

Defendant

- Fill in this form if you wish to dispute all or part of the claim and/or make a claim against the claimant (counterclaim).
- You have a limited number of days to complete and return this form to the court.
- Before completing this form, please read the notes for guidance attached to the claim form.
- Please ensure that all boxes at the top right of this form are completed. You can obtain the correct names and number from the claim form. The court cannot trace your case without this information.

How to fill in this form
- Complete sections 1 and 2. Tick the correct boxes and give the other details asked for.
- Set out your defence in section 3. If necessary continue on a separate piece of paper making sure that the claim number is clearly shown on it. In your defence you must state which allegations in the particulars of claim you deny and your reasons for doing so. **If you fail to deny an allegation it may be taken that you admit it.**
- If you dispute only some of the allegations you must
  - specify which you admit and which you deny; and
  - give your own version of events if different from the claimant's.

- If you wish to make a claim against the claimant (a counterclaim) complete section 4.
- Complete and sign section 5 before sending this form to the court. Keep a copy of the claim form and this form.

Community Legal Service Fund (CLSF)

You may qualify for assistance from the CLSF (this used to be called 'legal aid') to meet some or all of your legal costs. Ask about the CLSF at any county court office or any information or help point which displays this logo.

1. How much of the claim do you dispute?

☐ I dispute the full amount claimed as shown on the claim form

or

☐ I admit the amount of £ _____

If you dispute only part of the claim you must **either**:
- pay the amount admitted to the person named at the address for payment on the claim form (see How to Pay in the notes on the back of, or attached to, the claim form). Then send this defence to the court

or

- complete the admission form **and** this defence form and send them to the court.

☐ I paid the amount admitted on (date) _____

or

☐ I enclose the completed form of admission
(go to section 2)

2. Do you dispute this claim because you have already paid it? *Tick whichever applies*

☐ **No** (go to section 3)

☐ **Yes** I paid £ _____ to the claimant

on _____ (before the claim form was issued)

Give details of where and how you paid it in the box below (then go to section 5)

3. Defence

N9B Defence and Counterclaim (specified amount)(9.00) — Printed on behalf of The Court Service

Defence (continued)	Claim No.	

4. If you wish to make a claim against the claimant (a counterclaim)

If your claim is for a specific sum of money, how much are you claiming? £ ☐

- To start your counterclaim, you will have to pay a fee. Court staff will tell you how much you have to pay

- You may not be able to make a counterclaim where the claimant is the Crown (e.g. a Government Department). Ask at your local county court office for further information.

My claim is for *(please specify nature of claim)*

What are your reasons for making the counterclaim?
If you need to continue on a separate sheet put the claim number in the top right hand corner

5. Signed
(To be signed by you or by your solicitor or litigation friend)

*(I believe)(The defendant believes) that the facts stated in this form are true. *I am duly authorised by the defendant to sign this statement

delete as appropriate

Position or office held
(if signing on behalf of firm or company)

Date

Give an address to which notices about this case can be sent to you

Postcode

Tel. no.

if applicable

fax no.

DX no.

e-mail

Appendix A

Admission (unspecified amount, non-money and return of goods claims)	In the	
	Claim No.	
	Claimant (including ref.)	
	Defendant	

- Before completing this form please read the notes for guidance attached to the claim form. If necessary provide details on a separate sheet, add the claim number and attach it to this form.
- If you are not an individual, you should ensure that you provide sufficient details about the assets and liabilities of your firm, company or corporation to support any offer of payment made.

In non-money claims only
☐ I admit liability for the whole claim
(Complete section 11)

In return of goods cases only
Are the goods still in your possession?
☐ Yes ☐ No

Part A Response to claim *(tick one box only)*
☐ I admit liability for the whole claim but want the court to decide the amount I should pay / value of the goods

OR

☐ I admit liability for the claim and offer to pay [_____] in satisfaction of the claim
(Complete part B and sections 1- 11)

Part B How are you going to pay the amount you have admitted? *(tick one box only)*
☐ I offer to pay on (date) [_____]

OR

☐ I cannot pay the amount immediately because *(state reason)*
[_____]

AND

I offer to pay by instalments of £ [_____]
per (week)(month)
starting *(date)* [_____]

1 Personal details

Surname [_____]
Forename [_____]

☐ Mr ☐ Mrs ☐ Miss ☐ Ms
☐ Married ☐ Single ☐ Other *(specify)* [_____]

Age [_____]

Address [_____]
Postcode [_____]
Tel. no. [_____]

2 Dependants *(people you look after financially)*
Number of children in each age group

under 11 [__] 11-15 [__] 16-17 [__] 18 & over [__]

Other dependants *(give details)* [_____]

3 Employment

☐ I am employed as a [_____]
My employer is [_____]
Jobs other than main job *(give details)* [_____]

☐ I am self employed as a [_____]
Annual turnover is............... £ [_____]

☐ I am not in arrears with my national insurance contributions, income tax and VAT

☐ I am in arrears and I owe........... £ [_____]

Give details of:
(a) contracts and other work in hand [_____]
(b) any sums due for work done [_____]

☐ I have been unemployed for [__] years [__] months

☐ I am a pensioner

4 Bank account and savings

☐ I have a bank account
  ☐ The account is in credit by........ £ [_____]
  ☐ The account is overdrawn by.... £ [_____]

☐ I have a savings or building society account
  The amount in the account is.......... £ [_____]

5 Residence
I live in
☐ my own property ☐ lodgings
☐ jointly owned house ☐ rented property
☐ council accommodation

N9C - w3 Admission (unspecified amount and non-money claims) (8.99)   *Printed on behalf of The Court Service*

6 Income

My usual take home pay *(including overtime, commission, bonuses etc)*	£	per
Income support	£	per
Child benefit(s)	£	per
Other state benefit(s)	£	per
My pension(s)	£	per
Others living in my home give me	£	per
Other income *(give details below)*		
	£	per
	£	per
	£	per
Total income	**£**	**per**

7 Expenses

(Do not include any payments made by other members of the household out of their own income)

I have regular expenses as follows:

Mortgate *(including second mortgage)*	£	per
Rent	£	per
Council tax	£	per
Gas	£	per
Electricity	£	per
Water charges	£	per
TV rental and licence	£	per
HP repayments	£	per
Mail order	£	per
Housekeeping, food, school meals	£	per
Travelling expenses	£	per
Children's clothing	£	per
Maintenance payments	£	per
Others *(not court orders or credit debts listed in sections 9 and 10)*		
	£	per
	£	per
	£	per
Total expenses	**£**	**per**

8 Priority debts   *(This section is for arrears only. Do not include regular expenses listed in section 7)*

Rent arrears	£	per
Mortgage arrears	£	per
Council tax/Community Charge arrears	£	per
Water charges arrears	£	per
Fuel debts: Gas	£	per
Electricity	£	per
Other	£	per
Maintenance arrears	£	per
Others *(give details below)*		
	£	per
	£	per
Total priority debts	**£**	**per**

9 Court orders

Court	Claim No.	£	per
Total court order instalments		**£**	**per**

Of the payments above, I am behind with payments to *(please list)*

10 Credit debts

Loans and credit card debts *(please list)*

	£	per
	£	per
	£	per

Of the payments above, I am behind with payments to *(please list)*

11 Declaration   I declare that the details I have given above are true to the best of my knowledge

Signed

Date

Position or office held
(if signing on behalf of firm or company)

Appendix A 193

Defence and Counterclaim
(unspecified amount, non-money and return of goods claims)

In the	
Claim No.	
Claimant (including ref.)	
Defendant	

- Fill in this form if you wish to dispute all or part of the claim and/or make a claim against the claimant (a counterclaim)
- You have a limited number of days to complete and return this form to the court.
- Before completing this form, please read the notes for guidance attached to the claim form.
- Please ensure that all the boxes at the top right of this form are completed. You can obtain the correct names and number from the claim form. The court cannot trace your case without this information.

How to fill in this form
- Set out your defence in section 1. If necessary continue on a separate piece of paper making sure that the claim number is clearly shown on it. In your defence you must state which allegations in the particulars of claim you deny and your reasons for doing so. **If you fail to deny an allegation it may be taken that you admit it.**
- If you dispute only some of the allegations you must
   - specify which you admit and which you deny; and
   - give your own version of events if different from the claimant's.
- If the claim is for money and you dispute the claimant's statement of value, you must say why and if possible give your own statement of value.
- If you wish to make a claim against the claimant (a counterclaim) complete section 2.
- Complete and sign section 3 before returning this form.

Where to send this form
- send or take this form immediately to the court at the address given on the claim form.
- Keep a copy of the claim form and the defence form.

Community Legal Service Fund (CLSF)
You may qualify for assistance from the CLSF (this used to be called 'legal aid') to meet some or all of your legal costs. Ask about the CLSF at any county court office or any information or help point which displays this logo.

Community Legal Service

1. Defence

N9D Defence and Counterclaim (unspecified amount) (9.00)   *Printed on behalf of The Court Service*

Defence (continued)	Claim No.	

2. If you wish to make a claim against the claimant (a counterclaim)

If your claim is for a specific sum of money, how much are you claiming? £ ☐

- To start your counterclaim, you will have to pay a fee. Court staff will tell you how much you have to pay.

- You may not be able to make a counterclaim where the claimant is the Crown (e.g. a Government Department). Ask at your local county court office for further information.

My claim is for *(please specify)*

What are your reasons for making the counterclaim?
If you need to continue on a separate sheet put the claim number in the top right hand corner

3. Signed (To be signed by you or by your solicitor or litigation friend)	*(I believe)(The defendant believes) that the facts stated in this form are true. *I am duly authorised by the defendant to sign this statement *delete as appropriate	Position or office held (if signing on behalf of firm or company)	
Date			
Give an address to which notices about this case can be sent to you	 Postcode Tel. no.		if applicable
		fax no.	
		DX no.	
		e-mail	

5 FORM N211, INCLUDING FORMS N211A AND N211C – PART 20 CLAIM FORM

**Claim Form
(Additional claims-
CPR Part 20)**

In the

Claim No.

Claimant(s)

Defendant(s)

SEAL

Part 20 Claimant(s)

Part 20 Defendant(s)

Brief details of claim

Value

Defendant's name and address

	£
Amount claimed	
Court fee	
Solicitors costs	
Total amount	
Issue date	

The court office at

is open between 10 am and 4 pm Monday to Friday. When corresponding with the court, please address forms or letters to the Court Manager and quote the claim number.

N211 - w3 Claim Form (CPR Part 20 - additional claims)(4.99)   *Printed on behalf of The Court Service*

	Claim No.	

Particulars of Claim (attached)

Statement of Truth
*(I believe)(The Part 20 Claimant believes) that the facts stated in these particulars of claim are true.
* I am duly authorised by the Part 20 claimant to sign this statement

Full name _____

Name of Part 20 claimant's solicitor's firm _____

signed _____ position or office held _____
*(Part 20 Claimant)('s solicitor)(Litigation friend) (if signing on behalf of firm or company)
*delete as appropriate

Part 20 Claimant ('s solicitor's) address to which documents or payments should be sent if different from overleaf. If you are prepared to accept service by DX, fax or e-mail, please add details.

Notes for Part 20 claimant on completing a Part 20 claim form

- Please read all of these guidance notes before you begin completing the claim form. The notes follow the order in which information is required on the form. Unless you issue your Part 20 claim before or at the same time as filing your defence to the main claim, (in other words the claim being brought against you as defendant) you will first need to obtain the court's permission to do so.
- Court staff can help you fill in the claim form and give information about procedure once it has been issued. But they cannot give legal advice. If you need legal advice, for example about the likely success of your claim or the evidence you need to prove it, you should contact a solicitor or a Citizens Advice Bureau.
- If you are filling in the claim form by hand, please use black ink and write in block capitals.
- When you have completed the claim form, copy the claim form and the defendant's notes for guidance so that you have one copy for yourself, one copy for the court, one copy for the Part 20 defendant and a copy for each of the other parties to the main claim. Send or take the forms to the court office with the appropriate fee, the court will tell you how much this is.
- Unless the court has ordered otherwise, the Part 20 defendant should be served with the claim form within 14 days of your defence being filed, together with copies of all the statements of case filed in the main claim. The parties to the main claim must also at the same time be served with copies of the Part 20 claim form and particulars of claim, if these are separate from the claim.
- The defendant is added as a party to the main claim once served with the Part 20 claim form.

Notes on completing the claim form

Heading

The name of the court and the claim number will be the same as on the claim form in the main claim. You should copy those details on to your Part 20 claim form.

Claimant and defendant details

You should copy the claimant and defendant details from the main claim into the claimant and defendant boxes. You should enter your name into the Part 20 claimant box and the name of the person you are claiming against into the Part 20 defendant box. Claimants who are under 18 years old (unless otherwise permitted by the court), and patients within the meaning of the Mental Health Act 1983 must have a litigation friend to issue and conduct court proceedings on their behalf. Court staff will tell you more about what you need to do if this applies to you.

You must provide the following information about yourself **and** the Part 20 defendant according to the capacity in which you are suing and in which the defendant is being sued.

When suing or being sued as:-

an individual

All known forenames and surname, whether Mr, Mrs, Miss, Ms or Other (e.g. Dr) and residential address (**including** postcode, telephone and any fax or e-mail number) in England and Wales. Where the defendant is a proprietor of a business, a partner in a firm or an individual sued in the name of a club or other unincorporated association, the address for service should be the usual or last known place of residence **or** principal place of business of the company, firm or club or other unincorporated association.

Where the individual is:

under 18 write '(a child by Mr Joe Bloggs his litigation friend)' after the child's name.

a patient within the meaning of the Mental Health Act 1983 write '(by Mr Joe Bloggs his litigation friend)' after the patients name.

trading under another name

you must add the words 'trading as' and the trading name e.g. 'Mr John Smith trading as Smith's Groceries'.

suing or being sued in a representative capacity

you must say what that capacity is e.g. 'Mr Joe Bloggs as the representative of Mrs Sharon Bloggs (deceased)'.

suing or being sued in the name of a club or other unincorporated association

add the words 'suing/sued on behalf of' followed by the name of the club or other unincorporated association.

a firm

enter the name of the firm followed by the words 'a firm' e.g. 'Bandbox - a firm' and an address for service which is either a partner's residential address or the principal or last known place of business.

a corporation (other than a company)

enter the full name of the corporation and the address which is either its principal office **or** any other place where the corporation carries on activities and which has a real connection with the claim.

a company registered in England and Wales

enter the name of the company and an address which is either the company's registered office **or** any place of business that has a real, or the most, connection with the claim e.g. the shop where the goods were bought.

an overseas company (defined by s744 of the Companies Act 1985)

enter the name of the company and either the address registered under s691 of the Act **or** the address of the place of business having a real, or the most, connection with the claim.

Brief details of claim

Note: The facts and full details about your claim and whether or not you are claiming interest, should be set out in the 'particulars of claim' *(see note under 'Particulars of Claim').*

You must set out under **this** heading:
- a concise statement of the nature of your claim
- the remedy you are seeking

Value

Note:-
If you are issuing your Part 20 claim in the High Court, you do not have to give a statement of value.

If you are issuing in the county court and claiming a fixed amount of money (a 'specified amount') write the amount in the box at the bottom right-hand corner of the claim form against 'amount claimed'.

If you are not claiming a fixed amount of money (an 'unspecified amount') under 'Value' write "I expect to recover" followed by whichever of the following applies to your claim:
- "not more than £5,000" **or**
- "more than £5,000 but not more than £15,000" **or**
- "more than £15,000"

If your claim is for 'not more than £5,000' and includes a claim for **personal injuries**, you must also write "My claim includes a claim for personal injuries and the amount I expect to recover as damages for pain, suffering and loss of amenity is" followed by either:
- "not more than £1,000" **or**
- "more than £1,000"

If your claim is for 'not more than £5,000' and includes a claim for **housing disrepair** relating to residential premises, you must also write "My claim includes a claim against my landlord for housing disrepair relating to residential premises. The costs of the repairs and other work is estimated to be" followed by either:
- "not more than £1,000" **or**
- "more than £1,000"

"I expect to recover as damages in respect of repairs and other work" followed by either:
- "not more than £1,000" **or**
- "more than £1,000"

If you are not able to put a value on your claim, write "I cannot say how much I expect to recover".

Defendant's name and address

Enter in this box the full names and address of the Part 20 defendant receiving the claim form (ie. one claim form for each Part 20 defendant). If the defendant is to be served outside of England and Wales, you may need to obtain the court's permission.

Particulars of claim

You may include your particulars of claim on the claim form in the space provided or in a separate document which you should head 'Particulars of Claim'. It should include the names of the parties, the court, the claim number and your address for service and also contain a statement of truth. You should keep a copy for yourself, provide one for the court, one for each defendant and one for all other parties in the main claim. Separate particulars of claim **must** be served with the claim form. You should also attach copies of all statements of case already served in the main claim for service on the defendant.

Your particulars of claim must include
- a concise statement of the facts on which you rely
- a statement (if applicable) to the effect that you are seeking aggravated damages or exemplary damages
- details of any interest which you are claiming
- any other matters required for your type of claim as set out in the relevant practice direction

Address for documents

Insert in this box the address at which you wish to receive documents and/or payments, if different from the address you have already given under the heading 'Claimant'. The address you give must be either that of your solicitors or your residential or business address and must be in England or Wales. If you live or carry on business outside England and Wales, you can give some other address within England and Wales.

Statement of truth

This must be signed by you, by your solicitor or your litigation friend, as appropriate.

Where the claimant is a registered company or a corporation the claim must be signed by either the director, treasurer, secretary, chief executive, manager or other officer of the company or (in the case of a corporation) the mayor, chairman, president or town clerk.

Notes for defendant on replying to the Part 20 claim form

Please read these notes carefully - they will help you decide what to do about this claim.

- You must reply to this claim form within 14 days of the date it was served on you. If the claim was
    - sent by post, the date of service is taken as the second day after posting (see post mark).
    - delivered or left at your address, the date of service will be the day after it was delivered.
    - handed to you personally, the 14 days begins on the day it was given to you.
- You may either
    - pay the amount claimed
    - admit the truth of all or part of the claim or
    - dispute the claim
- If you do not reply, the court will consider that you have admitted the claim and judgment may be entered against you.
- The notes below tell you what to do and which forms to use for your reply.
- Court staff can help you complete the forms of reply and tell you about court procedures. But they cannot give legal advice. If you need legal advice, for example about the likely success of disputing the claim, you should contact a solicitor or a Citizens Advice Bureau immediately.

Registration of Judgments: If the claim results in a judgment being made against you in a **county court**, your name and address may be entered in the Register of County Court Judgments. This may make it difficult for you to obtain credit.
Costs and Interest: Additional costs and interest may be added to the amount claimed on the front of the claim form if judgment is entered against you. In a county court, if judgment is for £5,000 or more, or is in respect of a debt which attracts contractual or statutory interest for late payment, the claimant may be entitled to further interest.

Your response and what happens next

How to pay

Do not bring any payments to the court - they will not be accepted.

When making payments to the claimant, quote the claimant's reference (if any) and the claim number.

Make sure that you keep records and can account for any payments made. Proof may be required if there is any disagreement. It is not safe to send cash unless you use registered post.

Admitting the Claim

Claim for a specified amount
Complete Form N9A and send it to the claimant at the address given for payment on the claim form within 14 days. You should at the same time send a copy to all the other parties to the main claim (in other words the claim where the Part 20 claimant is the defendant).

Claim for an unspecified amount
Complete Form N9C and send it to the court within 14 days. A copy will be sent to the claimant.

What happens next
The claimant may apply to the court for judgment to be entered on your admission. The court will arrange a hearing and tell you and the claimant where and when to attend.

Disputing the claim

Complete the form of defence (either N9B if the claim is for a specified amount or N9D if the claim is for an unspecified amount) and return it to the court within 14 days. On receipt of your defence, the court will arrange a hearing and tell you and the claimant when and where to attend. At the hearing the judge will usually give directions as to the future case management of the claim but may make any other order, e.g. striking out all or part of a statement of case.

If you need longer than 14 days to prepare your defence, complete the acknowledgment of service Form N212 and return it to the court. This will allow you 28 days from the date of service of the claim form to file your defence.

Contesting the court's jurisdiction

Complete the acknowledgment of service Form N212 and return it to the court within 14 days. You should make an application to the court within 28 days of service of the claim. An application form (N244) can be obtained from the court and a fee may be payable.

If you do nothing

If you do nothing or you send an acknowledgment of service to the court but fail to send your defence, you will be considered to have admitted the claim and be bound by any judgment or decision made in the main claim where it relates to this claim against you.

Statement of truth

This must be signed by you, by your solicitor or your litigation friend, as appropriate.
Where the defendant is **a registered company or a corporation** the response must be signed by either the director, treasurer, secretary, chief executive, manager or other officer of the company **or** (in the case of a corporation) the mayor, chairman, president or town clerk.

N211C - w3 Notes for defendant (CPR Part 20) (4.99) *Printed on behalf of The Court Service*

6 FORM N150 – ALLOCATION QUESTIONNAIRE

Allocation questionnaire

To be completed by, or on behalf of,

who is [1st][2nd][3rd][   ][Claimant][Defendant] [Part 20 claimant] in this claim

In the	
Claim No.	
Last date for filing with court office	

Please read the notes on page five before completing the questionnaire.

You should note the date by which it must be returned and the name of the court it should be returned to since this may be different from the court where the proceedings were issued.

If you have settled this claim (or if you settle it on a future date) and do not need to have it heard or tried, you must let the court know immediately.

Have you sent a copy of this completed form to the other party(ies)? ☐ Yes ☐ No

A Settlement

Do you wish there to be a one month stay to attempt to settle the claim, either by informal discussion or by alternative dispute resolution? ☐ Yes ☐ No

B Location of trial

Is there any reason why your claim needs to be heard at a particular court? ☐ Yes ☐ No

If Yes, say which court and why?

C Pre-action protocols

If an approved pre-action protocol applies to this claim, complete **Part 1** only. If not, complete **Part 2** only. If you answer 'No' to the question in either Part 1 or 2, please explain the reasons why on a separate sheet and attach it to this questionnaire.

Part 1
please say which protocol

The* [_____] protocol applies to this claim.

Have you complied with it? ☐ Yes ☐ No

Part 2 No pre-action protocol applies to this claim.

Have you exchanged information and/or documents (evidence) with the other party in order to assist in settling the claim? ☐ Yes ☐ No

D Case management information

What amount of the claim is in dispute? £ [ ]

Applications

Have you made any application(s) in this claim? ☐ Yes ☐ No

If Yes, what for? [ ] For hearing on [ ]
(e.g. summary judgment, add another party)

Witnesses

So far as you know at this stage, what witnesses of fact do you intend to call at the trial or final hearing including, if appropriate, yourself?

Witness name	Witness to which facts

Experts

Do you wish to use expert evidence at the trial or final hearing? ☐ Yes ☐ No

Have you already copied any experts' report(s) to the other party(ies)? ☐ None yet obtained ☐ Yes ☐ No

Do you consider the case suitable for a single joint expert in any field? ☐ Yes ☐ No

Please list any single joint experts you propose to use and any other experts you wish to rely on. Identify single joint experts with the initials 'SJ' after their name(s).

Expert's name	Field of expertise (eg. orthopaedic surgeon, surveyor, engineer)

Do you want your expert(s) to give evidence orally at the trial or final hearing? ☐ Yes ☐ No

If Yes, give the reasons why you think oral evidence is necessary:

[ ]

Track

Which track do you consider is most suitable for your claim? Tick one box ☐ small claims track   ☐ fast track   ☐ multi-track

If you have indicated a track which would not be the normal track for the claim, please give brief reasons for your choice

[   ]

E Trial or final hearing

How long do you estimate the trial or final hearing will take? ____days ____hours ____minutes

Are there any days when you, an expert or an essential witness will not be able to attend court for the trial or final hearing?   ☐ Yes   ☐ No

If Yes, please give details

Name	Dates not available

F Proposed directions *(Parties should agree directions wherever possible)*

Have you attached a list of the directions you think appropriate for the management of the claim?   ☐ Yes   ☐ No

If Yes, have they been agreed with the other party(ies)?   ☐ Yes   ☐ No

G Costs

*Do **not** complete this section if you have suggested your case is suitable for the small claims track **or** you have suggested one of the other tracks and you do not have a solicitor acting for you.*

What is your estimate of your costs incurred to date?   £ [   ]

What do you estimate your overall costs are likely to be?   £ [   ]

In substantial cases these questions should be answered in compliance with CPR Part 43

H Other information

Have you attached documents to this questionnaire? ☐ Yes ☐ No

Have you sent these documents to the other party(ies)? ☐ Yes ☐ No

If Yes, when did they receive them?

Do you intend to make any applications in the immediate future? ☐ Yes ☐ No

If Yes, what for?

In the space below, set out any other information you consider will help the judge to manage the claim.

Signed _____ Date _____

[Counsel][Solicitor][for the][1st][2nd][3rd][   ]
[Claimant][Defendant][Part 20 claimant]

Please enter your firm's name, reference number and full postal address including (if appropriate) details of DX, fax or e-mail

			if applicable
	fax no.		
	DX no.		
Tel. no. Postcode	e-mail		
Your reference no.			

Notes for completing an allocation questionnaire

- If the claim is not settled, a judge must allocate it to an appropriate case management track. To help the judge choose the most just and cost-effective track, you must now complete the attached questionnaire.
- If you fail to return the allocation questionnaire by the date given, the judge may make an order which leads to your claim or defence being struck out, or hold an allocation hearing. If there is an allocation hearing the judge may order any party who has not filed their questionnaire to pay, immediately, the costs of that hearing.
- Use a separate sheet if you need more space for your answers marking clearly which section the information refers to. You should write the claim number on it, and on any other documents you send with your allocation questionnaire. Please ensure they are firmly attached to it.
- The letters below refer to the sections of the questionnaire and tell you what information is needed.

A Settlement

If you think that you and the other party may be able to negotiate a settlement you should tick the 'Yes' box. The court may order a stay, whether or not all the other parties to the claim agree. You should still complete the rest of the questionnaire, even if you are requesting a stay. Where a stay is granted it will be for an initial period of one month. You may settle the claim either by informal discussion with the other party or by alternative dispute resolution (ADR). ADR covers a range of different processes which can help settle disputes. More information is available in the booklet 'Resolving Disputes Without Going To Court' available from every county court office.

B Location of trial

High Court cases are usually heard at the Royal Courts of Justice or certain Civil Trial Centres. Fast or multi-track trials may be dealt with at a Civil Trial Centre or at the court where the claim is proceeding. Small claim cases are usually heard at the court in which they are proceeding.

C Pre-action protocols

Before any claim is started, the court expects you to have exchanged information and documents relevant to the claim, to assist in settling it. For some types of claim e.g. personal injury, there are approved protocols that should have been followed.

D Case management information

Applications
It is important for the court to know if you have already made any applications in the claim, what they are for and when they will be heard. The outcome of the applications may affect the case management directions the court gives.

Witnesses
Remember to include yourself as a witness of fact, if you will be giving evidence.

Experts
Oral or written expert evidence will only be allowed at the trial or final hearing with the court's permission. The judge will decide what permission it seems appropriate to give when the claim is allocated to track. Permission in small claims track cases will only be given exceptionally.

Track
The basic guide by which claims are normally allocated to a track is the amount in dispute, although other factors such as the complexity of the case will also be considered. A leaflet available from the court office explains the limits in greater detail.

Small Claims track	Disputes valued at not more than £5,000 except · those including a claim for personal injuries worth over £1,000 and · those for housing disrepair where either the cost of repairs or other work exceeds £1,000 or any other claim for damages exceeds £1,000
Fast track	Disputes valued at more than £5,000 but not more than £15,000
Multi-track	Disputes over £15,000

E Trial or final hearing

You should enter only those dates when you, your expert(s) or essential witness(es) will not be able to attend court because of holiday or other committments.

F Proposed directions

Attach the list of directions, if any, you believe will be appropriate to be given for the management of the claim. Agreed directions on fast and multi-track cases should be based on the forms of standard directions set out in the practice direction to CPR Part 28 and form PF52.

G Costs

Only complete this section if you are a solicitor and have suggested the claim is suitable for allocation to the fast or multi-track.

H Other Information

Answer the questions in this section. Decide if there is any other information you consider will help the judge to manage the claim. Give details in the space provided referring to any documents you have attached to support what you are saying.

7 FORM N242A – NOTICE OF PAYMENT INTO COURT

Notice of Payment into court (in settlement - Part 36)

In the	
Claim No.	
Claimant (including ref)	
Defendant (including ref)	

To the Claimant ('s Solicitor)

Take notice the defendant _____ has paid £ _____ (a further amount of £ _____) into court in settlement of
(tick as appropriate)

☐ the whole of your claim
☐ part of your claim *(give details below)*
☐ a certain issue or issues in your claim *(give details below)*

The (part) (issue or issues) to which it relates is(are): *(give details)*

☐ It is in addition to the amount of £ _____ already paid into court on _____ and the total amount in court now offered in settlement is £ _____ *(give total of all payments in court to date)*

☐ It is not inclusive of interest and an additional amount of £ _____ is offered for interest *(give details of the rate(s) and period(s) for which the amount of interest is offered.)*

☐ It takes into account all(part) of the following counterclaim: *(give details of the party and the part of the counterclaim to which the payment relates)*

☐ It takes into account the interim payment(s) made in the following amount(s) on the following date(s): *(give details)*

Note: This notice will need to be modified where an offer of provisional damages is made (CPR Part 36.7) and/or where it is made in relation to a mixed (money and non-money) claim in settlement of the whole claim (CPR Part 36.4).

242A Notice of payment into court (in settlement) (12.99)   The Court Service Publications Unit

For cases where the Social Security (Recovery of Benefits) Act 1997 applies

The gross amount of the compensation payment is £ _____

The defendant has reduced this sum by £ _____ in accordance with section 8 of and Schedule 2 to the Social Security (Recovery of Benefits) Act 1997, which was calculated as follows:

Type of Benefit   Amount

The amount paid into court is the net amount after deduction of the amount of benefit.

Signed [   ]   Position held [   ]
       Defendant('s solicitor)   *(If signing on behalf of a firm or company)*

Date [   ]

242A Notice of payment into court (in settlement) (4.99)   The Court Service Publications Unit

8 FORM N243A – NOTICE OF ACCEPTANCE AND REQUEST FOR PAYMENT

Notice of acceptance of payment into court (Part 36)

In the	
Claim No.	
Claimant (including ref.)	
Defendant (including ref.)	

Note: to the claimant
If you wish to accept the payment made into court without needing the court's permission you should:
- send this completed notice to the defendant not more than 21 days after you received this notice
- and at the same time send a copy to the court

Delete as appropriate I accept the payment into court totalling £ *(insert amount accepted)* in settlement of (the whole of)(part of)*(certain issue(s) in)* my claim set out in the notice of payment into court received on *(insert date)* (together with interim payment(s) of £ already received)

I declare that:-

☐ it is not more than 21 days since I received the notice of payment into court

or

☐ it is more than 21 days since I received the notice and I have agreed the following costs provisions with the other party(ies) *(give details below)*

or

☐ the defendant's payment was made less than 21 days before the start of the trial and I have agreed the following costs provisions with the other party(ies) *(give details below)*

And I request payment of the money held in court to be made to

claimant's (solicitor's) full name and address (and ref)

name of bank

sort code

title of account

account number

Signed

Claimant('s Solicitor)

Position held (If signing on behalf of a firm or company)

Date

N243A Notice of acceptance and request for payment (12.99)   The Court Service Publications Unit

9 FORM N170 – LISTING QUESTIONNAIRE

Listing questionnaire

In the

Claim No.

Last date for filing with court office

To

- The court will use the information which you and the other party(ies) provide to fix a date for trial (or to confirm the date and time if one has already been fixed), to confirm the estimated length of trial and to set a timetable for the trial itself. In multi-track cases the court will also decide whether to hold a pre-trial review.
- If you do not complete and return the questionnaire the procedural judge may
    - make an order which leads to your statement of case (claim or defence) being struck out.
    - decide to hold a listing hearing. You may be ordered to pay (immediately) the other parties' costs of attending.
    - if there is sufficient information, list the case for trial and give any appropriate directions.
- Separate estimates of costs incurred to date and those which will be incurred if the case proceeds to trial, should be given using Form 1 in the Schedule of Costs Forms set out in the Civil Procedure Rules. This form should be attached to and returned with your completed questionnaire. (This relates only to costs incurred by legal representatives.)

A Directions complied with

1. Have you complied with all the previous directions given by the court?   Yes   No

2. If no, please explain which directions are outstanding and why

Directions outstanding   Reasons directions outstanding

3. Are any further directions required to prepare the case for trial?   Yes   No
(If no go to section B)

4. If yes, please explain directions required and give reasons

Directions required   Reasons required

B Experts

1. Has the court already given permission for you to use written expert evidence?   Yes   No
(If no go to section B6)

2. If yes, please give name and field of expertise.

Name of expert   Whether joint expert   Field of expertise
                              (please tick, if appropriate)

3. Have the expert(s') report(s) been agreed with the other parties?   Yes   No

4. Have the experts met to discuss their reports?   Yes   No

5. Has the court already given permission for the expert(s) to give oral evidence at the trial?   *(If yes go to Q8)*   Yes   No

6. If no, are you seeking that permission?   Yes   No
   (If yes go to Q7)   *(If no go to section C)*

7. Give your reasons for seeking permission.

8. What are the names, addresses and fields of expertise of your experts?

Expert 1   Expert 2   Expert 3   Expert 4

9. Please give details of any dates within the trial period when your expert(s) will not be available.

Name of expert   Dates not available

C Other witnesses

(If you are not calling other witnesses go to section D)

1. **How many other witnesses (including yourself) will be giving evidence on your behalf at the trial?** *(do not include experts - see section B above)*

   (Give number)

2. **What are the names and addresses of your witnesses?**

   Witness 1   Witness 2   Witness 3   Witness 4

3. **Please give details of any dates within the trial period when you or your witnesses will not be available?**

   Name of witness   Dates not available

4. **Are any of the witness statements agreed?**   Yes   No
   (If no go to Q6)

5. **If yes, give the name of the witness and the date of his or her statement**

   Name of witness   Date of statement

6. **Do you or any of your witnesses need any special facilities?**   Yes   No
   (If no go to Q8)

7. **If yes, what are they?**

8. **Will any of your witnesses be provided with an interpreter?**   Yes   No
   (If no go to section D)

9. **If yes, say what type of interpreter e.g. language (stating which), deaf/blind etc.**

Appendix A 211

D Legal representation

1. Who will be presenting your case at the hearing or trial?   You   Solicitor   Counsel

2. Please give details of any dates within the trial period when the person presenting your case will not be available.

Name   Dates not available

E Other matters

1. How long do you estimate the trial will take, including cross-examination and closing arguments?   Minutes   Hours   Days

   If your case is allocated to the fast track the maximum time allowed for the whole case will be no more than one day.

2. What is the estimated number of pages of evidence to be included in the trial bundle?

   (please give number)

Fast track cases only

3. The court will normally give you 3 weeks notice in the fast track of the date fixed for a fast track trial unless, in exceptional circumstances, the court directs that shorter notice will be given. Would you be prepared to accept shorter notice of the date fixed for trial?   Yes   No

Signed

Claimant/defendant or Counsel/Solicitor for the claimant/defendant

Date

10 FORM N244 – APPLICATION NOTICE

Application Notice

In the	
Claim no.	
Warrant no. (If applicable)	
Claimant (including ref.)	
Defendant(s) (including ref.)	
Date	

You should provide this information for listing the application

1. How do you wish to have your application dealt with
   - a) at a hearing? ☐ ⎫
   - b) at a telephone conference? ☐ ⎬ *complete all questions below*
   - c) without a hearing? ☐   *complete Qs 5 and 6 below*

2. Give a time estimate for the hearing/conference
   _____(hours)_____ (mins)

3. Is this agreed by all parties?   ☐ Yes   ☐ No

4. Give dates of any trial period or fixed trial date _____

5. Level of judge _____

6. Parties to be served _____

Note You must complete Parts A **and** B, **and** Part C if applicable. Send any relevant fee and the completed application to the court with any draft order, witness statement or other evidence; and sufficient copies for service on each respondent.

Part A

1. Enter your full name, or name of solicitor

   I (We)$^{(1)}$ _____ (on behalf of)(the claimant)(the defendant)

2. State clearly what order you are seeking and if possible attach a draft

   intend to apply for an order (a draft of which is attached) that$^{(2)}$

3. Briefly set out why you are seeking the order. Include the material facts on which you rely, identifying any rule or statutory provision

   because$^{(3)}$

Part B

I (We) wish to rely on: *tick one box*

   the attached (witness statement)(affidavit) ☐   my statement of case ☐

4. If you are not already a party to the proceedings, you must provide an address for service of documents

   evidence in Part C in support of my application ☐

Signed _____   **Position or office held** _____
(Applicant)('s Solicitor)('s litigation friend)   (if signing on behalf of firm or company)

Address to which documents about this claim should be sent (including reference if appropriate)$^{(4)}$

	if applicable
fax no.	
DX no.	
Tel. no. _____ Postcode _____	e-mail

The court office at

is open from 10am to 4pm Monday to Friday. When corresponding with the court please address forms or letters to the Court Manager and quote the claim number.

N244 Application Notice (4.00)   *Printed on behalf of The Court Service*

Part C Claim No.

I (We) wish to rely on the following evidence in support of this application:

Statement of Truth

*(I believe) *(The applicant believes) that the facts stated in Part C are true
* *delete as appropriate*

Signed   **Position or office held**

(Applicant)('s Solicitor)('s litigation friend)   (if signing on behalf of firm or company)

                                              Date

11 FORM N260 – STATEMENT OF COSTS

Statement of Costs (summary assessment)

In the _____ Court

Case Reference _____

Judge/Master

Case Title

[Party]'s Statement of Costs for the hearing on *(date)*   *(interim application/fast track trial)*

Description of fee earners*
   (a) *(name) (grade) (hourly rate claimed)* _____
   (b) *(name) (grade) (hourly rate claimed)* _____

Attendances on   *(party)* _____
   (a) *(number)* ___ hours at £ ___   £ ___
   (b) *(number)* ___ hours at £ ___   £ ___

Attendances on opponents
   (a) *(number)* ___ hours at £ ___   £ ___
   (b) *(number)* ___ hours at £ ___   £ ___

Attendance on others
   (a) *(number)* ___ hours at £ ___   £ ___
   (b) *(number)* ___ hours at £ ___   £ ___

Site inspections etc
   (a) *(number)* ___ hours at £ ___   £ ___
   (b) *(number)* ___ hours at £ ___   £ ___

Work done on negotiations
   (a) *(number)* ___ hours at £ ___   £ ___
   (b) *(number)* ___ hours at £ ___   £ ___

Other work, not covered above
   (a) *(number)* ___ hours at £ ___   £ ___
   (b) *(number)* ___ hours at £ ___   £ ___

Work done on documents
   (a) *(number)* ___ hours at £ ___   £ ___
   (b) *(number)* ___ hours at £ ___   £ ___

Attendance at hearing
   (a) *(number)* ___ hours at £ ___   £ ___
   (b) *(number)* ___ hours at £ ___   £ ___
   (a) *(number)* ___ hours travel and waiting at £ ___   £ ___
   (b) *(number)* ___ hours travel and waiting at £ ___   £ ___

                                                              Sub Total £ ___

N260 Statement of Costs (summary assessment) (7.00)   *Printed on behalf of The Court Service*

Appendix A 215

| | | Brought forward £ | |

Counsel's fees *(name) (year of call)*
　　　　　　Fee for [advice/conference/documents]　　　　　£
　　　　　　Fee for hearing　　　　　　　　　　　　　　　£

Other expenses
　　　　　　[court fees]　　　　　　　　　　　　　　　　£
　　　　　　Others　　　　　　　　　　　　　　　　　　　£
　　　　　　(give brief description)

　　　　　　Total　　　　　　　　　　　　　　　　　　£
　　　　　　Amount of VAT claimed　　　　　　　　　　　£
　　　　　　　　　on solicitors and counsel's fees　　　　 £
　　　　　　　　　on other expenses　　　　　　　　　　 £
　　　　　　Grand Total　　　　　　　　　　　　　　 **£**

The costs estimated above do not exceed the costs which the *(party)*
is liable to pay in respect of the work which this estimate covers.

Dated　　　　　　　　　　　　　Signed

　　　　　　　　　　　　　　　　Name of firm of solicitors
　　　　　　　　　　　　　　　　[partner] for the *(party)*

* 3 grades of fee earner are suggested: (1) Solicitors with over 4 years post qualification experience (2) Other solicitors and legal executives and fee earners of equivalent experience (3) Trainee solicitors and fee earners of equivalent experience. 'Legal Executive' means a Fellow of the Institute of Legal Executives. Those who are not Fellows of the Institute are not entitled to call themselves legal executives and in principle are therefore not entitled to the same hourly rate as a legal executive. In respect of each fee earner communications should be treated as attendances and routine communications should be claimed at one tenth of the hourly rate.

N260 Statement of Costs (summary assessment) (7.00)　　　　　　　　　　*Printed on behalf of The Court Service*

12 FORM N265 – LIST OF DOCUMENTS

List of Documents:
Standard Disclosure

In the	
Claim No.	
Claimant (including ref)	
Defendant (including ref)	
Date	

Notes:
- The rules relating to standard disclosure are contained in Part 31 of the Civil Procedure Rules.
- Documents to be included under standard disclosure are contained in Rule 31.6
- A document has or will have been in your control if you have or have had possession, or a right of possession, of it **or** a right to inspect or take copies of it.

Disclosure Statement

I state that I have carried out a reasonable and proportionate search to locate all the documents which I am required to disclose under the order made by the court on [19][20].

(I did not search for documents -

1. pre-dating ....

2. located elsewhere than ....
....

3. in categories other than ....
....)

I certify that I understand the duty of disclosure and to the best of my knowledge I have carried out that duty. I further certify that the list of documents set out in or attached to this form, is a complete list of all documents which are or have been in my control and which I am obliged under the order to disclose.

I understand that I must inform the court and the other parties immediately if any further document required to be disclosed by Rule 31.6 comes into my control at any time before the conclusion of the case.

(I have not permitted inspection of documents within the category or class of documents (as set out below) required to be disclosed under Rule 31(6)(b)or (c) on the grounds that to do so would be disproportionate to the issues in the case.)

Signed		**Date**	

(Claimant)(Defendant)('s litigation friend)

Position or office held
(if signing on behalf of firm or company) Please state why you are the appropriate person to make the disclosure statement.

continued overleaf

N265 List of Documents: Standard Disclosure (4.99)   *Printed on behalf of The Court Service*

List and number here, in a convenient order, the documents (or bundles of documents if of the same nature, e.g. invoices) in your control, which you do not object to being inspected. Give a short description of each document or bundle so that it can be identified, and say if it is kept elsewhere i.e. with a bank or solicitor	I have control of the documents numbered and listed here. I do not object to you inspecting them/producing copies.
List and number here, as above, the documents in your control which you object to being inspected. (Rule 31.19)	I have control of the documents numbered and listed here, but I object to you inspecting them:
Say what your objections are	I object to you inspecting these documents because:
List and number here, the documents you once had in your control, but which you no longer have. For each document listed, say when it was last in your control and where it is now.	I have had the documents numbered and listed below, but they are no longer in my control.

13 FORM N252 – NOTICE OF COMMENCEMENT OF ASSESSMENT OF BILL OF COSTS

Notice of commencement of assessment of bill of costs

In the	
Claim No.	
Claimant (include Ref.)	
Defendant (include Ref.)	

To the claimant(defendant)

Following an .... *(insert name of document eg. order, judgment)* dated .... (copy attached) I have prepared my Bill of Costs for assessment. The Bill totals *£ .... If you choose to dispute this bill and your objections are not upheld at the assessment hearing, the full amount payable (including the assessment fee) will be £ .... (together with interest *(see note below)*). I shall also seek the costs of the assessment hearing

Your points of dispute must include

- details of the items in the bill of costs which are disputed
- concise details of the nature and grounds of the dispute for each item and, if you seek a reduction in those items, suggest, where practicable, a reduced figure

You must serve your points of dispute by .... *(insert date 21 days from the date of service of this notice)* on me at:- *(give full name and address for service including any DX number or reference)*

You must also serve copies of your points of dispute on all other parties to the assessment identified below *(you do not need to serve your points of dispute on the court).*

I certify that I have also served the following person(s) with a copy of this notice and my Bill of Costs:- *(give details of persons served)*

If I have not received your points of dispute by the above date, I will ask the court to issue a default costs certificate for the full amount of my bill *(see above*)* plus fixed costs and court fee in the total amount of £

Signed .... **Date** ....
(Claimant)(Defendant)('s solicitor)

Note: Interest may be added to all High Court judgments and certain county court judgments of £5,000 or more under the Judgments Act 1838 and the County Courts Act 1984.

The court office at

is open between 10 am and 4 pm Monday to Friday. When corresponding with the court, please address forms or letters to the Court Manager and quote the claim number.

N252 Notice of commencement of assessment of bill of costs (12.99) *The Court Service Publications Unit*

Appendix B

OTHER DOCUMENTS

1. Overview of the five stages of litigation
2. Determining jurisdiction where the defendant is domiciled in an EU or EFTA state
3. Judgment by consent
4. *Tomlin* order
5. Consequences of Part 36 Payment
6. Consequences of offer made by claimant under r 36.2
7. Model bill of costs for detailed assessment (Precedent A from the Practice Direction to Parts 43–48 – Schedule of costs precedents)

1 OVERVIEW OF THE FIVE STAGES OF LITIGATION

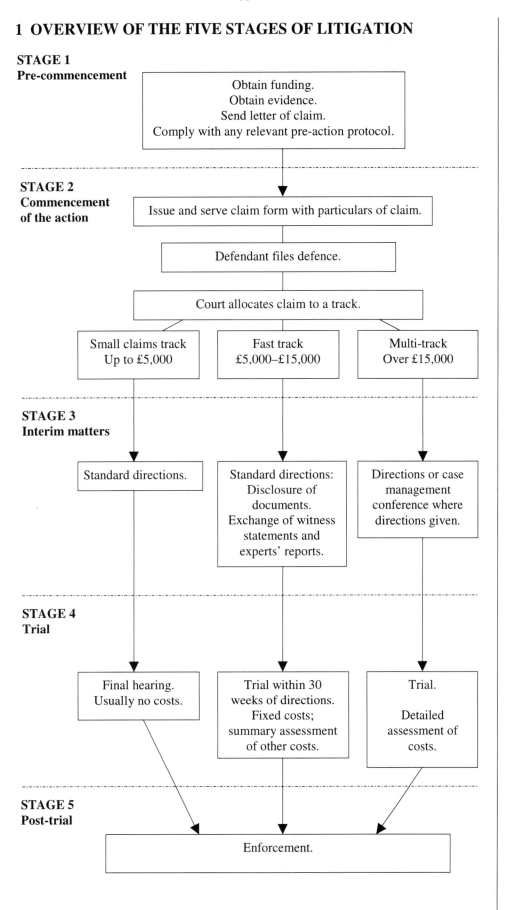

2 DETERMINING JURISDICTION WHERE THE DEFENDANT IS DOMICILED IN AN EU OR EFTA STATE

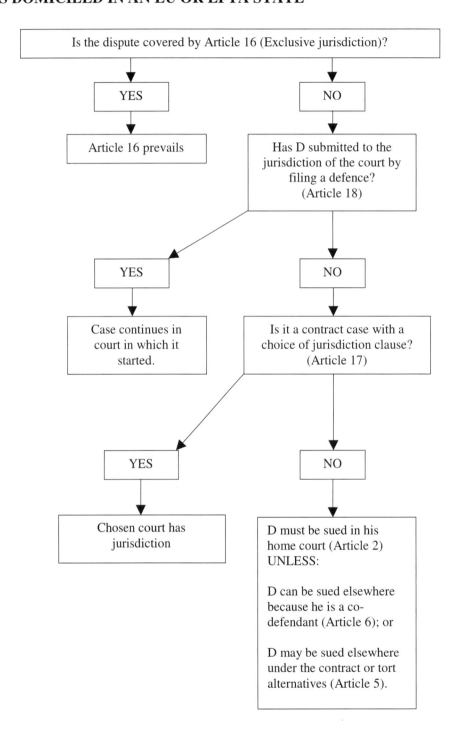

3 JUDGMENT BY CONSENT

IN THE WEYFORD COUNTY COURT Claim No: WF 01 067
BETWEEN

BENJAMIN RICHARD DAVIES
and
PORTLAND MUSIC LIMITED

JUDGMENT BY CONSENT

BY CONSENT, the parties having agreed terms of settlement, IT IS ORDERED THAT–

1. The Defendant shall pay the Claimant on or before 12 November 2001 the sum of £12,000 (inclusive of interest to that date).

2. The Defendant shall pay the Claimant's costs, to be assessed by detailed assessment if not agreed.

Dated ....

We consent to a judgment in the above terms

....
Collaws, Solicitors for the Claimant

....
Advocate & Co., Solicitors for the Defendant

4 *TOMLIN* ORDER

IN THE HIGH COURT OF JUSTICE   HQ 00 1242
QUEEN'S BENCH DIVISION

BETWEEN

LA BOULE S.A.   Claimant

and

CHRISTALINE LIMITED   Defendant

ORDER BY CONSENT

UPON the parties having agreed terms of settlement

BY CONSENT IT IS ORDERED THAT:

1. All further proceedings in this action shall be stayed upon the terms set out in the attached schedule, except for the purpose of carrying such terms into effect.

2. Each party shall have liberty to apply to the court if the other party does not give effect to the terms set out in the schedule.

3. The Defendant do pay the Claimant the sum of £10,000 in respect of costs.

Dated: ....

We consent to the making of an order in the above terms.

....
Swallows & Co., Solicitors for the Claimant

....
Singleton Trumper & Co., Solicitors for the Defendant

SCHEDULE

1. The Claimant shall pay or cause to be paid to the Defendant the sum of £50,000 on or before 14 August 2001 in full and final satisfaction of all claims arising in this action.

2. In the event of late payment, the Claimant will pay interest at a daily rate equal to 3% above the base lending rate of Barcloyds Bank plc as at 14 August 2001.

3. The Claimant and the Defendant have entered into a distribution agreement dated 1 August 2001 as part of the compromise of this action.

4. The Defendant will, at its own expense, attend and display the Claimant's 'Stella Star' range at the International Distributors' Licensed Products Fair in Paris during the week beginning 8 October 2001.

5 CONSEQUENCES OF PART 36 PAYMENT

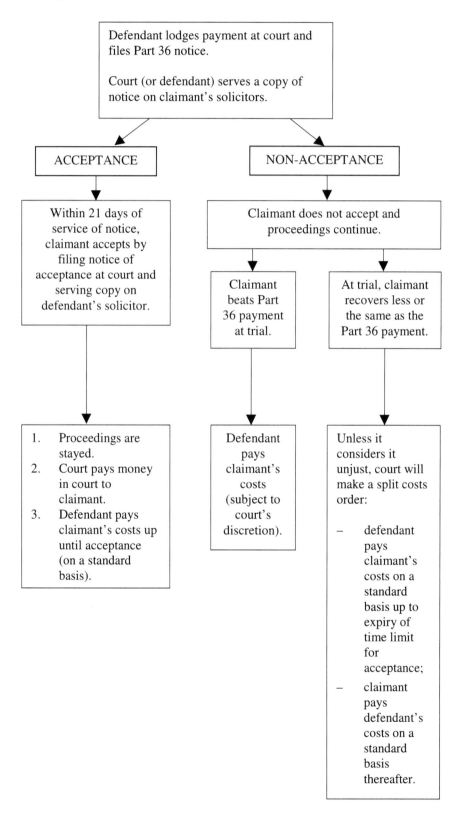

6 CONSEQUENCES OF OFFER MADE BY CLAIMANT UNDER r 36.2

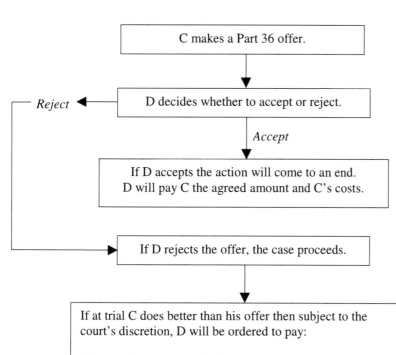

C makes a Part 36 offer.

D decides whether to accept or reject. — *Reject*

Accept

If D accepts the action will come to an end. D will pay C the agreed amount and C's costs.

If D rejects the offer, the case proceeds.

If at trial C does better than his offer then subject to the court's discretion, D will be ordered to pay:

(a) the damages awarded;

(b) plus the 'normal' interest and costs up to the last date when D could have accepted C's offer without the permission of the court;

(c) plus penalty interest on the damages from the day after the last date for acceptance;

(d) plus C's costs on an indemnity basis from that date together with penalty interest on those costs.

Penalty interest = up to 10% per annum above the base rate.

If C is awarded **the same or less** than his offer, D pays the damages awarded to C and (subject to the court's discretion) costs on the standard basis.

If C **loses** at trial he received no damages and (subject to the court's discretion) has to pay D's costs on the standard basis.

7 MODEL BILL OF COSTS FOR DETAILED ASSESSMENT (PRECEDENT A FROM THE PRACTICE DIRECTION TO PARTS 43–48 – SCHEDULE OF COSTS PRECEDENTS)

SCHEDULE OF COSTS PRECEDENTS
PRECENDENT A
IN THE HIGH COURT OF JUSTICE   2000 - B - 9999
QUEEN'S BENCH DIVISION
BRIGHTON DISTRICT REGISTRY

BETWEEN

AB   Claimant

– and –

CD

Defendant

CLAIMANT'S BILL OF COSTS TO BE ASSURED PURSUANT TO THE ORDER DATED 26TH JULY 2000

V.A.T. No. 33 4404 90

In these proceedings the claimant sought compensation for personal injuries and other losses suffered in a road accident which occurred on Friday 1st January 1999 near the junction between Bolingbroke Lane and Regency Road, Brighton, East Sussex. The claimant had been travelling as a front seat passenger in a car driven by the defendant. The claimant suffered severe injuries when, because of the defendant's negligence, the car left the road and collided with a brick wall.

The defendant was later convicted of various offences arising out of the accident including careless driving and driving under the influence of drink and drugs.

In the civil action the defendant alleged that immediately before the car journey began the claimant had known that the defendant was under the influence of alcohol and therefore consented to the risk of injury or was contributorily negligent as to it. It was also alleged that, immediately before the accident occurred, the claimant wrongfully took control of the steering wheel so causing the accident to occur.

The claimant first instructed solicitors, E F & Co, in this matter in July 2000. The claim form was issued in October 2000 and in February 2001 the proceedings were listed for a two day trial commencing 25th July 2001. At the trial the defendant was found to be liable but the compensation was reduced by 25% to take account of contributory negligence by the claimant. The claimant was awarded a total of £78,256.83 plus £1,207.16 interest plus costs.

The claimant instructed E F & Co under a conditional fee agreement dated 8th July 2000 which specifies the following base fees and success fees.

    Partner – £180 per hour plus VAT
    Assistant Solicitor – £140 per hour plus VAT

Other fee earners – £85 per hour plus VAT
Success fees exclusive of disbursement funding costs: 40%
Success fee in respect of disbursement funding costs: 7.5%
(not claimed in this bill)

Except where the contrary is stated the proceedings were conducted on behalf of the claimant by an assistant solicitor, admitted November 1999.

E F & Co instructed Counsel (Miss GH, called 1992) under a conditional fee agreement dated 5th June 2001 which specifies a success fee of 75% and base fees, payable in various circumstances, of which the following are relevant

Fees for interim hearing whose estimated duration is up to 2 hours: £600
Brief for trial whose estimated duration is 2 days: £2,000
Fee for second and subsequent days: £650 per day.

Item No.	Description of work done		V.A.T.	Disbursements	Profit Costs
	8th July 2000 – E F & Co instructed				
	22nd July 2000 – AEI with Eastbird Legal Protection Ltd				
1	Premium for policy		–	£120.00	
	7th October 2000 – Claim issued				
2	Issue fee		–	£400.00	
	21st October 2000 – Particulars of claim served				
	25th November 2000 – Time of service of defence extended by agreement to 14th January 2001				
3	Fee on allocation		–	£80.00	
	20th January 2001 – case allocated to multi-track				
	9th February 2001 – Case management conference at which costs were awarded to the claimant and the base costs were summarily assessed at £400 (paid on 24th February 2001)				–
	23rd February 2001 – Claimant's list of documents				
	12th April 2001 – Payment into court of £25,126.33				
	13th April 2001 – Filing listing questionnaire				
4	Fee on listing		–	£400.00	
	28th June 2001 – Pre-trial review: costs in case				
	Engaged 1.5 hours	£210.00			
	Travel and waiting 2.00 hours	£280.00			
5	Total solicitor's base fee for attending				£490.00
6	Counsel's base fee for pre-trial review (Miss GH)			£600.00	
	25th July 2001 – Attending first day of trial: adjourned part heard				
	Engaged in Court 5.00 hours	£700.00			
	Engaged in conference 0.75 hours	£105.00			
	Travel and waiting 1.5 hours	£210.00			
7	Total solicitor's base fee for attending				£1,015.00
8	Counsel's base fee for trial (Miss GH)			£2,000.00	
9	Fee of expert witness (Dr IJ)		–	£850.00	
10	Expenses of witnesses of fact		–	£84.00	
	26th July 2001 – Attending second day of trial when judgment was given for the claimant in the sum of £78,256.53 plus £1207.16 interest plus costs				
	Engaged in Court 3.00 hours	£420.00			
	Engaged in conference 1.5 hours	£210.00			
	Travel and waiting 1.5 hours	£210.00			
11	Total solicitor's base fee for attending				£840.00
12	Counsel's base fee for second day (Miss GH)			£650.00	
	To summary		£–	£5,184.00	£2,345.00
13	**Claimant** 8th July 2000 – First instructions: 0.75 hours by Partner: base fee Other timed attendances in person and by telephone – See schedule 1				£135.00

14	Total base fee for Schedule 1 – 7.5 hours			£1,050.00
15	Routine letters out, and telephone calls – 29 (17 + 12) total base fee			£406.00
	Witnesses of Fact Timed attendances in person, by letter out and by telephone – See schedule2			
16	Total base fee for Schedule 2 – 5.2 hours			£728.00
17	Routine letters out, emails and telephone calls – 8 (4 + 2 + 2) total base fee			£112.00
18	Paid travelling on 9th October 2000	£4.02	£22.96	
	Medical expert (Dr IJ)			
19	11th September 2000 – long letter out 0.33 hours: base fee			£46.20
20	30th January 2001 – long letter out 0.25 hours base fee			£35.00
21	23rd May 2001 – telephone call 0.2 hours base fee			£28.00
22	Routine letters out and telephone calls – 10 (6 + 4) total base fee			£140.00
23	Dr IJ's fee for report	–	£350.00	
	Defendant and his solicitor			
24	8th July 2000 – timed letter sent 0.5 hours: base fee			£70.00
25	19th February 2001 – telephone call 0.25 hours: base fee			£35.00
26	Routine letters out and telephone calls – 24 (18 + 6) total base fee			£336.00
	Communications with the court			
27	Rountine letters out and telephone calls – 9 (8 + 1) total base fee			£126.00
	Communications with Counsel			
28	Routine letters out, emails and telephone calls – 19 (4 + 7 + 8) total base fee			£266.00
	Work done on documents Timed attendances – See Schedule 3			
29	Total base fees for Schedule 3 – 0.75 hours at £180, 44.5 hours at £140, 12 hours at £85			£7,385.00
	Work done on negotiations 23rd March 2001 – meeting at offices of Solicitors for the Defendant			
	Engaged 1.5 hours	£210.00		
	Travel and waiting	£175.00		
30	Total base fee for meeting			£385.00
	Other work done Preparing and checking bill			
	Engaged: Solicitor – 1 hour	£140.00		
	Engaged: Costs Draftsman – 4 hours	£340.00		
31	Total base fee on other work done			£480.00
	To summary	£4.02	£372.96	£11,763.20
32	Success fee on solicitor's base fee on interim orders which were summarily assessed (40% of £400) plus VAT at 17.5%	£28.00		£160.00
33	VAT on solicitor's other base fees (17.5% of £14,108.20)	£2,468.94		
34	Success fee on solicitor's other base fees (40% of £14,108.20) plus VAT at 17.5%	£987.58		£5,643.28
35	VAT on Counsel's base fees (17.5% of £3,250)	£568.75		
36	Success fee on Counsel's base fee (75% of £3,250) plus VAT at 17.5%	£426.57	£2,437.50	
	To summary	£4,479.84	£2,437.50	£5,803.28
	SUMMARY			
	Page 3	£–	£5,184.00	£2,345.00
	Page 4	£4.02	£372.96	£11,763.20
	Page 5	£4,479.84	£2,437.50	£5,803.28
	Totals:	£4,483.86	£7,994.46	£19,911.48
	Grand total:			£32,389.80

INDEX

References are to paragraph numbers and Appendix.

Accounts
    order to prepare and file   9.6
Acknowledgement of service   5.1, 5.3
    disputed jurisdiction, and   5.3
Adjournment
    court power   8.2
Admiralty Court   4.1
Admission   5.1, 5.5
    claimant's response to   5.5.1–5.5.4
    defence, in   6.3
    full claim, specified amount   5.5.1
    part claim, specified amount   5.5.1
    rate of payment   5.5.1, 5.5.5
        interest   5.5.6
        redetermination application   5.5.5
        varying   5.5.7
    unspecified amount
        no offer   5.5.3
        offer   5.5.4
Affidavit evidence   9.2.5, 11.7
    bankruptcy petition, verifying   14.5.6
    meaning   11.7
    search order and freezing injunction, for   9.6, 11.7
Agent
    document, holding   10.4
    enquiry   14.3, 14.4.1
Allocation
    criteria for   8.5.1
    defended cases   8.5
    hearing   8.5.2
    questionnaire   8.5, App A(6)
        completing   8.5.1
        contents   8.5.1, 11.13.2
        dispensing with, court power   8.5
        failure to file   8.5.2
    sanctions for default of party   8.5.2
    track, to   1.3, 4.1, 4.3, 8.6
        factors for court   8.6
        fast, *see* Fast track
        multi, *see* Multi-track
        Part 8 claim   7.3
        small claims, *see* Small claims track
        time for   8.6
    value, determining   8.5.1
Alternative dispute resolution   2.3.1, 2.8.2, 15.1 *et seq*
    ADR group   15.5
    advising client   15.7, 15.8
    breach of agreement for
        contractual breach   15.3.2
        court jurisdiction   15.3.1
    CEDR   15.4.5, 15.5
    conciliation, by   15.4.1
    confidentiality   15.6.3
    consent order, agreement as   15.3.2
    contract clauses for   15.6, 15.8
    cost   15.2.1, 15.8
    courts encouraging use   2.8.2
    disclosure limitations   15.3.3
        contract clauses dealing with   15.6.1, 15.6.2
    distinguished from other resolutions   15.1.1
    enforcement   15.3.2, 15.8
    expert
        appraisal   15.4.4
        determination   15.4.6
    final offer arbitration   15.4.7
    flexibility of   15.2.2
    independent third party   15.1.2, 15.2.4, 15.8
        appointment   15.6.3
    judicial appraisal   15.4.5
    litigation, in conjunction with   15.7
    meaning   15.1
    Med-arb   15.4.2
    mediation, by   15.4.1, 15.4.2
    mini-trial   15.4.3
    non-binding nature   15.3.1
    organisations providing   15.5, 15.8
    privacy, preserving   15.2.3
    refusal to try, sanctions   15.8
    representatives' authority to settle   15.6.3
    speed of   15.2.1, 15.8
    structured settlement   15.4.3
    unsuitability, cases   15.3.4
Appeal
    interim order, against   9.4
Applicant   9.2
Application to court   9.1 *et seq*
    appeal against order made   9.4
    application notice (general)   9.2, App A(10)
        content   9.2.2
        documents to be filed with   9.2.4
        documents to be served with   9.2.5
        service   9.2.5
        statement of truth   9.2.2, 9.2.4
    charging order
        land, on   14.5.2
        securities, on   14.5.3
    costs   9.3
    court   9.2.1
    default judgment, to set aside   9.5.1
        human rights challenge to   9.9
    evidence in support   9.2.4, 11.7
    further information, for   9.5.3
    non-attendance of respondent   9.2.7

Application to court *cont*
   oral, at hearing   9.2.7
   oral examination, for   14.4
   order
      consent, procedure for   9.2.6
      draft/disk copy   9.2.3
   summary judgment for   9.5.2
      application notice   9.5.2
      directions   9.5.2
      human rights challenge   9.9.2
   telephone hearing   9.2.8
   urgent   9.2.7
   without notice, circumstances and procedure   9.2.7
Arbitration   2.8.1
   ADR distinguished   15.1.1, 15.4.6
   Chartered Institute of Arbitrators   15.5
   enforcement   2.8.1
   'final offer'   15.4.7
   Med-arb   15.4.2
Assessor
   costs appeal, for   13.3.7
   court   11.14
Assets, *see* Property
Attachment of earnings order   14.5.5
Attendance
   court power to require   8.2

Bank
   garnishee proceedings against   14.5.4
Bankruptcy   14.5.6
Barrister, *see* Counsel
Branch   2.7.1
Building society
   garnishee proceedings against   14.5.4
Bundle, *see* Trial bundle
Burden of proof   2.3.2

Capacity   4.4
Case, statement of, *see* Statement of case
Case management   1.1, 1.3, 4.2, 8.1 *et seq*
   see also Allocation; Striking out
   conference   8.6.3
   court duty   1.1, 8.1
   court powers   8.2, 11.1
   hearing, at   8.5.2
Centre for Dispute Resolution   15.4.5, 15.5
Charging order
   holder as secured creditor   14.5.6
   land, on   14.5.2
      notice and registration   14.5.2
   securities, on   14.5.3
Child
   see also Litigation friend
   claimant   2.2.4, 4.4.1

   claims involving   12.5
   defendant   4.4.1
   money recovered for   4.4.1
   settlement of case   4.4.1, 7.3
   witness   13.2.4
Civil procedure
   flowchart   1.3
   new Rules
      applicability and exclusions   1.2
      as code   1.1
   'old' rules, retention of   1.2, 14.1
   overriding objective   1.1, 2.3.1, 11.1
      furthering, court power   8.2
   pre-action protocol   3.7
Claim
   discontinuance of   12.6
   form
      forms served with   5.1
      lodging   4.3
      not received by defendant   9.5.1
      specimen   App A(1)
   letter of   3.8
   merits   2.3.1, 2.5.6
   particulars of, *see* Particulars of claim
   service, *see* Service
   verification   4.3, 6.2.3
Claimant
   see also Party
   closing speech   13.2.5
   meaning   4.3
   opening speech and evidence   13.2.3
   statement of case, *see* Statement of case
Client
   duties to   2.5, 2.6
   instructions, confirming   3.1
Commencing proceedings   4.1 *et seq*
Commercial Court   4.1
Committal to prison
   debtor, of   14.5.5
Community legal service   2.5.6
Companies Court   4.1
Company, limited
   branch in EU   2.7.1
   domicile   2.7.1
   party, as   4.4.4
   search   2.3.1, 4.4.4
   security for costs order against   9.8
   service on   4.4.4, 4.5.4
   winding up   14.5.6
Compensation   2.8.6–2.8.8
   court power on sentencing   2.8.8
   Criminal Injuries Compensation Authority   2.8.7
Computer disk
   copy of draft order   9.2.3
   document, as   10.3
Conciliation   15.4.1

Conditional fee agreement   2.5.2, 13.3.7
   community legal service funding, and   2.5.6
   costs, liability for other side's   2.5.2
   disbursement   2.5.2
   drafting   2.5.2
   insurance cover   2.5.2
   success fee   2.5.2
Conditional order   9.5.2
Conduct
   costs, effect on   13.3.4, 13.3.6, 13.3.7
Confidentiality   2.6.1
   ADR, and   15.6.3
Conflict of interest   2.6.2
Consent
   discontinuance of claim, to   12.6.1, 12.6.2
   order   9.2.6
      ADR agreement as   15.3.2
   without notice application   9.2.7
Contingency fee   2.5.3
Contract
   dispute resolution clauses   15.6, 15.8
Contract action
   EU, within   2.7.1
   limitation   2.2.1, 2.2.2, 2.2.5
   particulars of claim   6.2.1, 6.2.2
   proof, burden of   2.3.2
   remedies   2.4
Contribution claim   7.1, 7.2.2, 7.2.3
   see also Part 20 claim
   directions   7.2.7
   service   7.2.5
Corporation
   service on   4.5.4
Costs   2.5
   advising client   2.5, 3.1
   appeal   13.3.7
   application to court   9.3
   basis of assessment   13.3.3
      indemnity basis   13.3.3
      standard basis   13.3.3
   between the parties   2.5.1, 13.3.7
   bill of costs   13.3.7, App B(7)
      challenge   13.3.7
   conditional fee agreements   13.3.7
   conduct, effect on   13.3.4, 13.3.6, 13.3.7
   default costs bill   13.3.7
   delay, effect on   13.2.7, 13.3.7
   detailed assessment   13.3.5, 13.3.7
   discontinuance, on   12.6.3
   discretion of court   13.3.2
   factors for court   13.3.4
   fast track   13.3.6
   fixed   9.5.2
   garnishee proceedings, of   14.5.4
   general rule   13.3.2
   human rights challenge on grounds of   2.9.1
   in any event   9.3
   in the case/application   9.3
   indemnity principle   13.3.1
   insurance   2.5.2, 2.5.4
   multi-track   13.3.7
   no order   9.3
   order   13.8
      chart   9.3
   Part 36 offer, and   13.3.7
   payment on account   14.2.1
   public funding, *see* Public funding
   reserved   9.3
   sanction, as   8.5.2, 15.8
   security for   9.8
   solicitor and client   2.5.1
   statement of costs   9.3
   summary assessment   9.3, 9.5.2, 13.3.5, 13.3.6
      conditional fee agreements   9.3.1
      interim application   9.3.1
   summary judgment application   9.5.2
   wasted, order   8.6.3
Counsel   3.6
   brief to   13.1.1
   conference   3.6.2, 13.1.1
   fees   13.1.1
   instructions to   3.6.2, 13.1.1
   legal professional privilege, scope   10.11.1
   use of   3.6.1, 13.1.1
Counterclaim   6.3, 7.1, 7.2 *et seq*
   see also Part 20 claim
   costs   13.3.2
   defence and counterclaim, one form   7.2.1
   filing   7.2.1
   judgment on   13.2.6
   parties, description of   7.2.8
   permission, *see* Permission of court
   response of claimant   7.2.1
   service   7.2.5
   succeeding   13.2.6, 13.3.2
County court   4.1
   attachment of earnings order application   14.5.5
   bailiff   14.5.1, 14.5.5
   charging order application   14.5.2
   debt action, example particulars of claim   6.2.1
   examination of debtor, procedure   14.4.2
   execution of judgment   14.5.1
   garnishee proceedings   14.5.4
   judgment, interest on   14.2.2
      certificate, need for   14.2.2
      enforcement proceedings, effect of   14.2.2
Court
   allocation to track, *see* Allocation
   application, for   9.2.1
   choice   4.1
   control of litigation   1.1, 1.3, *see also* Case management

Court *cont*
   costs, factors for assessment   13.3.4
   county, *see* County court
   High, *see* High Court
   jurisdiction, see Jurisdiction
   overriding objective
      duty   1.1
      powers to further   8.2
      see also Case management
   payment into, *see* Payment
   personnel   4.2
   solicitor's duties   1.1, 2.6.3
   venue for trial   13.2.1
Court forms   App A, *see also* Claim form; Response pack
Creditor
   judgment, *see* Judgment debt: enforcement
   secured   14.5.6
Criminal Injuries Compensation Authority   2.8.7

Damages
   claim for   6.2.1, 6.2.2
   interest   2.4.3, 6.2.2, 13.2.7, 14.2, *see also* Interest
   payment on account, *see* Interim payment
   provisional   5.6.1, 6.2.1
   quantum   2.4.1
Debt action   2.4.2, 2.4.3, 3.8
   defence to
      method for   6.3
      non-compliance with Rules etc   8.3.2
      statements of case, inadequate   8.3.1
      striking out   8.3
   particulars of claim   6.2.2
      example   6.2.1
   payment on account, *see* Interim payment
Debt, judgment, *see* Judgment debt
Declaration, interim   9.6
Default judgment   5.1, 5.6
   co-defendants   5.6.6
   human rights challenge to   5.7
   interest   5.6.5
   non-availability   5.6.1
   Part 20 claim   7.2.6
   procedure   5.6.2
   setting aside   5.6.7, 9.5.1
      application procedure   9.5.1
   specified amount   5.6.3
   unspecified amount   5.6.4
Defence   5.1, 5.4, 6.3
   admission in   6.3
   allocation of case   8.5
   contents   6.3
   copy documents with   6.3
   counterclaim with   7.2.1
   example   6.3
   form for   5.4
   reply by claimant   6.1, 6.4
   striking out   8.3
   time for filing   5.4
   verification   6.3
Defendant
   see also Party
   co-defendant
      contribution or indemnity claim   7.2.2
      default judgment   5.6.6
      EU, in   2.7.1
   counterclaim, *see* Counterclaim
   defence, *see* Defence
   evidence   13.2.3
   letter to   3.8
   meaning   4.3
   no response to claim   5.6, *see also* Default judgment
   payment by, *see* Payment
   response to claim   5.1–5.5, App A(4), *see also* Admission; Defence
   security for costs order   9.8
   solvency of   2.3.1, 14.1
   whereabouts   2.3.1, 14.3
Delay   8.6.2, 8.6.3, 13.2.7, 13.3.7
Deposit-taking institution
   garnishee proceedings against   14.5.4
Directions
   expert evidence, on   11.13.2
   fast track   8.6.2
      agreeing   8.6.2
      failure to comply   8.6.2
      listing   8.6.2
   multi-track   8.6.3
   small track   8.6.1
   summary judgment application, in   9.5.2
Disability, person under   2.2.4
Disclosure   10.1 *et seq*
   definition   10.2
   document
      copy, as separate   10.5
      copy, for inspection   10.7
      definition   10.3
      'party's control', in   10.4
   expert, instructions to   11.13.3
   expert report   3.4.1, 11.13.4
   failure   10.13
   inspection
      limits on   10.7
      right   10.7
      specific, order for   10.15
      withholding   10.11
   non-party, against   10.16
   obligation   3.3, 10.9
      continuing   10.10
   pre-action   10.16
      application for order   3.9
      interim order   9.6

Disclosure *cont*
  privilege and waiver of   10.11
    inadvertent disclosure   10.11.5
  public policy   10.11
  self-incrimination, and   10.11
  solicitor's duty   10.9
  specific   10.15
  standard   10.4–10.10
    disclosure statement   10.9
    list of documents   10.8, App A(12)
    reasonable search requirement   10.6
    subsequently found documents   10.10
  use of disclosed document   10.14
Discontinuance   12.6
  consent to   12.6.1, 12.6.2
  costs liability   12.6.3
  notice of   12.6.2
  permission of court   12.6.1
Dismiss
  court power   8.2
District judge   4.2, 9.2.1
Document
  see also Trial bundle
  agent holding   10.4
  copy with particulars of claim   6.2.1
  disclosure, *see* Disclosure
  meaning   3.3
  notice to prove   11.12
  preservation   3.3
  service, *see* Service
  witness summons for production   13.1.2
Document exchange   4.5.1
Domicile   2.7.1

Electronic service   4.5.1
E-mail   4.5.1
Employer
  attachment of earnings order   14.5.5
Enforcement
  ADR   15.3.2, 15.8
  judgment, of, *see* Judgment debt
Ethics   2.6
European Union
  discrimination   9.8
  jurisdiction between States   2.7.1
  service in   4.5.4(1)Evidence   11.1 *et seq*
  admissibility   11.1 *et seq*
    hearsay, *see* 'hearsay' *below*
    opinion   11.8
    plan, photo etc   11.10
    witness statement   3.2
  admission of facts   11.11
  affidavit, *see* Affidavit evidence
  application notice, with   9.2.4, 9.6
  claimant's   13.2.3
  court control   11.1
  defendant's   13.2.3
  document proof   11.12
  exchange of   8.6.2
  expert, *see* Expert(s)
  failure to challenge opponent's   13.2.3
  hearsay   11.9
    admissibility   11.9.2
    competence and credibility, and   11.9.3
    cross-examination right   11.9.3
    definition   11.9.1
    first-hand   11.9.1
    human rights implications   11.15.2
    multiple   11.9.1
    notification of proposed use   11.9.2
    previous inconsistent statement   11.9.3
    weight to, guidelines to court   11.9.3
  human rights challenges   13.4
  opinion   3.4.3, 11.8
  oral   11.2, 11.4, 13.2.3, *see also* Witness
  order of   13.2.3
  plan, photo or model, use of   11.10
  preservation, *see* Search order
  video link   11.2
  witness statement, *see* Witness
  witness summary   11.5
    non-service   11.6
Examination of debtor   14.4.2
Exclusion of issue
  court power   8.2
Execution   14.5.1
  court for   14.5.1
  exempt items   14.5.1
  motor vehicle   14.5.1
  walking possession   14.5.1
Exhibit   11.3, 11.7
Expert(s)   3.4, 11.13
  appraisal by, for dispute resolution   15.4.4
  assessor   11.14
  determination   15.4.6
  directions   8.6.2, 11.13.2, 11.13.7
  discussion between   11.13.7
  duty to court   11.13.1, 11.13.5
  fees   3.4.1, 11.13.2
  form   11.13.4
  human rights implications   11.15.1
  instructing   3.4.1, 11.13.3
    disclosure of letter   11.13.3
  joint   11.13.8
  opinion evidence   3.4.3, 11.13
  oral evidence   11.13.2
  permission of court for evidence of   3.4.4, 11.13.2
    time for grant   11.13.2
  plan, photo etc in   11.10
  report   3.4.1, 3.4.2, 11.13.4
    contents   11.13.5, 11.13.6
    directions as to exchange, fast track   8.6.2

Expert(s) *cont*
   report *cont*
      disclosure   3.4.1, 11.13.4
      statement of truth   11.13.5
      restriction of evidence, court power   11.13.2
   witness summons   13.1.2
   written questions to   11.13.6

Fact, notice to admit   11.11
Failure to comply
   allocation questionnaire   8.5.2
   directions   8.6.2, 8.6.3
   fees   8.4
   relief from sanctions, court powers   8.4
Fast track   1.3, 8.6, 8.6.2
   see also Allocation
   costs   13.3.6
   counsel's fees   13.1.1
   directions   8.6.2
      failure to comply   8.6.2
   evidence, exchange of   8.6.2
   hearing   8.6.2
   listing questionnaire   8.6.2
   statement of costs, filing   13.3.6
   timetable   8.6.2
   trial
      bundle and case summary   8.6.2
      venue   13.2.1
   varying directions   8.6.2
Fax
   service by   4.5.1
Fee
   counsel's   13.1.1
   non-payment   8.4
Foreign element   2.7
   service   4.5.5 Freezing injunction   9.6, 11.7
Funding, *see* Costs
Further information
   court order   6.6.1, 6.6.4, 9.5.3
      application   9.5.3
   no response to request   6.6.4
      reasons for   6.6.3
   request, formalities   6.6.1
   response to request   6.6.2
Garnishee order   14.5.4
   bank or building society, against   14.5.4
   costs   14.5.4
Goods
   delivery up, order for   9.6
   seizure and sale   14.5.1

Hearing
   allocation   8.5.2
   application at   9.2.7
   costs, detailed assessment   13.3.7

   court power to alter date   8.2
   fast track, circumstances for   8.6.2
   multi-track, circumstances for   8.6.3
   notice of   8.2
   oral examination of debtor   14.4
   small claims track, final   8.6.1
   telephone, *see* Telephone
Hearsay, *see* Evidence
High Court   4.1
   charging order application   14.5.2
   defence, example   6.3
   defence and counterclaim, example   7.2.1
   divisions   4.1
   examination of debtor, procedure   14.4.2
   execution of judgment   14.5.1
   garnishee proceedings   14.5.4
   judgment, interest on   14.2.1
   sheriff's office   14.5.1
Human rights challenges   1.4, 2.9, 9.9, 10.18
   default judgment   5.6.7
   evidence   11.15, 13.4
      expert   11.15.2
      hearsay   11.15.1
   funding   2.9.1
   limitation   2.9.1
   orders made without notice   9.9.1
   privilege   10.18
   public access   9.9.4
   security for costs   9.9.3
   statement of case struck out   8.7
   summary judgment   9.9.2

Indemnity basis
   cost assessment   13.3.3
Indemnity claim   7.1, 7.2.2
   see also Part 20 claim
   service   7.2.5
Information
   property subject of freezing order, on   9.6
   further, *see* Further information
Injunction
   freezing   9.6, 11.7
   interim   9.6
Insolvency
   defendant, of, check on   2.3.1
   petition   14.5.6
Inspection
   documents, *see* Disclosure
   property, interim order   9.6
   site   3.5
Instalment   14.2.2
Insurance   2.8.5, 2.8.6
   litigation costs, for   2.5.2, 2.5.4
   notification of insurers   2.8.5
   pre-event   2.5.4

Interest
    admission, after, conditions   5.5.6
    award of   2.4.3, 5.5.6, 5.6.5, 13.2.7
    claim for   2.4.3, 6.2.1
        basis in particulars of claim   4.3, 6.2.1
    default judgment including   5.6.5
    judgment, after   13.2.7
    judgment debt, on   14.2
    overpayment, on   9.7.3
    rate   13.2.7, 14.2.1, 14.2.2
Interim payment   9.6, 9.7
    interest on overpaid amount   9.7.3
    order   9.6, 9.7
        amount   9.7.2
        application notice   9.7.1
        conditions for   9.7.2
        evidence in support   9.7.1
        time for application   9.7
    repayment or reimbursement, order for   9.7.2
    voluntary   9.7
Interim remedies   9.6
Interim application, *see* Application to court
Interview
    first, with client   2.1 *et seq*
    witness, with   3.2

Judge   4.2
    see also District judge
    former, appraisal by   15.4.5
Judgment
    consent, by   App B(3)
    court power after preliminary decision   8.2
    debt, enforcement, *see* Judgment debt
    default, *see* Default judgment
    request for   5.5.1
    setting aside   8.2, 8.3, 9.2.7
    striking out of defence, after   8.3
    summary   8.5.1, 8.5.2, 9.5.2
        application grounds and procedure   9.5.2
        court's own initiative   9.5.2
        orders court may make   9.5.2
    trial   13.2.6
Judgment debt   14.1 *et seq*
    enforcement methods   14.5
        attachment of earnings   14.5.5
        bankruptcy or winding-up petition   14.5.6
        charging order on land   14.5.2
        charging order on securities   14.5.3
        execution   14.5.1
        garnishee proceedings   14.5.4
    enquiry agent, use of   14.3, 14.4.1
    insolvent debtor   14.5.6
    interest   14.2
        county court judgment   14.2.2
        'enforcement proceedings', and   14.2.2
        High Court judgment   14.2.1
    means of debtor, investigation methods   14.4
    oral examination of debtor   14.4.2, 14.5.4
        county court procedure   14.4.2
        High Court procedure   14.4.2
    tracing   14.3
Jurisdiction
    clause in contract   2.7.1
    dispute as to   5.3
    EU   2.7.1
        determining   App B(2)
    issues   2.7
    outside EU   2.7.2
    security for costs, where claimant outside   9.8

Land
    charging order   14.5.2
        order for sale   14.5.2
    entry, order authorising   9.6
    possession order   7.3
Landlord and tenant repair case   8.6
Legal advice, see Counsel; Solicitor
Legal professional privilege   10.11
    advice privilege   10.11.1(1)
    inadvertant disclosure of documents   10.11.5
    litigation privilege   10.11.1(2), (3)
Limitation period   2.2
    date of knowledge   2.2.2
    human rights challenge   2.9.1
    statement of case, amendment outside   6.5.4
    summary, table   2.2.5
Listing
    directions   8.6.2
    hearing   8.6.3
    questionnaire   8.6.2, 8.6.3, App A(9)
        witness's availability   13.1.2
Litigation
    Overview of five stages of   App B(1)
Litigation friend   4.4.1
    authority or certificate of suitability   4.4.1
    cessation of appointment   4.4.1
    requirement   4.4.1

Master   4.2, 9.2.1
Med-arb   15.4.2
Mediation   15.4.1, 15.4.2
    contract clause for   15.6
Mediation UK   15.5
Medical report   3.4.1, 3.4.2
Mental Health Act patient
    see also Litigation friend
    claimant   2.2.4, 4.4.1
    defendant   4.4.1
    money recovered for   4.4.1
    settlement of case   4.4.1, 7.3

Mitigation duty 2.4.1, 2.4.2
Model 11.10
Money claim
   see also Debt action
   claim form 4.3
   defence 6.3
   enforcement of judgment 14.1 *et seq*, *see also* Judgment debt
   interest in particulars of claim 6.2.1
Motor Insurers Bureau 2.8.6
Motor vehicle
   see also Road traffic
   seizure for execution 14.5.1
Multi-track 1.3, 8.6, 8.6.3
   see also Allocation
   case management conference 8.6.3
   case summary 8.6.3
   costs 13.3.7
      bill of costs 13.3.7, App B(7)
   directions 8.6.3
      variation and non-compliance 8.6.3
   listing questionnaire 8.6.3
   pre-trial review 8.6.3
   trial
      bundle 8.6.3
      venue 13.2.1

Negligence
   expert, in ADR determination 15.4.6
   insurance against claim 2.8.5
   interest on damages 2.4.3
   jurisdictional issues 2.7.2
   limitation 2.2.1–2.2.5
      latent damage 2.2.3
   proof 2.3.2
   remedies 2.4
Negotiations 2.8.4, 3.10.1, 12.1
   ADR distinguished 15.1.1
   basis of 12.1.2
   solicitor's authority 3.10.1, 12.1.1
   without prejudice 3.10.1, 12.1.2
Non-party
   see also Third party
   disclosure against 10.17
Notice
   application without, circumstances 9.2.7
   discontinuance, of 12.6.2
   documents, to produce 11.12
   facts, to admit 11.11
   hearsay evidence, of 11.9.2
   prior chargees, to, of charging order 14.5.2
   trial bundle, in 13.1.3

Offer
   Part 36 12.4
      alternatives to 12.4.7
      assessing the terms 12.4.5
      claimant's offer 12.4.4
      consequences of App B(5), App B(6)
      costs, and 13.3.7
      defendant's offer 12.4.3
      defendant's payment 12.4.2
      pre-action offers 12.4.1
      secrecy 12.4.6

   pre-action 3.10.2
Opinion evidence 3.4.3, 11.8
Oral examination of debtor 14.4.2
Order
   see also Judgment; Setting aside order; Variation
   appeal against 9.4
   application for 8.3, 8.6.3, 9.1 *et seq*, *see also* Application to court
   conditional 9.5.2
   consent 9.2.6
   court power to make 8.2, 8.3
   disclosure, for 10.4, 10.15–10.17
   draft 9.2.3
   enforcement of judgment debt, for 14.5
   interim 9.6
   interim payment 9.7
   provisional 8.2
   sale of land, for chargeholder 14.5.2
   security for costs 9.8
   setting aside, *see* Setting aside order
   summary judgment application, available on 9.5.2
   variation 8.2, 9.2.7
   without notice 8.2, 9.2.7
      human rights challenge to 9.9.1

Part 8 claim 7.3
   availability 7.3
   multi-track, allocation to 7.3
   no default judgment 5.6.1, 7.3
Part 20 claim 7.1 *et seq*
   see also Third party
   contribution, *see* Contribution
   counterclaim, *see* Counterclaim
   defence 7.2.7
   description of parties 7.2.8
   directions 7.2.7
   form App A(5)
   indemnity, *see* Indemnity claim
   judgment in default 7.2.6
   meaning 7.1
   permission for 7.2.1, 7.2.3
      application notice 7.2.4
   service 7.2.5

Part 20 claim *cont*
   title   7.2.8
Part 36 offer or payment, *see* Offer
Particulars of claim   4.3, 6.1, 6.2
   contents   6.2.1, 6.2.2
   contract action   6.2.1, 6.2.2
   debt action   6.2.2
      example   6.2.1
   function of   6.2.1
   interest, basis for   6.2.1
   Practice Direction   6.2.1
   prayer for relief   6.2.2
Partnership
   party, as   4.4.2
   service on   4.5.4
Party
   see also Claimant; Company, limited; Defendant; Partnership
   capacity   4.4
   overriding objective of court, duty   1.1, 2.3.1
   tracing   14.3
Patents Court   4.1
Patient, *see* Mental Health Act patient
   claims involving   12.5
Payment
   interim, order for   9.6, 9.7
      order for   9.6
   rate of
      admission, after, *see* Admission
      default judgment   5.6
Permission of court
   application for   7.2.1, 7.2.4
      delay, explanation of   7.2.4
      matters for court   7.2.4
   application without notice, for   9.2.7
   discontinuance of claim, for   12.6.1
   expert evidence   3.4.4, 11.13.2
Personal injury action
   claim form   4.3
   court for   4.1
   interim payment
      application   9.7.1
      conditions for order   9.7.2
   limitation   2.2.2, 2.2.5
Photograph   3.5, 11.10
Plaintiff, *see* Claimant
Plan   3.5, 11.10
Police
   witness, as   13.1.2
Possession order   7.3
Post
   service by   4.5.1
Pre-action disclosure, *see* Disclosure
Pre-action protocol   3.7
   compliance   8.5.1
Pre-action settlements   12.2
   costs   12.2.1
   interest   12.2.1

   recording of   12.2.2
Pre-trial review   8.6.3
Privilege
   challenging   10.11.4
   inadvertent disclosure of documents   10.11.5
   withholding inspection of document for   10.11
Procedure, *see* Civil procedure
Proceedings
   issue, *see* Claim
   order of   13.2.3, *see also* Trial
Property
   see also Goods; Land
   detention or preservation, order for   9.6
   income from, order for   9.6
   inspection, order for   9.6
   recovery of personal   9.6
   sale, order for   9.6
   sample or experiment on, order for   9.6
Proportionality principle   10.6, 13.3.3
Provisional order   8.2
Public access
   human rights challenge to   9.9.4
Public funding   2.5.6
   certificate
      counsel, copy to   3.6.2
   Community Legal Service   2.5.6
   Community Legal Service Fund   2.5.6
   conditional fee agreement, and   2.5.2
   counsel's fee   12.3
   Legal Services Commission   2.5.6
   statutory charge   2.5.6
Public policy
   withholding inspection for   10.11

Relief
   sanctions for failure to comply, from   8.4
Remedy
   see also Damages; Injunction
   interim   9.6
   particulars of claim, in   6.2.2
Reply to defence   6.1, 6.4
Report
   assessor, by   11.14
   expert, by, *see* Expert(s)
Research
   law, into   3.11
Respondent   9.2
   without notice application, rights   9.2.7
Response pack   5.1, 5.3, 5.4, 5.5, App A(4)
Road traffic
   see also Personal injury action
   contribution claim   7.1
   expert report   3.4.1
   insurance, minimum   2.8.5
   MIB   2.8.6

Sale, order for   14.5.2
Sanctions   8.4, *see also* Costs; Failure to comply
Search order   9.6, 11.7
Securities
    charging order on   14.5.3
Security
    costs, for, application for order   9.8
        human rights challenge to   9.9.3
    debt, for, charging order on land   14.5.2
Self-incrimination
    privilege, and   10.11
Service   4.5
    address for   4.5.4, 5.3
    application notice   9.2.5
    certificate of suitability   4.4.1
    claim   5.1
    counterclaim   7.2.5
    court, by   4.5.3
    defence, of   5.4
    electronic/e-mail   4.5.1
    forms with particulars of claim   5.1
    individual, on   4.5.4
    methods   4.5.1
    personal   4.5.1
    post   4.5.1, 4.5.3
    time for, of claim form   4.6
    witness statement/summary, sanction for failure   11.6
    witness summons   13.1.2
Setting aside order   8.2, 9.2.7
    default judgment   9.5.1
        human rights challenge to   5.6.7
Settlement   2.8.4
    see also Alternative dispute resolution; Arbitration; Negotiations; Offer; Pre-action settlements
    child or patient, case involving   4.4.1
    encouragement of   8.5.1
    stay for   8.5.1
Settlement after issue of proceedings   12.3
    consent orders   12.3.1
    judgments   12.3.1
    Tomlin orders   12.3.2, App B(4)
Site visit   3.5
Small claims track   1.3, 8.6, 8.6.1
    see also Allocation
    costs   8.6.1
    hearing   8.6.1
    standard directions   8.6.1
Sole trader   4.4.3
Solicitor
    ADR, advice on   15.7, 15.8
    confidentiality   2.6.1
    conflict of interest   2.6.2
    costs, duty to client   2.5, 3.1
    disclosure, duty to client   10.9
    legal professional privilege   10.11
    negotiations, *see* Negotiations
    not to mislead   2.6.3
    overriding objective, duty   1.1
    preliminary steps   3.2
    presentation of case, duty   2.6.3
    service on   4.5.4
Statement of case   6.1 *et seq*
    amendment to   6.5
        after service, with permission   6.5.2, 6.5.3
        before service   6.5.1
        directions following   6.5.3
        limitation period, outside   6.5.4
        statement of truth   6.5.5
    application notice, with   9.2.4
    claimant's
        first, *see* Particulars of claim
        reply to defence   6.1, 6.4
    defendant's, *see* Counterclaim; Defence
    rules for   6.1
    striking out, court power   8.3
        human rights challenge to   8.7
Statement of costs   9.3
    filing, fast track   13.3.6
    form   App A(11)
Statement of truth   4.3, 6.2.3
    amendment to statement of case, for   6.5.5
    application notice/evidence, verifying   9.2.2, 9.2.4
    expert report, in   11.13.5
    response to information request, verifying   6.6.2
    witness statement, in   11.3
Statutory charge, *see* Public funding
Stay of order   8.2
Stay of proceedings   8.5.1
    extension   8.5.1
Striking out
    court power   8.3, 8.5.2, 8.6.2, 8.6.3
    failure to pay fee   8.4
Summary assessment, *see* Costs
Summary judgment, *see* Judgment

Telephone
    hearing, court power   8.2, 9.2.8
    mediation by   15.4.1
Time-limits   5.2–5.5, 7.2.1
    appeal against interim order   9.4
    computation for   5.2
    court power to extend or reduce   8.2
Timetable
    fast-track case   8.6.2, 13.2.2
    multi-track case   8.6.3, 13.2.2
Third party
    ADR, for   15.1.2, 15.4
    claim against   7.1, 7.2.3
        service   7.2.5

Third party *cont*
  communications with   10.11
Tomlin orders   12.3.2, App B(4)
Tort action
  EU, within   2.7.1
  limitation   2.2.1–2.2.5
  remedies   2.4
Tracing party   14.3
Track, *see* Allocation
Trade scheme   2.8.3
Trade union
  funding from   2.5.5
Transfer, automatic   8.5
Trial
  bundle, *see* Trial bundle
  closing speeches   13.2.5
  cross-examination of witnesses   11.4, 11.9.3, 13.2.3
  fast track
    court   13.2.1
    date sacrosanct   8.6.2
    deadline   8.6.2
    notice of   8.6.2
  judgment   13.2.6
  leading questions   13.2.3
  multi-track
    court   13.2.1
    date for   8.6.3
    date sacrosanct   8.6.3
  opening speech by claimant   13.2.3
  timetable   13.2.2
  venue   13.2.1
  witness statement and evidence   11.4
Trial bundle
  contents   13.1.3
    agreeing   13.1.3
  copies   13.1.3
  fast track   8.6.2
  multi-track   8.6.3
  preparation and filing   13.1.3

UK
  jurisdictions   2.7.1

Value of claim
  allocation, for   8.5.1
  costs award in fast track trial, for   13.3.6
Variation
  directions   8.6.2, 8.6.3
  order made without notice   8.2, 9.2.7
  rate of payment   5.5.7

Verification   4.3
  see also Statement of truth
  defence, of   6.3
Video link
  use for evidence   11.2
Video tape
  document, as   10.3

Waiver of privilege   10.11
Walking possession   14.5.1
Winding up   14.5.6
Witness
  availability   13.1.2
  character   13.2.3
  child   13.2.4
    sworn evidence   13.2.4
  compelling   3.2, 13.1.2
  competence   11.9.3
  credibility   11.9.3, 13.2.3
  cross-examination   11.4, 11.9.3, 13.2.3
  exhibits, verification etc   11.3
  expert, *see* Expert(s)
  hostile   13.2.3
  interviewing   3.2
  opinion, admissibility   11.8
  oral evidence   11.2, 11.4, 11.6, 11.9.2
  re-examination   13.2.3
  statement   3.2
    amplification in court   13.2.3
    application notice, with   9.2.4
    directions as to exchange, fast track   8.6.2
    evidence-in-chief, as   11.4, 11.9.3
    form and contents   11.3
    heading   11.3
    hearsay evidence in   11.4, 11.9.2, 11.9.3
    non-service   11.6
    statement of truth   11.3
    use at trial   11.4, 13.2.3
  previous inconsistent statement   11.9, 13.2.3
  summary   11.5
    non-service   11.6
  summons   13.1.2
    expert, for   13.1.2
    pay, offer with   13.1.2
Without notice
  application to court   9.2.7
    interim remedy, for   9.6
'Without prejudice'   3.10.1
Woolf Report   1.1
  implementation   1.1
Writ of fieri facias   14.5.1